Jane Dunn describes herself as a wife, mother, and grandmother with an overwhelming love of the freedom of the open road. She and her husband are experienced campers and enjoy nothing more than setting off on another magical trip with, as she says, “our house on our back”.

The author pursues interests in chamber music and opera, and loves to haunt antique shops. Gardening, cooking, and interior design and decoration are abiding passions, and she enjoys heated discussions on politics around the dining table. Future plans include another motorhome tour of New Zealand to visit the places missed on the last trip, and a caravan tour of Spain.

MOTORHOME MAGIC:

Paradise Found in New Zealand

Jane Dunn

MOTORHOME MAGIC:

Paradise Found in New Zealand

Vanguard Press

VANGUARD PAPERBACK

A CIP catalogue record for this title is
available from the British Library.

ISBN: 978 1 84386 367 0

DISCLAIMER

All prices quoted were correct at the time of writing.

Vanguard Press is an imprint of
Pegasus Elliot MacKenzie Publishers Ltd.
www.pegasuspublishers.com

First Published in 2007

Vanguard Press
Sheraton House Castle Park
Cambridge England

Printed & Bound in Great Britain

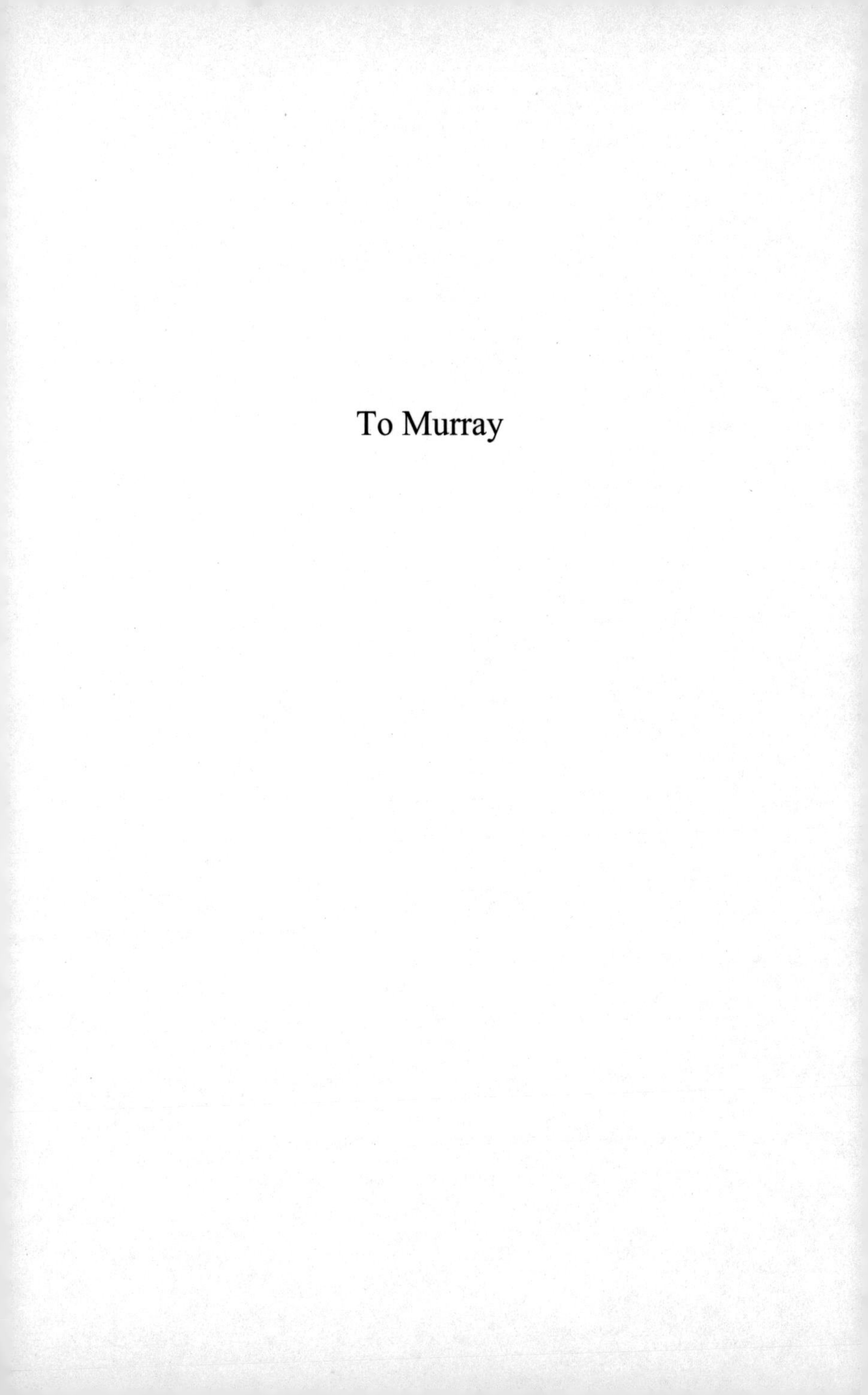

To Murray

ACKNOWLEDGMENTS

I am indebted to the following publications, which I used daily on tour, for their important contribution to the success and enjoyment of our holiday:

Kiwi Pathfinder – New Zealand Travellers Road Atlas, 5th Edition.
Designed and published by C.A. Boot, Kiwimaps Limited, Christchurch.

Driving Scenic New Zealand. A Guide to Touring New Zealand by Road, 2nd Edition, by Dave Chowdhury. Craig Potton Publishing, Nelson, 2004.

The New Zealand Camping Guide, North Island 2005, and *The New Zealand Camping Guide, South Island 2005, 13th Revised Editions*, by Gay Kerr. Gay Kerr, Plimmerton.

The Lord of the Rings Location Guidebook, Revised Edition 2003, by Ian Brodie. HarperCollins Publishers.

Maui Motorhomes 2005. AA Guides Limited, NZ Automobile Association.

I relied on the following publications for help with historical and descriptive information:

The Companion Guide to the North Island of New Zealand, and *The Companion Guide to the South Island of New Zealand*, by Errol Brathwaite. William Collins Publishers, Auckland, 1974 reprints.

Tales of Pioneer Women, 2nd and Revised Edition, edited by H.E. Woodhouse. Whitcombe and Tombs Limited, 1940.

New Zealand's Heritage: The Making of a Nation, Vols. 1-4. Paul Hamlyn Limited, Wellington, 1972.

Mobil World Heritage Highway Guide, South Westland and Haast Pass. Published by the West Coast Conservancy, Department of Conservation, Hokitika.

The following poems were quoted:

Elegy Written in a Country Churchyard by Thoms Gray. *A Pageant of English Verse*, edited by E.W. Parker, Longmans, Green and Co. Ltd., London. Second Impression 1951.

The Rime of the Ancient Mariner by Samuel Taylor Coleridge. *Fifteen Poets*, Oxford University Press, London, 1951 Reprint.

AUTHOR'S NOTE

The esteemed British publication *MMM Motorcaravan Motorhome Monthly* refers to road touring vehicles as motorvans, campervans, motorcaravans, and motorhomes. All the names are interchangeable and depend for their selection on the preference of the person writing the article. My own preference is for the nomadic-sounding 'motorcaravan', an apt description of the wandering activity carried out in one, particularly since the art of taking such a vehicle on tour is called 'motorcaravanning'.

However, most New Zealanders call them campervans, and because our two-berth vehicle with its sleek streamlined shape, and minus the ubiquitous top deck overhanging the driving cab, did indeed look like a large van, I have referred to it as such, even though 'van' is too plain a description for the sophistication it contained. Larger four and six-berth vehicles, because of their boxy 'house' shape and top deck, have been referred to throughout as motorhomes so that you can picture easily their distinctive appearance.

NORTH ISLAND OF NEW ZEALAND

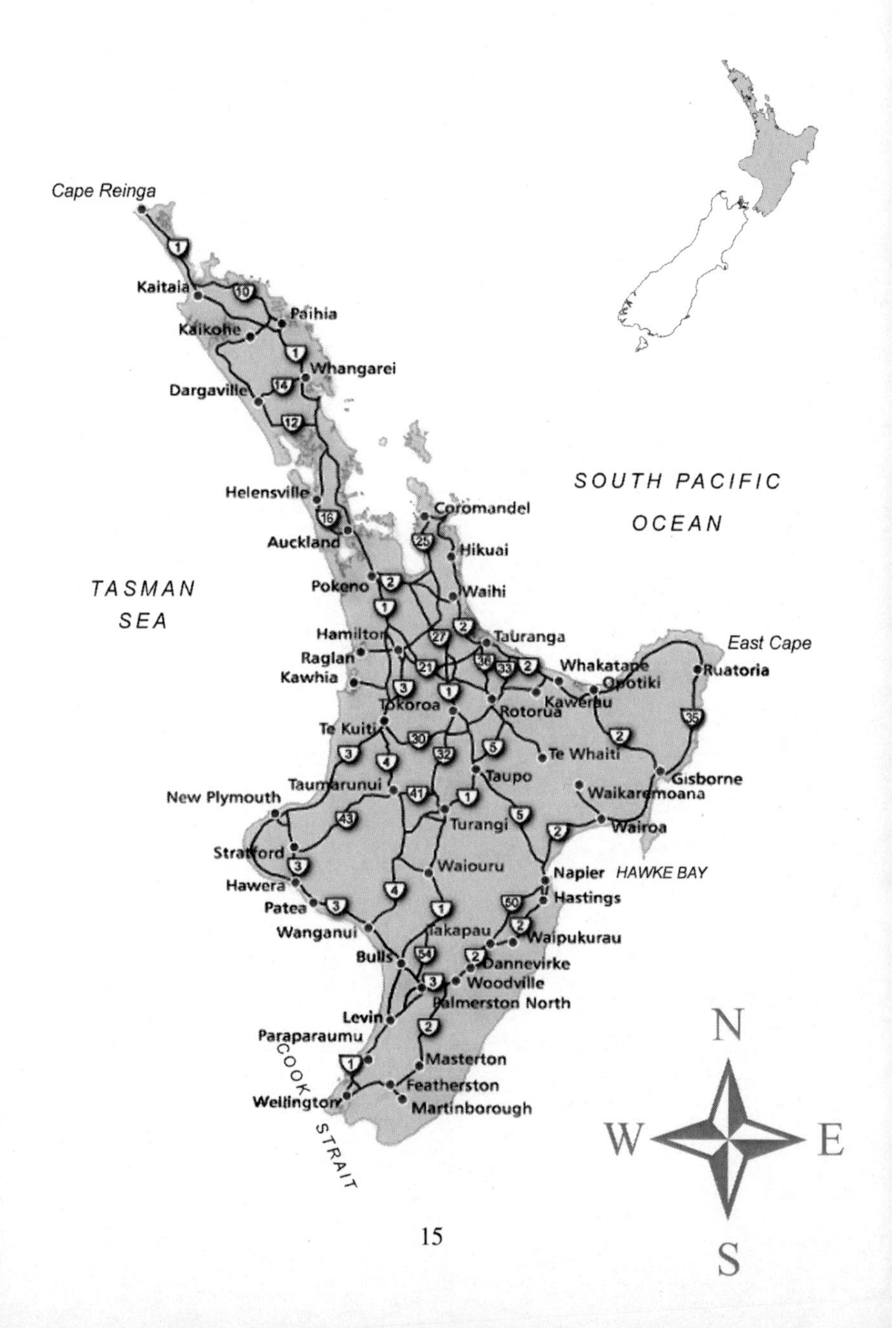

SOUTH ISLAND OF NEW ZEALAND

CONTENTS

CHAPTER 1

WHY MOTORHOME?

Not one of our friends can understand why we love life on the road – not even our own children!

'Er, you don't seem the *type* to camp…' 'Why do you go to all that trouble (*trouble*?) when you could fly everywhere and stay in hotels?' 'I can't imagine you roughing it…' (we don't), and the comments continue to come. 'Look, just have a month in Surfers Paradise and you'll feel great again.' (We do, often.) Occasionally there is a wistful '…but I've always thought I'd like to do it one day…' and that is where the conversation ends. What a pity.

I want to dispel notions of our insanity and cussedness, and reassure readers that we are two of the millions of people around the world who see camping/motorhoming/caravanning – call it what you will – as the most relaxing way to holiday, the way that brings us up close to a place and its people *in a more comfortable way* than cycling, horse-trekking, train travel, walking, motoring or any of the other land-based options that abound. With our home on our back, we can go anywhere, do anything, and see everything! It is impossible to remain detached from the surrounding environment when shopping for local produce in a local supermarket, using public transport, sharing communal facilities in the campgrounds, talking there to visitors from abroad and finding out their views on New Zealand, and seeing first-hand what they are seeing, what activities they are undertaking, and often doing the same thing ourselves.

We found on this trip that a typical motorhomer from overseas visits the Bay of Islands if time permits, sees a few major attractions in Auckland, 'does' Rotorua, and Wellington briefly on the way to the Cook Strait ferry crossing, and then tours the South Island, prime destinations there being Aoraki Mount Cook and

Queenstown. Major attractions on the way are the Waitomo Caves in the North Island, the West Coast of the South Island and the Southern Alps, anything in Queenstown and the surrounding region, Milford Sound, and the Royal Albatross Colony in Dunedin. These are the famous sightseeing attractions that appear in overseas publications.

But, as we discovered on this journey, visiting many places we'd never been to in all our decades of living here, there is so much more to New Zealand than that. Like all New Zealanders, we know a good beach when we see one, we worship the richness of our native forests and bush, and we are proud of the places, many of them right off the beaten track, that mirror our unique culture and heritage. There are plenty of extras on offer in New Zealand, and we found that our time on the road was not long enough to do justice to all of them. However, we tried, and travelled long distances some days in our effort to see what we could. When I look back on our holiday I realise we couldn't have covered the ground, done as much, and really lived life to the full unless we'd toured by motorhome.

Four challenging weeks on the road as tourists in our own country changed us for the better, gave us an enhanced appreciation of New Zealand's spine-tingling natural beauty unduplicated elsewhere, but which is too easy to take for granted, gave us admiration for the kindness, the spirit and the humour of hardworking New Zealanders engaged in the tourist and service industries, and gratitude for the achievements of the nineteenth century pioneers who set up this great little country to be the microcosm of much that is finest in the world today. We had a month full of re-awakened delight in the simple pleasures of life – fresh, pure air, unparalleled views, great food (even the sausages and pies were sensational), hot showers, splendid wine, grass underfoot, and deep sleep. It was the best holiday we've ever had, and one that we can't stop talking about.

So what made us do it?

M. and I are members of British camping organizations The Caravan Club and The Camping and Caravanning Club. We are experienced caravanners and have undertaken three extensive tours of Europe in the last 30 years. We want to tour again to revisit favourite places, and to have the excitement of exploring countries not yet seen. But should we tow a caravan again or, in view of our senior status, take the physically easier option of travelling by motorhome?

Caravanning has suited us very well and has the overwhelming advantage that a caravan can be set up in a camp, leaving us free to drive the car off to sightsee, shop, and dine, secure in the knowledge that we can return to base and have a very comfortable roof over our heads for the night. However, the benefits of motorcaravanning are many. First of all, progress is always forward because it is not necessary to return to a fixed base. Secondly, there are no setting-up rituals to go through other than connecting the electric power cable to a socket, and putting on the kettle, and you can act on impulse and depart from a camp within two minutes if you want to. Thirdly, the manoeuvrability of a motorhome gives greater licence to free camp in a field, beside a lake, in a quiet country lay-by, even in a town square. We are cautious types and would never free camp in Europe, but we know New Zealanders who have, many times, in perfect safety. A motorhome is preferable also if one is tackling dubious-looking country roads because the driver can extricate the vehicle easily if the going gets tough, and it is always an advantage to be able to pull up in a roadside rest place to make a cup of tea and a sandwich without having to wind down the caravan steadies for balance.

The pros and cons of caravanning versus driving a motorhome next time in Europe had hung over our heads for a few years and eventually, in 2004, after many enjoyable discussions planning routes and destinations with a European road atlas in front of us, we decided to hire a motorhome in England and test-drive it through Spain. The distances in Spain are vast, and much of the terrain is arid and rather boring. We had already crossed the country in a caravan in 1973, rather an exciting trip considering that Spain was still ruled by General Franco and the Spain we saw then was the 'old Spain', but had found the landscape one to cover quickly. This we could accomplish more easily in a motorhome, and if we didn't like the mode of travel we would return the van to England and repeat the previous activities which had served us so well, buying a suitable towing car and a nearly new caravan, and setting off again.

Fortunately, commonsense prevailed. Why on earth had we suffered all this indecision when the obvious course of action was to test-drive a motorhome through *New Zealand*! With the minimum of fuss, in our own surroundings, we would find out which sort of long-term casual travel we preferred. Everything fell into place.

Arrangements started auspiciously with my phone call to Maui Rentals, New Zealand's largest motorhome rental company, in July 2004 to enquire about the availability and the cost of hiring a motorhome for two people during February/March 2005. The efficient and pleasant response to that one phone call by the helpful company representative was a benchmark for the excellence to follow.

'The type of vehicle that will suit you and your husband best is the Spirit 2T/S,' she replied. 'We have plenty of them and you will not need to make your decision to hire until early November. Our present prices will hold firm until the end of March 2005, and we will require a deposit when you book.'

I asked her what the average length of hire time was for a Maui motorhome.

'Most tourists do New Zealand in three weeks!' she said.

I thought it didn't seem long enough to tour New Zealand properly, and she agreed, but said that travellers from the northern hemisphere often did New Zealand first before moving on to tour Australia, and because of the relative size of the two countries they allotted less time to New Zealand. It seemed a perfectly reasonable explanation.

‘What about Australians who do a Maui tour?’ I asked.

‘It’s about the same length of time, too, because they’re using their annual leave to do it.’

Our planned month on the road seemed luxurious in comparison; little did we know that one could tour New Zealand for at least two months and still feel there was more to see and do.

At the end of October 2004, on a quiet Sunday morning, we drove to the Auckland branch of Maui Motorhomes and Rental Cars at 36 Richard Pearse Drive, Mangere, a five minute drive from the Auckland International Airport terminal. The company’s address turned out to be in the middle of a light industrial area, one which we, and almost every other Aucklander, were never likely to visit. We had no idea what to expect.

We drove through the entry barrier arm to the visitor parking lot and stared in utter disbelief. Facing us was a large, ultra-modern building fronted with huge plate glass windows through which we could see a crowd of people. To the left was a long, laned forecourt for returning vans, with petrol and diesel pumps, and beyond that a row of hangar-like vehicle workshops. On the right was a line-up of Britz and Maui vans and motorhomes, ready for inspection or for immediate take-off in the departure lane, and we glimpsed an area at the rear, which looked half the size of a rugby field and held dozens and dozens of vehicles lined up neatly in rows. The evident scale of the operation was breathtaking. Our amazement was reinforced when we entered through automatic glass doors into a cavernous, air-conditioned business area, which was dominated in the centre by a semi-circular desk, staffed by three very busy receptionists. I saw Internet connections for the customers, a foreign exchange facility, cold drinks and snacks cabinets, comfortable seating, racks of literature on New Zealand tourist attractions, plenty of space to park luggage and camping packs while being attended to, and the orderly bustle of a top-flight and well-staffed organisation moving nearly 30 newly-arrived tourists and their baggage quickly and efficiently into their pre-booked vehicles, or supplying them with their camping equipment. The tourists had evidently arrived on flights early that morning and taken advantage of the complimentary transfer from the airport. (One of the disadvantages of the time distance between New Zealand and the northern hemisphere is that long haul flights often land at an ungodly hour). I had the feeling that although we had decided to look at other hire companies, we were most likely to settle for this one.

We were directed to the Customer Service Enquiries Office upstairs and told Jocelyn Jacobs, the wonderfully efficient and friendly sales representative, of our requirements, and our firm dates of travel – 12 February to 12 March 2005 – and she whisked us downstairs to inspect the various vehicles. To me, this is always the fun part, while I play imaginary housekeeper, decide whether the living arrangements will suit me, and check out the storage; M. is the one who kicks the tyres and asks about the engine. Jocelyn agreed with my suggestion that a Spirit 2T/S would suit us, and said that we wouldn't achieve much by booking the next size up, a Spirit 4, and paying an extra $45 on average per day, or $1,305 for our intended 29-day hire. She was right, although there were times we would have welcomed the 35 centimetre extra vehicle width, and the sleeping space above the driving cab to use as a top locker, always the easiest to get to. She also recommended hiring a Maui van over one of the company's Britz branded vans because the Maui fleet was very up-to-date, and said she would reserve one of the newest vans for us. In no time at all she had secured our details, noted our decision to drop the campervan off at their depot in Christchurch at the end of the holiday so that we could fly from there directly back to Auckland, worked out the standard hire rate for 17 days in February of $236 per day at $4,012, minus $119 for long-hire discount, and for 12 days in March at $155 per day at $1,860 minus $36 for long-hire discount (long-hire being 5 to 20 days), plus $180 one-way fee for depositing the van in Christchurch and not bringing it back to the Auckland base, for a total charge of

$5,897 including GST. Should we decide to take this offer, a deposit of $1,143.40 would have to be made on booking.

Jocelyn also suggested that we take out the Excess Reduction 2 insurance cover which gave us complete cover without excess for damage to the vehicle or the property of a third party, but said this and the other insurance options available didn't need to be decided until we collected the van on 12 February.

Our vehicle was noted on the quotation form as a Spirit 2 Deluxe 2BTSM, could be collected from 7 a.m. onwards on the day of departure, and had to be returned in Christchurch by 5 p.m. on 12 March. She also said we would be liable on return of the van for the Government-imposed Diesel Tax Recovery fee, which for our vehicle would be $2.47 per 100 kilometres.

It was strongly recommended that we decide fairly soon if we were going to proceed with the booking. She clicked her computer and said that Maui Rentals still had 197 vans available for the dates in question, but that November was upon us and with it the annual upsurge in bookings for the summer.

On the way out we were given an AA-published Maui Motorhome Guide, a thick volume with excellent information on what to see and do, where to stay, and essential operating instructions in English and German for the Maui vehicles, and a comprehensive booklet giving all the vehicle types, with diagrams of the daytime and sleeping layouts, vehicle specifications, equipment provided and extra items for hire, branch locations and opening hours, international sales offices, extra service benefits and insurance options, and the terms and conditions of hire. We were even provided with a disc with which to open the exit barrier. Everything had been thought of. We were to discover later that Jocelyn's friendliness, super-efficiency, patience and sheer *niceness* were symptomatic of all our subsequent dealings with the company.

We hadn't expected anything like it. Our English experiences of sizing up various makes of motorhome and caravan and of actually buying three caravans to tour with on different holidays had sometimes been difficult. Perhaps it was the fact that the Maui organisation is geared particularly for inbound tourism that made it all such a slick and easy operation for us, but that doesn't explain the 'people' factor. Perhaps we did indeed need to discover our own country through a tourist's eyes, for that Sunday's experience was repeated every day, in every aspect of the tourist industry that we covered, for the month we travelled – warm service and friendly smiles, with no supercilious waiters, no rip-offs, no bribery or shoving to get to the head of a queue, no restaurateurs mysteriously upping the price of a meal, all tips gratefully received with thanks, taxis that took the direct route, and drivers who delighted in recommending a moderately-priced restaurant and saying as we got out of the cab '…and tell them I sent you!'

We drove out onto the road in a daze, utterly dumbfounded at the scale and expertise of the enterprise. Tourism statistics and visitor arrivals are always the subject of reports in the newspapers and are read with interest because the New Zealand economy depends greatly on incoming tourist dollars, but until one encounters an operation such as we did that Sunday morning, set up entirely for one kind of massive tourism, the topic has little meaning; the New Zealanders we know are, like us, more actively concerned with their own departures for vacations overseas than with what is occurring here. No right-minded business sets up a large-scale operation unless circumstances warrant it, and we were to discover during our month on the road that what we had seen at the Maui headquarters is just the tip of the tourism iceberg.

We had planned to visit two other motorhome rental firms that day, Pacific Horizon Travelhomes whose Auckland branch is situated at Aintree Avenue, Mangere, a two minute drive from the Maui depot, and Kea Campers (New Zealand) Limited, at Glenfield on Auckland's North Shore. We had decided not to argue with the excellence of the operation at Maui, but it was prudent to make a comparison with another company. Pacific Horizon Travelhomes was the closest, so we called there.

Pacific Horizon's brochure gave just one address, that of its Wellington office, and it was immediately obvious on arriving at Aintree Avenue that we were at a branch, which seems odd when you consider that Auckland is the main international airport. The yard was unpaved for the most part, and a small office building in the corner was in a state of slight disarray. We were the only customers there. The pleasant receptionist said they were in the process of upgrading and re-organising, and escorted us to a row of vans, two of which we were able to view, the others having been returned recently and not yet cleaned and ready for inspection. We examined a 2+1-berth van, the equivalent of the one we had been quoted on at Maui, and a 4+2-berth van. They were attractive vehicles, very well appointed and with all the expected features, but the Eclipse 2+1-berth van was considerably smaller overall than the Maui vehicle. The next size up, the Eclipse 4+2-berth, had a pull-down handbasin in the shower/toilet, and I knew from our 1997 caravan tour of Europe, where we towed a large Lunar Clubman caravan, how nice it is to have a handbasin to oneself, but it was not an essential item for two people who were planning to spend only a month away. Next to Maui motorhomes, the Pacific Horizon motorhomes were the most popular on the road and I believe that if you dealt only with that company, and did not wish to investigate further, you would be delighted with your choice. We came away from the Pacific Horizon yard with their booklet giving all details of price, layouts, vehicle specifications and equipment, and over the next few days I weighed up the relative merits of each deal. We didn't investigate Kea Campers. If Maui and Pacific Horizon, in competition with each other, were as closely aligned in product, service and price as they seemed to be, we could see little point in visiting a third company. However, it is important to know that although we didn't visit Kea Campers, it was the Supreme Award Winner and Major Category Winner for Tourism and Transportation Services in 2005 at the Annual Tourism New Zealand awards, and their campervans, particularly the smaller ones, were the ones most often seen after Maui and Pacific Horizon vans as we toured around the country.

Details of Maui Motorhomes, Pacific Horizon Travelhomes and Kea Campers are given in the Appendix. A close perusal of their extensive websites is strongly recommended, and you will find the information given in this chapter, plus other relevant and important information such as van layout and the fine print of rental agreements, on your screen for printing out in ready reference format.

The visit to Maui had made up our minds. If we were contemplating a motorcaravan trip through Spain to see whether we liked that sort of touring and wanted to continue around Europe with it, we would be utterly *mad* not to sort out the pros and cons of such a venture in New Zealand first, where we had a formidable company infrastructure supporting us to take care of any problems, where there was no language barrier, no devastating mileage to cover in a relatively short time, and, we hoped, perfect late summer weather. One knows the ropes in one's own country.

I spent a pleasurable 10 days re-reading the brochures. There were subtle differences in the details. Pacific Horizon's fridges ran off gas, as well as 12 volt battery and 240 volt electricity, their heaters/coolers ran off gas, and the hot water was heated by gas. It was therefore possible to free camp 'without dependence on a holiday park connection'. However the Maui fridge operated well from the 12 volt battery as we soon discovered when our electric cable developed a fault just two days into the trip.

Pacific Horizon Travelhomes does not charge for Road Diesel Tax, but I presume it is built into the overall price, and nor does it charge one-way fees, or charge for the LPG gas used. Like Maui Motorhomes, the company allows unlimited mileage. An electric jug, toaster and frypan is provided with all the other kitchen utensils, but not by Maui Motorhomes, which provides on request a toaster and a coffee plunger as part of the kitchen kit, but no electric jug or frypan, and one has to boil up a kettle on the gas stove for a cup of tea. Both companies operate a Freephone service. Pacific Horizon charges $55 for mobile phone hire, but includes a $20 pre-pay card. Maui does not charge for mobile phone hire, but you have to load your own credit using your credit card, or you can pay $20, with $20 of credit pre-loaded. Pacific Horizon charges $15 for the hire of a table and $5 for each chair, whereas Maui charges $22 for the table and $12 for each chair. Pacific Horizon has gas barbecues for hire at $45, or charcoal ones for $35, TVs for $60, bike racks for $55, snow chains for $35, port-a-cots for $55, and child safety sleep nets for $15. Maui provides snow chains free of charge, but has none of the other options listed in its brochure. Both companies hire baby car seats and child booster seats for $25 per rental.

It is possible to take out an all-inclusive package with Maui that includes the Excess Reduction 2 insurance option, one-way fee (if applicable), the Diesel Tax Recovery fee, a pre-purchase gas option, a picnic table and two chairs, and one baby car or booster seat.

Both companies provide a Starter Pack, the contents of which are not mentioned in Pacific Horizon's brochure, but which, with Maui, consist of a toilet roll, two packets of toilet chemical crystals, matches, miniature toilet soap, facial tissues, dishwashing detergent, and a pair of light rubber gloves to be used when emptying and rinsing out the toilet cassette. The items are very handy for use during the first two days until you have sorted out all your requirements.

Pacific Horizon Travelhomes provides a copy of the New Zealand Traffic Rules with each vehicle. I didn't notice that in the Maui van we hired, but it may have been there on the driver's side. Pacific Horizon Travelhomes also supplies a New Zealand road atlas, but Maui's road atlas is available for purchase only at $24.95. I, as the navigator on our journeys, am extremely fussy about the quality of my maps and would never use a road atlas provided by someone else unless I had established that it was the very best for my purpose, so that provision didn't interest me. Importantly, for inbound tourists, Maui Motorhomes has free luggage storage at their Auckland and Christchurch branches.

There was no mention in the Pacific Horizon brochure of tents and other camping equipment for hire, which didn't bother me, of course, but I mention Maui's offerings here in case it is of interest. Their tents, suitable for two to four people, cost $75 per rental. They also have a Camping Kit, which consists of tent, breadboard, kettle, teapot, frying pan, knives, can opener, serving utensils, clothes pegs, a torch, pots, a vegetable peeler, cutlery, crockery and sleeping equipment. The charge for all that is $20 per day, with a maximum charge of $200 for two persons.

And what of the vehicle hire prices? Here they are.

As I've written, our Maui Motorhomes price per day for a 2+1 person campervan was $236 from 12-28 February in the peak season, and dropped off to $155 per day from 1-12 March. Discounts for long-term hire for the two periods totalled $155, making the total price payable for those dates $5,717.

Pacific Horizon's per day charges for the same period were $210 for 17 days in February, and $188 for 12 days in March. Their long-hire discount, from 21-28 days, was 3 per cent, and from 29-39 days was 5 per cent. With the $52.50 discount calculated for nine days of hire, the total of $5,826 dropped to $5,773.50, only $56.50 more expensive than the rate from Maui minus their discount.

So basic price was *not* a factor in choosing between these two companies over our hire period. What *were* the factors? First of all, with Pacific Horizon Travelhomes, we were required to pay $10 per day, or $290 for us, to reserve one of the newest vehicles under 18 months old with cab air-conditioning, low mileage, and a CD player, all of which were important to us, but which were provided free of charge at Maui. We didn't see why we should have to pay extra for any of these things. It would have been more comfortable to have had carpet underfoot, which I missed greatly, but I could do without it and anyway the Maui vans we had inspected had well-laid vinyl in a tasteful blue. The reason we chose to hire our motorcaravan from Maui Motorhomes was because of the readily apparent size and organisation of the company, and the supreme excellence of the staff we encountered that Sunday morning.

On 11 November I telephoned Jocelyn and said we wished to confirm our booking with her company, paid the $1,143.40 deposit by credit card, and that was that! She reiterated that she would make sure we got a new model van, warned us not to delay booking for our Cook Strait ferry crossing, and wished us well.

I immediately booked our airfares from Christchurch to Auckland on the early afternoon of 13 March, which would give us a well-deserved night in a hotel after we had returned the van to the Maui depot at 5 p.m. on 12 March. Although we were able to get a 'free' flight on Air New Zealand because of accumulated air points, there was still a surcharge of $39.80 each for fuel and security costs.

The next day we left for a few weeks' holiday in Queensland, Australia, and by the time we returned the Christmas rush was upon us, so it was the middle of January before I made the booking for the Cook Strait ferry service which plies between the North and South Islands. But before I could nominate the day of travel, I had to prepare a rough North Island itinerary and it was not easy to do. Who could tell what we would enjoy, how long we might want to stay in a place, or how quickly leave? Murray wanted to drive on the sand along the Ninety Mile Beach at the top of the North Island (he later found out that he couldn't), and visit Cape Reinga again, we both wanted to get as far up the Coromandel Peninsula as possible, I wanted to travel to the Hawkes Bay and do a food and wine tour, and I had an unexpected yearning to revisit the Wairarapa on our way to Wellington and the ferry. I hadn't been there for 40 years!

There was no easy solution, and in the end we decided to divide the time away equally between the two islands, so on 13 January 2005 I booked the 8 a.m. sailing on the *Lynx* ferry on 25 February. Three ferries cross Cook Strait daily from Wellington to Picton and return, on what is described on the Interislander website as 'one of the world's most scenic ferry journeys', a claim I endorse; the *Aratere* and the *Arahura,* which are large, 'traditional' ferries, and take three hours to cross, and the smaller *Lynx*, a catamaran, which covers the journey in two and a quarter hours. Up to six return sailings cross Cook Strait daily in the peak season. Three types of fare are offered, but if you are booking from outside New Zealand your bookings will be limited to the most flexible fare type, called 'Easy Change Fares', which allows passengers to cancel, without any cancellation fees, right up to the time of check-in.

I had only just made the booking in time. I looked at the website two days later, and all the crossings for 25 February, six weeks away, were full. The cost for the one-way sailing for two people over 60 years old plus vehicle length of 6.60 metres was $290. Had I known then our preferred date to cross, I could have booked through Maui at the time of confirming our trip. However the Internet has changed the face of the travel industry and made it simple to have a hands-on approach. Five minutes after I had logged in all the application and payment details for the ferry crossing, the email reply came back: 'Your booking arrangements have been confirmed. Booking Number: W64266; Password: Magi.' What could be easier? I felt we were under way!

CHAPTER 2

VEHICLE SPECIFICATIONS

Our 2.5L Turbo Diesel campervan had a Volkswagen engine, 5-speed manual transmission, and power steering. The fuel tank held 75 litres, and fuel consumption per 100 kilometres was expected to be about 10 litres. The fresh water tank held 85 litres, as did the grey or wastewater tank. The power supply was provided through a 12 volt battery which recharged itself as we drove, and a 240 volt mains supply which we hooked into on arrival in a camp. A large capacity LPG gas cylinder was fitted into a locker accessible from the outside only.

There were two batteries in the vehicle, one under the bonnet for starting the engine, and the other, located at the rear in a locker under a divan, operated the lights, refrigerator and water pump. These automatically switched onto the 240 volt circuit when we plugged into a power socket at a camping ground. We never needed to heat water, but the operations manual at the rear of the Maui Motorhomes 2005 guidebook lists it as being gas-operated.

The hot and cold water supply was pressurised. The driving cab had air-conditioning and heating, and the main cab had 240 volt heating.

The stainless steel sink had a good tap, and the benchtop at the side was of stainless steel, ridged for drainage. The cupboard underneath the sink held cutlery and crockery drawers, which pulled out smoothly on runners, and there was a moderately-sized storage space underneath the bottom drawer. The under-benchtop microwave ran off 240 volt power, and was positioned above the 60 litre fridge/freezer, the usual size for a touring vehicle. The two-burner gas stove situated opposite had a grill unit. There was no separate oven. On a wall adjacent to the gas stove were two power plugs for use with electrical appliances. The pot cupboard under the gas stove was very roomy, and the bottom shelf held plenty of bulky items like the washing powder, sliced bread, the toaster, extra tinned food which I bought from time to time, a small supply of potatoes, and cake and biscuit tins. A cupboard to the side of this, over the heater, was perfectly suited to drinks storage and held the gin, a few bottles of wine, a six-pack of beer and one of tonic water, bottled water in case we had an emergency, soft drinks, and tall items like cooking oil and flyspray which didn't fit anywhere else.

The wardrobe space was lamentable, not nearly wide enough even for just two people, and our polar fleece jackets and my rain jacket almost filled it up. There were only two overhead lockers, the sort I always prefer because I don't have to bend down to use them. I filled one with the tea, coffee, basic tinned food, our vitamins, and other supplies of small size, and the one adjacent was used for the torches, CDs, reading material, spare reading glasses, the mobile phone recharger, and all the other small everyday items which didn't fit anywhere else but needed to be stored safely. A boxed-in shelf above the wardrobe held our toilet bags, and our large medical kit, without which we never travel, was pushed for easy access into the bottom of the wardrobe.

The toilet/shower cubicle was spacious enough and lined with shiny white plastic, and the chemical toilet, a Thetford, was extremely efficient.

The excellent, roomy driving cab had fully adjustable seats, and plenty of door storage on my side for maps, camping guides, and information booklets, my water bottle, and a folding umbrella. M. had an ingenious drink holder fitted above the floor behind his seat, where he could reach down without danger while driving and pull out his bottle of water. The dining table was clipped in securely behind his seat for travelling, and the fire extinguisher had its special slot behind my seat.

To the rear of the campervan on either side of the 'hallway' were two single divans measuring 1.84 metres x 0.60 metres, with four lift-up lockers underneath of which only two could be used for bedding and clothing storage. One locker was filled with the rear battery, which had so many important-looking bits to it that we decided not to pack anything in around it in case we damaged a vital part; the other rear locker held the power cable when travelling, the hoses for water and drainage, a bucket, broom, brush and shovel, pegs, and the stretcher-style third bed for a child which could be fitted above one of the divans. We used this rear space as our shoe locker. Shoes take up a lot of space, are always dirty when you camp, and can't be packed alongside other articles.

The gap between the divans was bridged at night with the dining table and an extra wooden base which folded away neatly during the day. The upholstered back rests fitted across the gap and formed a very comfortable double bed measuring 1.84 metres x 1.74 metres.

The vehicle was well-equipped with navy blue cotton curtains which fastened back during the day, and we felt very private at night. The divan seats and backrests were covered with a pleasantly patterned and sturdy dark blue fabric, which sponged down well if food got spilt, and, as I have said, the floor was fitted with blue vinyl. The driving seats and the floor of the cab were coloured a soft grey, and the fronts of the cupboard doors were of light-coloured imitation wood. The decoration of the interior was harmonious and restful.

Fortunately for me, there were interior holds at both sides of the large sliding door behind my seat so that I could hoist myself into the van, and I was very glad they were there. Our campervan had double doors at the rear which we never used, but if you camped by a beach or lake it would be nice to open them and put your table and chairs directly outside. We decided not to hire a table and chairs – we were going to be away for just one month, most of which would be spent on the road to cover the distance we had set ourselves. As we were to discover, all the Top 10 camps had barbecue-style picnic tables dotted around the grounds, sometimes one table to every two pitches, so we never felt as though we had to be trapped indoors.

If we were to do a similar trip again, we would hire the Spirit 4 motorhome (booking code 4BM), which sleeps four adults, and would use the extra bed space above the cab for storage. The 4-berth vehicle also has a wider wardrobe, fly screens on all windows in the living area, and it is 35 centimetres wider. We found it annoying to have to move out of each other's way all the time in the narrow kitchen area. We are both quite thin; it would be hellish if you were plump.

The 4 and 6-berth motorhomes both have 2.2L Turbo Diesel Mercedes engines and a choice of manual or automatic transmissions, and hold 68 litres of fuel. The fuel consumption for both vehicles is given as 15 litres per 100 kilometres.

Our campervan's dimensions were: length 6.60 metres, width 1.90 metres, outside height 2.57 metres, and interior height 1.85 metres. The 4 and 6-berth motorhomes both had the same width, 2.25 metres, outside height 2.95 metres, and interior height of 2.0 metres, but the 4-berth was 6.10 metres long, and the 6-berth the same as ours at 6.60 metres long. If you are booking your Cook Strait ferry crossing yourself, you will need to give the length of your vehicle.

Maui Motorhomes have a smaller 2+1-berth campervan which has 5-speed manual transmission, takes unleaded petrol, and has power steering, but there is no cab air-conditioning, which we found an absolute lifesaver for the first two weeks of our tour, and there is no shower, toilet or microwave. The fresh water tank holds 35 litres, and supplies cold water only. It is too basic for us, and we never considered it, but we saw quite a few on the road during our travels.

Here are relative hire prices for the other three vehicles besides ours in the Maui stable, for the period of our trip. You already have our totals in the previous chapter, together with the comparisons with Pacific Horizon Travelhomes.

Spirit 2, Booking Code 2BM

Peak season	17 days @ $186 per day	$3,162
Off-peak shoulder	12 days @ 120 per day	$1,440
		$4,602

Spirit 4, Booking Code 4BM

Peak season	17 days @ $282 per day	$4,794
Off-peak shoulder	12 days @ $199 per day	$2,388
		$7,182

Spirit 6, Booking Code 6BM

Peak season	17 days @ $307 per day	$5,219
Off-peak shoulder	12 days @ $221 per day	$2,652
		$7,871

The over-all discount for our hire of 29 days, on peak and off-peak days, was $155 or 2.64%. Applying the same rate of percentage discount, the hire prices for the three vehicles above would be $$4,481, $6,993, and $7,664. The difference isn't huge, and shouldn't be a factor in weighing up your choice of a campervan or motorhome.

CHAPTER 3

WHAT TO PACK

Appearances aren't important in a camping ground. The splendid feature of stepping out of your vehicle looking a little shabby is that everyone else does too, that's the nature of the holiday. Campers are not snobs. The fact that you are *there* is enough to guarantee acceptance by fellow travellers. It's the reverse of 'keeping up appearances', just 'appearance' by a different definition, that of your presence, and a refreshing and relaxing change from the sartorial regimentation of one's normal life.

At home in Auckland I sometimes change my clothes four times a day to suit my various activities. This is a nuisance when travelling and it won't be necessary if you take the right gear. Ideally, at the end of a busy day's travel and sightseeing, all you should need to do is swap your old shorts, skirt, or trousers for a better skirt, or trousers, keep the same shirt or top on, change your shoes, and go out for the evening. Although you mightn't look as glamorous as usual, you will not be refused admission anywhere. New Zealand is not a country where you need to dress up, and I can say that I had all the better a holiday for it.

There are certain clothes for both men and women that travel well when camping – shorts, jeans, and dark coloured shirts and tops. I have a preference for taking away only black, navy or denim clothes, and nothing that has to be ironed, of course. However I do possess a shirt and matching shorts in light blue Tencel, a marvellous fabric which seems to shed dirt and can easily cope without an iron. The shorts are baggy and held up with an elastic waistband which is starting to give way and I never wear them in Auckland, but for a camping trip they are fine! I wore them almost every day for over two weeks in the baking hot weather at the start of the trip, changing at night for dinner into a pair of old beige chinos. I packed a pair of jeans for the cooler South Island temperatures, and a pair of smart black drip-dry Valentino jeans which have seen long service for my ‘good’ trousers. I took seven tops and shirts, all in black or dark colours, and a pale blue T-shirt to wear with my black jeans. I only wore four of the tops, plus the Tencel shirt. For shoes, really the most important items to pack because the success of any holiday depends on having the right shoes for the different occasions, I took an old pair of Nike trainers, some sandals for the hot North Island weather, black cotton rope-soled espadrilles which were very comfortable in the van when we were driving along, a pair of stoutish waterproof Ecco lace-ups for colder, or wet weather, and Nike plastic slides for wearing in the shower. I also took a pair of Sebago moccasins which look appropriate with almost all casual wear, especially shorts and jeans, and are an excellent shoe for travelling as they are comfortable worn on bare feet. In London in the mid 1990s I had gone to Russell and Bromley in Bond Street to look at shoes, and during a chat with the saleswoman she said that if there was one pair of shoes which should be in every woman’s travelling wardrobe it was brown Sebagos. She had recently toured New Zealand and Australia and had spent the entire holiday in her Sebagos without suffering sore feet, corns or blisters, and was now an ardent advocate of their comfort and versatility.

I packed a black cashmere v-neck sweater, warm and very light, and took the precaution of including some thermal vests because the weather in the South Island can be quite chilly in March. I retrieved an old navy blue polar fleece jacket and a lightweight hooded rain jacket from the back of the hall cupboard, and took a baseball cap and a battered pack-flat sunhat in which I looked so dreadful that I discarded it early on, much to M.’s relief. Like my clothes, my jewellery was minimal – a plastic Swatch watch with an easy-read dial, my wedding ring, and some small pearl stud earrings which I never wore.

M. wore his dark navy blue cotton shorts for the first two weeks and alternated three Polo shirts in black, navy and blue, and in Wellington he changed into some navy blue cotton chinos which he kept on for another two weeks. He took a pair of crease-resistant navy microfibre trousers for best. He packed a heavy cable knit sweater and a navy polar fleece jacket, alternated his footwear between tennis trainers during the day and black leather slip-ons at night, and took his Nike slides for use in the showers. When I packed up our gear to come home, I found in the hose and broom locker a bag with three extra pairs of shoes which he hadn't worn – brown leather Sebagos, spare trainers, and heavy waterproof Ecco lace-ups. He said he'd forgotten about them.

Keeping up with our laundry was never a problem. All the Top 10 camps we stayed in had large laundries with new coin-operated Maytag commercial washers and dryers, and an ironing board and iron were always available if I had wanted to use them. On the journey I saw plenty of middle-aged women religiously ironing their husband's cotton shirts. Old habits die hard, I know, but there comes a time when a line has to be drawn under those habits. If you pack clothes made from the right sort of fabrics, all they need is a quick smooth down when they come out of the dryer. After all, *you* are roughing it, and so should your clothes!

If you decide to invest in a new pair of trainers or similar sports shoes for sightseeing comfort, I recommend strongly buying these in a practical dark colour. Many of the most enjoyable sights and activities in New Zealand involve a walk through damp forest, or across steaming volcanic rocks and soil, or dusty tussockland, and along stony, wet foreshores. I checked in the Foot Locker and Stirling Sports stores at the Westfield Shopping Centre in Riccarton, Christchurch and saw several designs. Indeed New Zealand, with its emphasis on outdoor life, is the ideal place to buy every type of sports and casual footwear, so do not despair if you have to leave home without anything suitable.

There is no need to pack a bulky towelling dressing gown, or a white satin robe, two unnecessary items of clothing I happened to notice on campers during this trip. If you must shower in the mornings, then dress properly first before leaving your van. Seasoned campers shower on arrival at their camp in the late afternoon, or at night after dinner, and avoid the morning queues and the uncomfortable feeling of entering a wet shower stall immediately after a complete stranger has occupied it. In the morning, all you have to do is jump into your travelling clothes, have a quick breakfast, put out the rubbish, and depart.

As a rule of thumb, before you pack, lay out your shorts, skirts or trousers and jeans on the bed and make sure that you have three tops which will make a harmonious combination with each of your bottoms. Because of the excellent laundry facilities at Top 10 camps, you will need just one item of sleepwear, and the minimum of underwear.

The items of clothing we should have taken away were our swimming togs. We dawdled on the most magnificent beaches in Northland and on the Coromandel Peninsula where it would have been a pleasure to have pulled the curtains in the van for privacy, changed quickly, and run across the warm, soft pale sand into the limpid turquoise water (yes, the beaches really were like that!). We're not fans of public thermal pools, but New Zealand has some very good complexes at the popular tourist spots of Rotorua in the North Island, and Hanmer Springs north of Christchurch in the South Island, and it's a pity to miss the opportunity for a soak if you've never done it before.

Now to the campervan itself. Included in our information brochure was a list of the items in the various kits we would be issued with.

Personal Kit
Pillow and pillow case
Doona/Duvet, sheet
Towel and tea towel

General Equipment
Toilet paper and toilet chemicals
Pegs
Dustpan and brush
Fire extinguisher
Bucket and hose
Broom
Matches
Ice cube tray

Kitchen Kit
Plates and bowls
Cups and glasses
Knives, forks, spoons
Bottle and can opener
Mixing bowls
Saucepans
Frying pan
Cooking utensils
Chopping board
Kettle, teapot
Coffee plunger (on request)
Toaster (on request)

You will notice that no coathangers are supplied. I took an assortment of old wire dry cleaning hangers and disposed of them before returning home.

In November, when I confirmed our booking, I asked for the two pillows and pillowcases and the duvet to be omitted from the personal kit. I had a hunch that the pillows would be uncomfortable, and I don't like duvets. Before departure M. and I went to the Rebel Sports Store at the Manukau Supa Centa in Cavendish Drive, South Auckland, and bought two splendid Domex sleeping bags for $110 each, of heavy duty navy blue nylon, filled with polyester non-allergenic multifil, and lined with pale blue polycotton, always the most warm and cosy fabric to slide into as it doesn't create arctic reaches at the bottom of the bag in cold weather. They will be useful to lend to our grandsons when they are old enough to go on their own camping trips. We both had our own elderly pillows which we found very comfortable, but which I had intended to replace for some time, so I took them on the trip and dumped them without regret in a waste collection bin on the last day.

I was glad to have inspected the vehicles before we booked, because the first thing I had noticed was the absence of comfortable bolsters on the divans. There's nothing quite as relaxing as putting your feet up in the late afternoon with a drink in one hand, and a trashy magazine in the other, but you do need something to lean against. I had two cushions which had seen better days so I took those also, and they copped the same fate at the end as the pillows.

You cannot manage on one bath towel if you intend to swim, either in the ocean or the excellent public swimming pool complexes which exist in New Zealand. At some of the thermal baths, notably at Rotorua, you will be able to hire towels, but you cannot rely on that service at all places.

I took four hand towels to use at ablution blocks in older camps that might not have a hand-drying facility, and was glad I did. They were very useful in the campervan, too, because I packed a small pump bottle of anti-bacterial liquid soap and kept it by the sink to use before and after preparing food. The sink was never used for ablutions, which took place in the proper facility, or for dishwashing, either, firstly because we used cheap plastic disposable plates, glasses and cups, and secondly because one of M.'s greatest loves is to take the frying pan and saucepan over to the kitchen at night and wash them there in the company of other men deputed to the same chore. There are some rituals of life on the road that are really worthwhile!

We already had a large heavy-duty torch bought for use during the Millennium changeover when the computerised electricity networks were supposed to break down. I found it useful at night when we arrived back at the campervan from dinner and I had to unlock the side locker to turn the gas supply off until the morning – a wise safety precaution, especially as my head was closest to the cylinder! As a safeguard, M. bought a large box-shaped torch which could rest on the ground should we find ourselves travelling at night and need to change a tyre. We never did, but it is a peace of mind article, and could be useful to have on hand if you think you might be free camping in the countryside.

I had a small, shabby radio on my kitchen windowsill which I had been meaning to replace for years, so we took that, used it only once, and it followed the cushions into the bin at the end of the trip. We bought the local newspaper most mornings and that did us for news; we didn't miss it, and our days were so full and entertaining that what was happening in the outer world seemed irrelevant, for a change.

I never travel anywhere, even in New Zealand, without taking a few excellent small utensils, so I packed my bottle opener, my reliable can opener, a pair of kitchen scissors to cut the resistant tops off the plastic bags inside microwaveable meals, my favourite potato peeler, and had a debate with myself as to whether to include my foolproof champagne bottle opener which takes the terror out of that task, but decided to be practical – this was not shaping up to be that sort of holiday.

I have excellent small kitchen knives with serrated edges of the Swiss Victorinox brand, very lightweight and inexpensive, definitely available in the United Kingdom and probably world wide. In Auckland they are stocked by the chefs' shop, House of Knives, at 24 Mt. Eden Road, and cost $10. They are viciously sharp, multifunctional, and are the perfect knife to travel with. I took two with me. They will trim fat off raw meat, carve a roast, slice fruit, vegetables, and French loaves, and butter the bread because they have a rounded tip. I use them to chop onions and garlic finely because the blade is straight, and they make excellent steak or emergency dinner knives. I have even used one to joint a small chicken. I have three, they are all in use all the time in my kitchen, because I cook a lot, and I cannot manage without them.

The kitchen utensils supplied by Maui were of cheap quality, but adequate for their purpose – a bread knife and a carving knife, large serving spoons, a turning fork and a pair of tongs, useful if you barbecue on the facility provided at Top 10 camps, a wooden spoon, the usual array of knives, forks, dessert spoons and teaspoons, a can opener, bottle opener, vegetable peeler, and a small paring knife. I recommend taking your own preferred utensils, as I did.

We had three plastic dinner plates (our campervan was officially designated as a two-adult-one-child van), three bread and butter plates, three mugs and three glasses. There were no bowls. We never used what was provided, because this holiday had to be *easy*. Before departure I went to our local Remuera New World supermarket and stocked up with disposable plastic dinner plates, pudding bowls, beer, wine and water glasses, and insulated foam plastic throwaway cups for tea and coffee. I bought too many dinner plates – we dined out almost every night – and not nearly enough of anything else, and every week I had to top up supplies. I also bought plastic dessertspoons and teaspoons. It was so marvellous in the mornings to make the first cup of tea, prepare our bowls of chopped fresh fruit, open the yoghurts, and throw everything we had used into a rubbish bag and dump it in a bin before departing from the camp. The only item which needed washing was my knife, which I rinsed out quickly under the tap, dried on the tea towel supplied, and put back in the drawer, a task of scarcely 10 seconds.

I packed my own plastic breadboard. I have a horror of using a 'public' one. I have plenty of similar boards, so chucked this one out before flying back. I debated whether or not to take my electric jug, but I like it, it is nearly new, and I would have to bring it back in the plane. In the end I decided to suffer hardship and boil the kettle supplied in the van.

An item which was not supplied with our campervan, but which should be available on request for older campers like me, is an outdoor stepping stool. I am never the fittest of people. We used the wide sliding side door for access when we were camped, and the step up was far too high for my comfort. I should, of course, have stopped at a hardware store and bought a cheap stool, but I thought I should try to improve my fitness and I must confess that after four weeks of travel my leg muscles had strengthened considerably. I noticed that other older travellers had bought stools, and some motorhomes had a small pull-down step at the side door to assist people.

While at the New World supermarket I bought necessary pantry supplies; Twinings Earl Grey, English Breakfast and Peppermint tea bags, Lavazzo ground espresso coffee, a tin each of red salmon, beetroot and asparagus for an emergency meal should the occasion ever arise (which it never did), small sized salt and peppers, Paul Newman's Classic Vinaigrette, Heinz Tomato Ketchup, the incomparable Kato garlic mayonnaise, half a dozen organic eggs which I never cooked and threw out at the end, some Edam cheese, a six-pack of Monteith's Gold beer, and one of Schweppes tonic water to go with our gin, Anchor spreadable butter, Vegemite, a jar of jam, a loaf of sliced toast bread, various yoghurts, vine tomatoes, and plenty of fruit, including two lemons to slice for the G and Ts. Everything fitted properly into the fridge, cupboards or overhead locker. The tall cupboard to the left of the pot cupboard was especially useful, as I have said, for the wine we bought en route and tall soft drink and water bottles. I bought a packet of Persil laundry detergent, a new pair of rubber gloves, sponge cloth bench wipes, and a paper kitchen towel roll. I decanted a small amount of dishwashing liquid into an old bottle and M. used that on the three or four occasions he washed the frying pan, etc.

I have given all this information, which I know is not absolutely necessary, to assist tourists arriving from overseas who need some idea of what they may want to provide themselves. It is not easy to disembark after a long flight, collect one's campervan or motorhome, and be faced immediately with the job of supplying extras particularly if you are not an experienced camper.

If you arrive in New Zealand at Auckland International Airport and collect your vehicle from the depot at Mangere, your best plan is to drive immediately to the Westfield Shopping Centre in Manukau City, a large mall complex with ample outdoor parking, and a journey of only 15 to 20 minutes allowing for a few wrong turns. The Foodtown supermarket, as its name suggests, stocks everything you are likely to need, and the Farmers Department Store has reasonable quality, moderately-priced household items. Here you can buy towels, pillows and pillowcases, and cushions. The Manukau Supa Centa in Cavendish Drive, five minutes' journey from the Westfield mall, has nearly 30 large-format stores specialising in housewares of every type. We bought our excellent sleeping bags here, at Rebel Sports. If you are planning particular outdoor sporting activities during your holiday, this is a good store in which to seek your items.

Visitors landing at Christchurch International Airport who wish to stock up on essential items immediately should drive to the Westfield Shopping Centre at Riccarton, 15 minutes away, where they will find everything they need.

Throughout New Zealand, The Warehouse operates a chain of cut-price variety stores which stock everything imaginable including clothing, toys, gifts, stationery, appliances, household and home entertainment items, and some of the newer stores stock food. The 'big red sheds', as they are known, are worth a visit, and there is one in every major centre in New Zealand. Auckland has several. The chain is renowned for its toys, and if you are travelling with children and need a bucket and spade for the beach, or an on-tour birthday gift, this is the place to visit. If I want to give my young grandsons a treat I take them there and let them choose what they want, with a limit of $10!

This last paragraph applies only to tourists who have hired a van-type vehicle without overhead cab space, and who are dropping the campervan off at another depot. In this case, it is essential to travel with soft luggage which can be folded flat and stored for the duration of your trip in one of the floor lockers. If you are returning your vehicle to the depot from which you hired it, then your unwanted luggage will have been stored there and you can reclaim it and repack your clothes and other belongings. We were provisioning our van in Auckland and depositing it in Christchurch, so I took the precaution of packing five large, soft bags, enough, I hoped, to bring back our bulky sleeping bags, clothing, and essentials. If you hire a motorhome with overhead cab space you will have room to store your luggage and this dilemma will be avoided.

CHAPTER 4

ON THE ROAD AT LAST

Just three weeks before departure we had a major set-back to our travel plans; M. was required to attend a business conference to be held from 20-22 February at Puka Park Lodge in the holiday resort town of Pauanui on the Coromandel Peninsula. It forced a major rethink of our itinerary. No matter how I juggled dates and distances, I could not fit in our proposed three-day tour of the east cape of the North Island, the city of Napier with its famous art deco buildings, and a food and wine odyssey in the Hawkes Bay. The date of our crossing of Cook Strait, 25 February, couldn't be changed – the ferries were all booked out – and the only remedy was to begin our trip three days earlier. Alas, Maui Motorhomes were booked out, too. The best a sympathetic Jocelyn could do was to make a campervan available on 11 February, just one day earlier. We took her offer – one day was better than nothing.

The forthcoming conference created another dilemma, that of *wardrobe*! I knew that the hanging space in the campervan was severely limited, but my presence at the conference would require smart resort clothes, a dinner dress, and proper shoes, handbag and jewellery, none of which are items one wishes to take on a camping trip. I was trying to avoid, for those precious four weeks, best clothes, smart hair, nail polish, and make-up. I decided not to attend, and said firmly that I would live instead in the camping ground at Pauanui while M. enjoyed the conference. I could have a self-indulgent break, slop around in my old clothes, go for walks and sunbathe on the beach, read a book, write up my journal, and catch up on laundry after 10 days on the road. M. said he would spend the day at the lodge with his colleagues, but would return to the campervan after dinner at night and depart early each morning for breakfast back at the lodge; no one except his close associates would be aware of his evening whereabouts. It was an ideal solution and it worked well in practice, but it still meant that the Hawkes Bay trip with its food and vineyards would have to wait until some other time.

At 7 a.m. on 11 February we arrived in my car at Maui Motorhomes at Mangere to collect our campervan, and found a booking agent ready behind her desk for our arrival. We were, of course, required to pay for one extra day's hire, and we also decided not to bother to return a full gas cylinder but to pay a fill-up fee of $25. We undertook to return the campervan with a full tank of diesel fuel, and we took out the Excess Reduction Option 2 insurance policy recommended by Jocelyn at a cost of $38 per day (with a maximum charge of $1,900). It was straightforward, and covered us for everything. Our final bill looked like this:

Description	Hire Period	Currency	Amount
Spirit 2 Deluxe	30 day	NZD	5,946.00
Excess Reduction 2	30 day	NZD	1,140.00
Vehicle Security Bond	1	NZD	220.00
One-way NZ Fee	1	NZD	180.00
Prepaid Gas		NZD	25.00
			7,511.00
	Minus deposit		1,143.40
	Paid on collection		$6,367.60

The $220 Security Deposit was taken as an Amex Imprint, refundable at the conclusion of the trip if the van was returned in good order. The amount of the Vehicle Security Deposit is determined by the insurance package selected. If we had taken out the Standard Excess Insurance Policy, the security deposit would have been $5,000 payable on pick-up, and if we had taken out

Excess Reduction 1 the amount immediately payable would have been $2,500. You will need your own personal travel insurance while in New Zealand, as legislation provides limited coverage for personal injury.

We returned the campervan in suitable condition at the Maui depot in Christchurch and our Amex Imprint was waiting there to be given back to us, an excellent piece of organisation, we thought.

With the $220 deducted from the tally, the final cost for 30-day hire, insurance, pre-paid gas, and one-way collection fee was $7,291, or $243 per day. In the last chapter I will give a full breakdown of the other costs incurred as we travelled around New Zealand.

With the financial transactions completed, the representative collected our van from the rear lot and parked it in the departure lane, and gave us (M., really!) a lesson in how to empty the toilet cassette, rig up the electric power cable, fill and empty the water tanks, and work the pump and the electricals. All I was concerned about was the gas cylinder, which is always my best friend on a camping trip because a cup of tea so often depends on its satisfactory operation. The tuition took 15 minutes; she gave us the keys and a travel information pack, and wished us well on our journey. She spoke English with a slight accent and I asked her if she was Swiss, so clear and thorough had been her run-down on the workings of the van. She said she was German, actually, but had been called Norwegian and South African often by other clients.

I got into my car to drive home, and in the rear window I could see M. in the campervan cautiously changing into first gear to move off. It was at least 30 years since he had driven a vehicle with a manual transmission, and to my certain knowledge he had never driven a van of any sort in his life!

It was as well that we had collected the campervan at 7 a.m. when the depot opened, because the roads leading into Auckland are clogged with commuter traffic from 7.45 a.m. onwards. We arrived at our apartment building, parked the campervan in the drive where it looked very much at odds with the svelte surroundings, and M. went off to a day of meetings.

I packed the van, crammed into the wardrobe the three business shirts which were now necessary for M. to take for his forthcoming conference, and at 3.45 p.m. we set off for our first night's stop, the Baylys Beach Holiday Park just north of Dargaville on the west coast of the North Island (details in Appendix), exiting from the northern motorway at the turnoff to the north-western motorway, Helensville and State Highway 16.

I rate map-reading as one of the happiest of travel experiences, whether it takes the form of unfolding a large map on the table after dinner and deciding where to go the next day, or of opening a road atlas when setting off in the vehicle and plotting the best route to take to that night's destination. To me, as the navigator, *nothing* is more important than a good road atlas. On previous caravan tours of Europe I had devoted considerable time in London to the selection of suitable guides published by Michelin, Philips, or the Automobile Association and had been happy each time with my choice, but I had never bought a similar atlas in New Zealand. I have become finicky. A road atlas for me must not only number and grade the roads and give distances, but must define the topography, mark recreational activities, and pinpoint historical sites and places of particular interest to the tourist; it must also provide city and town maps which situate airports, information centres, public buildings and emergency services, shopping centres, churches and parking places. In the case of New Zealand, with its extensive and important coastline, the information needs to be detailed. The index has to match up to the wealth of information provided in the maps.

I had gone to the large Whitcoulls bookstore in Queen Street, Auckland, one quiet Sunday afternoon to examine their travel section and see what guides were available. With good memories of my previous European road atlases, I wondered whether I would be able to find a New Zealand publication of similar quality. In trepidation I picked up the first one, the *Kiwi Pathfinder New*

Zealand Travellers Road Atlas, and knew immediately that I didn't have to search further. This remarkable road atlas fulfils every possible requirement and nothing else in the way of a navigation aid needs to be bought. The maps are of outstanding clarity, the best I have ever encountered. It is user-friendly, being ring-bound and small enough to fit nicely across one's knees when travelling, and should always be kept, for it is an invaluable education aid and scanning the maps is almost like reading a history book of the development of this new country.

So it was with pleasurable anticipation that I opened the atlas and checked our route to Baylys Beach. I had plenty of time to do so, for the evening rush of traffic had started and it took over three-quarters of an hour to clear the bumper-to-bumper traffic on the north-western motorway. While we were stuck, at times barely able to move, I phoned the campground to check that they had a vacancy with a powered site.

'Oh, yes, there are plenty to choose from,' replied the friendly receptionist. 'I'll be here in the office until about 8.30 tonight, so you don't need to worry about arriving late.' I said I thought we should be there by 7.30 p.m., and enquired about the nearby licensed café mentioned in the camping guidebook.

'It's just through the back fence,' came the cheerful reply. 'Shall I book you a table? It's likely to be full tonight, being a Friday.'

'Two people for 8 o'clock, please,' and I rang off, thinking that the evening augured well.

The New Zealand Camping Guidebooks were my Bibles for the next four weeks and I could not have managed without them. We knew absolutely nothing about the quality of the many campsites in New Zealand and were not inclined to arrive in a strange town and take pot luck with an overnight stop. These well-researched books for the North and South Islands list all the camping grounds in New Zealand and take the guesswork out of one's selection. Their information is reliable and up-to-date. A stay in a poor camp can be a dreadful experience, even if you are just there for the night and your vehicle is fully self-contained, and we have struck camps in Europe so awful that we still sweat when we think about them.

I had selected Baylys Beach for our first night's stop because it would put us well on our way that day. Even though our departure from Auckland was later than intended, the distance of 240 kilometres was achievable because the State Highways we were taking would be quite deserted in the late afternoon. And so it proved, once clear of the Massey turnoff at the end of the north-western motorway. We sped along State Highway 16, past the many excellent roadside fruit and vegetable orchard outlets where prices for in-season produce are usually ridiculously cheap. I make a pilgrimage to this five kilometre stretch of road every year, in late summer, and buy large beefsteak tomatoes, bags of red capsicums, courgettes, Spanish onions, a long plait of garlic, aubergines, and any stone fruits I fancy, and spend a pleasurable few days processing everything into tomato soup, pasta sauces, ratatouille, red onion jam, aubergine lasagnes, and fruit pie fillings to shove into the freezer. This stretch of road held many good memories. When our children were young we used to drive here for annual picnics, to buy cases of apples which we had watched being sorted on the rollers in an apple shed for their school lunches, and to climb ladders in a favourite orchard to pick our own peaches.

The drive along State Highway 16 is a pleasant one, through semi-rural, rolling countryside, past Kumeu with its extensive vineyards, red roses planted at the end of rows, and past the country restaurants of Allely House and Gracehills Vineyard Restaurant at Kumeu, and The Hunting Lodge at Waimakau, all favourite weekend destinations for Aucklanders for a long Sunday lunch. Kumeu is a busy regional centre serving the surrounding countryside, typical of most such places in New Zealand, and the area is noted for its wineries – Coopers Creek, Nobilo, Kumeu River, and Matua Valley – all of which provide wine tastings.

The weather was humid and large raindrops splashed occasionally on the windscreen, but the single lane highway, named the Twin Coast Discovery Highway because it takes the traveller up the west coast to Kaitaia and down the east coast back to Auckland, had been upgraded recently. From Huapai onwards the road was empty and we made good time to Helensville.

Living in Auckland, as I do, where New Zealand's distinctive, fine colonial architecture exists in quantity in just a few inner city and early seaside suburbs, I always anticipate eagerly the pleasure of travelling through country towns and seeing the many excellent old buildings still standing, a remarkable feat when you consider that so many of them are built of wood. Churches, hotels and parish halls, country stores, old farmhouses and cottages, courthouses and other public buildings abound, and give great character to centres that are now approached from all sides by petrol stations, car yards, farm machinery and implement suppliers, hardware and paint stores, fast food outlets, panel beaters, garden suppliers, marine shops, and light industrial enterprises. It is a pleasure to see the old Helensville Post Office, now an antique store but with the exterior still intact, and the nearby Grand Hotel which could stand as the template for other large early hotels in New Zealand.

The early commercial and trading history of this region can be seen in the logging and sawmilling yard at the entrance to Helensville. The Kaipara Harbour was the major port for the export of kauri timber in the nineteenth century, and more timber was exported from there than from all the other ports of New Zealand combined. Rafts of kauri logs were floated down the northern Wairoa River and its many tributaries to sawmills to be processed, and then loaded onto the ships waiting in the estuary. Together with kauri gum, the timber was the main source of income for early settlers for many years until, in the early 1920s, supplies of both ran out.

The Kaipara Harbour is the largest in New Zealand, with an indented coastline of over 3,000 kilometres, and provided the sole access to many Northland settlements for passengers, postal services, and supplies. It was not until the early 1940s, when the railway reached Dargaville to the north, that the Kaipara Harbour ceased to be a commercial and trading hub.

We drove quickly through Kaukapakapa (pron. co-copper-copper), past its delightful colonial hotel, and at last had what we wanted – our first glimpse of the Kaipara Harbour. It is what I call a flat and serene harbour, but its placidity belies the entrance bar and its strong currents, which were responsible for the groundings and strandings of many vessels during the early years. All ships, whether cutters, schooners, full-rigged ships, or steamers, had to enter or leave the harbour on the full tide.

Although the harbour was a busy hub, large development never occurred in this part of the North Island. The settlers who arrived at Port Albert in the 1860s faced great hardships because of the inaccessibility by land of the district, and the unsuitability of the land for farming, a fact which was exacerbated by the early pioneers being townspeople with little knowledge of how to break in land. The only roads until the latter part of the nineteenth century were rough bush walking tracks, and flour and other vital supplies had to come from Mangawhai about 30 kilometres away on the opposite coast. The journey took at least two days each way, with the stores being carried on the backs of the men. Not surprisingly, the first settlers faced starvation and were dependent for survival on fish, wild pigs in the surrounding bush, and fuschia berries which they used for fruit tarts, even though the lack of butter, for at first they had no cows, meant that the pie crust had to be made of damper.

None of these early travails showed as we continued north, thrilled to have an empty road through excellent scenery on which to get used to the campervan. Native bush on the hillsides was juxtaposed with pine plantations, and the winding, undulating road passed coastal smallholdings with sheep and cattle grazing in the paddocks, and scenic lookouts where one could stop for a few minutes' appreciation of the beauty of the harbour and the landscape.

The main route north out of Auckland follows State Highway 1 on the east coast of the island. We have always thought that this western road is the better of the two to take because although the driving distance is a little longer, the comparative lack of traffic and the unspoilt scenery make up for everything.

At Wellsford the Discovery Highway linked up with State Highway 1 for the 30 kilometres to our turnoff to Dargaville on State Highway 12. Wellsford is a large, bustling town and should you want a rest stop, there is a handy bakery-cum-café on the left hand corner as you enter the main highway, with ample parking in the side street for touring vehicles.

At Brynderwyn we turned left onto State Highway 12 and the so-called Kauri Coast, and met a patched and bumpy road surface. The winding and rather hilly road was quite a contrast to the smooth highway we had just come off, but at Matakohe the road surface and marking improved to what you would expect of a State Highway, and so did the quality of the farms. I noticed a sign pointing to a kauri and pioneer museum which I would dearly have loved to visit, but it was past the closing time of 5.30 p.m. The next day, at the information centre in the Waipoua Forest, I discovered a brochure on the museum and saw what a treat we had missed. The Kauri Museum at Church Road, Matakohe (www.kauri-museum.com) is large, highly educational, and divided into wings featuring fine kauri furniture, timber panels and carving, and real equipment for felling trees, milling the timber, and for collecting kauri gum. The Smith Wing even has a blacksmith's workshop, a gumdigger's nikau hut and a model dam, and the Sterling Wing is described as 'A quality six room c.1900 home, fully furnished, original décor, dressed models, a fascinating insight'. There is a real steam sawmill, a wood workshop, early pioneering photographs, and what is said to be the world's best kauri gum display. Outdoor buildings include the old local post office, made of kauri, and a pioneer church built in 1867.

The heady country smells of cow bails, manure and pasture filled the air as we neared the township of Ruawai, with small, modest homes lining the highway. The lowering, dark grey sky threatened rain. I can't bear to set up camp in the rain, even if all we had to do was click in the power cable, so I urged M. on and we whipped alongside the wide and muddy Wairoa River, bypassed Dargaville which is worth a look because of its old main street which typifies much of the nineteenth century style of New Zealand towns, and four kilometres further on turned left towards Baylys Beach and our camp for the night.

If you look at a map you will see why I chose this place to stop. Twelve years ago, when we last drove up to the Waipoua Forest, we stopped in Dargaville to buy some sandwiches and a Lotto ticket, and headed on north hoping to find a picnic spot to have lunch. 'Baylys Beach 15 km' said the signpost, so we decided to spend a peaceful hour there with our food and the newspaper. Well, you don't go to Baylys Beach for peace and quiet. It might say 'seaside resort' on the map, but it is actually a small part of one of the mightiest stretches of coastline in New Zealand, running straight from the Kaipara Harbour entrance up to the South Head of the Hokianga Harbour. The flat sands are accessible in part by 4WD vehicles, but much of the beach is for walkers only. We ate our sandwiches to the thunderous accompaniment of mountainous waves, which had gathered up steam on their unbroken progress across the Tasman Sea to land crashingly on the beach in front of us. It was majestic and awesome, a little frightening, and the last place in the world I would want to paddle, let alone swim. I just had to see it again, hence this choice of our overnight stop.

We pulled up outside the camping ground office where I met the charming woman to whom I'd spoken on the phone some three hours earlier. She charged us $24, we could choose any powered site we fancied, and the Funky Fish Café was expecting us shortly.

We were starving. After a quick handwash we bounded through the gap in the back fence, along a shell path and through a slightly overgrown garden, past a garishly painted outbuilding which said 'Dunny', and into the café. We didn't know at the time, although I had my suspicions later on because of the excellence of the food, that this is the premier restaurant in the area. Being a Friday night, the inside room was full, and we were invited to sit outside at what seemed like the biggest kauri dining table in New Zealand, milled from a solid slab, planed smooth but with all the knots and barky indentations along the side left intact, a table which could seat 20 people but which this night held a party of six, and us.

I relaxed immediately in the unusual and very informal surroundings. After the early 5.30 a.m. awakening, the somewhat strenuous task of loading up the van, the late departure and the trauma of Auckland's gridlocked traffic, and the race against time to reach Baylys Beach before the campground closed, I felt quite wrung out and I think M. did too, though he was at pains not to show it.

You meet the most interesting people when touring. We shared the table with a local resident, there with his family and some friends. He had left New Zealand as a young man and spent 14 years working in London, the Middle East, and Melbourne, and during all his time away was homesick for the beach. Baylys Beach and this part of the world had everything he ever wanted, he said, and he couldn't wait to return. He looked remarkably content, with his attractive wife and two very well-behaved children alongside him. His little girl, aged about seven years, wore a stylish ruby red velvet Rembrandt beret and in-between mouthfuls of food drew accurate portraits of everyone at the table. He asked where we were travelling to the next day, and when we said Ninety Mile Beach, immediately told us to stay at the Top 10 Holiday Park at Waipapakauri (pron. wy-poppa-co-ree).

'Top 10?' asked M. 'Never heard of it.'

'They're the best chain of camping grounds in New Zealand, excellent standard, and in all the best spots,' our new friend replied. 'I'll be there myself in 10 days, had my booking for a year.'

Now this was interesting stuff. A 12 month booking for a *campsite*?

'Yep,' he continued. 'I'm gonna drag a 40 foot line off the beach tomorrow when the tide's right and bring in some mullet – they make the best bait for snapper.'

'But why?'

'It's the annual fishing contest up there and I never miss it. Look forward to it all year!'

It seemed that the owner of The Park Top 10 at Waipapakauri runs a famous five day snapper fishing contest off the beach each year, called the Lion Red Ninety Mile Beach Snapper Competition, charging $250 per entrant but limited to 1,000 tickets sold within New Zealand, with proceeds going to a Charitable Trust, and hefty prizes donated by local firms. This would be the 24th annual contest, and the prize for the heaviest snapper over-all was $50,000 cash with a total of $80,000 given out in cash prizes during the event. This year the major spot prizes were two Ford Ka motorcars, a Ford Courier Double Cab 4 x 4, and a Ramco Ranger 350 dinghy with outboard motor plus a Voyager trailer.

This is the biggest and richest fishing contest in the country and attracts competitors from all over Australia and New Zealand. The Park Top 10 camp is next to the competition headquarters. Contact information is included in the Appendix at the end of the book.

Our friend was a mine of information on the Far North, and said that Fullers runs the best coach tours from Paihia in the Bay of Islands up to Cape Reinga, and we could pick up a tour at the Waipapakauri camp. We'd taken the all-day tour 12 years ago and rated the bus drive along the sands of Ninety Mile Beach as the highlight of our Northland holiday, and M. was keen to go again. The fine print in our contract with Maui Motorhomes forbids driving their vehicles on this beach, so we would have to take the organised tour again. I thought it was a waste of a day that could be spent doing something new, and the idea lapsed. We were recommended to stop at Awanui when we left the Ninety Mile Beach to view the staircase hollowed out of the massive trunk of a 45,000-year-old kauri tree. He said it would 'blow our minds'.

Recommendations which one receives on the road from locals and like-minded travellers are always the best, and shouldn't be ignored. We were thrilled to visit the Ancient Kauri Kingdom two days later and find that our friend was right. While we were being regaled with suggestions for our tour, the rain, which had been promising to fall all afternoon, came down in torrents. Our table was sheltered by a green corrugated plastic awning, but a miniature river developed behind my chair so we all shifted cosily together along the trestled seating, hoping the wind wouldn't change and blow the rain onto us. The waitress placed a low candle alongside each diner and there, with total strangers, in the pouring rain which drummed noisily on the awning, our feet avoiding the puddles, at this unique table and by the light of the small candles which guttered in the wind, in such unpromising circumstances, we had the most delicious dinner! I gave a long 'Mmmm' of appreciation when I tasted my prawn and dory spring rolls, accompanied by a perfectly-dressed salad,

'The chef's a local boy,' we were told. 'He's cooked all over the world but decided to come back and do his own thing here. It's the best place to eat for miles around.'

Lucky locals! I ordered a scotch fillet steak with kumara and herb mash, and buttered zucchini and carrot strips, to follow, and every mouthful was a well-flavoured and tender delight, the sort of food you think you could cook at home but much prefer to have someone else do for you. Murray ordered the kumara and mussel fritters (it's hard to get away from kumara, the New Zealand sweet potato, in the Far North where it grows so abundantly) and battered fish and chips with salad. We chose one of the more expensive wines from the list, a Nelson Old Coach Road Chardonnay 2002 for $32, an excellent choice as the wine was soft, with a buttery fullness and came served at exactly the right temperature – NOT TOO COLD!

At 10 o'clock we said goodnight to our table companions and tottered through the back fence to the camp. We were so tired that we rolled into bed without showering, and, as we always do when we are camping, slept soundly until eight o'clock the next morning. It had been a very busy day for the pensioners.

CHAPTER 5

WAIPOUA FOREST AND THE KAURI TREES, A CAR FERRY TRIP ACROSS THE HOKIANGA HARBOUR, AND THE NINETY MILE BEACH

Sparkling sunlight poured in when I pulled back the curtains the next morning and we finally had a good look at our camping ground. It was everything the camping guidebook had said, with pleasant level lawn sites, 22 with power and some with hard stands and taps, and excellent kitchen and barbecue facilities, a laundry with an automatic washer and dryer, and clean ablutions. We could have booked Waipoua Kauri Forest trips, horse treks, 4WD beach trips and fishing trips from the camp, had we wished. If there is one thing which endears me to a camp, it is thick, closely mown grass. We live in an apartment building in Auckland, and if I want grass I have to visit my daughter and enjoy her large back lawn, or drive to the nearby Auckland Domain. I stepped outside as soon as I was dressed and relished the feel of my feet on the soft, slightly damp green surface, and the salty smell of the air.

We still felt tired and not inclined to hurry away, so after a breakfast of sliced fruit and yoghurt, washed down with plenty of tea, a slightly meagre effort because we discovered the toaster didn't work, M. walked along the road until he found a dairy-cum-newsagent on the corner and bought *The New Zealand Herald* and we propped our feet up on the divans and read what was happening in the rest of the world. It all seemed very far away, and this feeling of disengagement was to be a hallmark of the next month.

We eventually rolled up the electric power line, climbed into the cab, and drove off. I had had a look at the showers, but had decided to stay dirty until we got to the fabled campground at Waipapakauri. As a precaution I phoned the camp to enquire if we could book a power site for that night; it would be too awful if we drove so far and were turned away.

'There's tons of room,' replied the well-spoken young man in the camp office. I asked if the restaurant advertised in my camping guidebook would be open, and if we would need to book.

'Oh yes, it's open, just say you'll be in for dinner when you check in!'

With that urgent piece of business settled, we took the three minute drive to the beach, parked the van, and walked along a foot track between shoulder-high flax bushes to My Beach. It hadn't changed! The area is well-peopled with real Kiwi baches or holiday homes as well as permanent residences yet, again, there wasn't a soul to be seen and the sense of vast isolation was so overpowering that I had the feeling I could die here and my body might never be discovered. The contrast with the eastern beaches and bays we were to visit over the next few days couldn't have been greater. M. took a photo of me standing on the sands, but a small print cannot convey the power of that place.

We headed north on State Highway 12. M. said he was getting used to the diesel engine and manual transmission, and I could tell he was enjoying the driving more today. The road was good and well-marked and we were never very far from glimpses of the Tasman Sea. The countryside was rural, and pretty, with pleasant vistas everywhere, pine forests on the hills, and cattle grazing on the rolling farmland. A kiwi bird sign, the picture, not the words, warned that kiwis cross the road here, and since they are a nocturnal bird would be a driving hazard at night. I would hate to run over a kiwi.

It was a busy Saturday morning. M. pulled over several times to let long streams of cars towing small craft overtake in safety. They were on their way to the Kai Iwi Lakes for a day's boating. It was tempting to follow them off the main highway, particularly when I looked closely at my map and saw the National Walk sign, a large white W on a red background, and a guarantee of a manageable track and exceptional scenery, but we pressed on to Waipoua and the giant kauri trees (*Agathis Australis*). The short distance through the forest to view the trees might have to suffice as our walk for the day. A road sign advertising a turnoff to the right to the Trounson Kauri Park Scenic Reserve was another reminder that we weren't allocating enough time to this part of the trip. The Park has a 40 minute walk through kauri forest, and offers guided night-time walks which give a chance to see kiwi in their natural habitat.

We entered the Waipoua Forest, and 18 kilometres of very winding and narrow hill road, and I tried not to look down into the steep gullies on my side. M. remarked several times that he was glad he wasn't towing a caravan, a refrain I was to hear often on our tour of New Zealand. This is a beautiful and precious drive, the real forest and bush, the way New Zealand used to be until the early settlers cleared so much of it for farmland, a rich green glade with large native trees closing in, and thickets of feathery ferns overlapping onto the edges of the road. I wound down my window and inhaled great lungfuls of air. I love the unique smell of a New Zealand forest – damp, earthy, and a little mouldy, and not, obviously, a scent to be found in the city.

Trees seem to evoke a country, or a particular place; perhaps they are a little Proustian for me. I look at a flowering cherry, and immediately recall a trip to Japan and the wonderful cloud of palest pink frothy blossoms, outlined against the sky, on the double avenue of trees lining the main thoroughfare of a town. To me, the rich Tuscan landscape of Italy is drawn into scale by the punctuation marks of its dark green cypress trees. The association of those trees with Italy and its architecture is so strong that I cringe when I drive past a brand new Italianate mansion in suburban Auckland and see planted a rhododendron or two, a few pittosporums and some mondo grass.

The desolation and vastness of the Australian outback is accentuated by its forlorn stands of eucalyptus trees, with dusty drooping leaves and bark sharding off the trunks, land and tree a perfect foil for each other. The mountainside fir trees in Switzerland look sombre and colourless when dusted with snow in winter, but in summer they stand in tight, stiff ranks keeping the countryside around in good and tidy order. As soon as I see a picture of a coconut palm leaning over the white sand of a tropical beach, I recall Fiji, or Rarotonga, and feel the heat of the sun and hear the islanders singing. Tall, straight palm trees say 'sunny boulevard' and 'French Riviera' to me. Canada loves its maple trees so much that it has put a leaf on the national flag, and the giant redwood trees of California are celebrated in film. I recall flying into New York one October a few years ago. We were banked up in a long holding pattern, so the pilot announced that while we were waiting our turn to land he was going to take us on a little side trip up-State so we could admire the wonderful fall colouring on the trees below!

I see a willow tree and remember immediately punting on the Cam at Cambridge; a spreading oak tree and I think of England, a sycamore tree and I am again swinging as a child on the one in our front garden. If in London in the spring, I delight in making a pilgrimage around my neighbourhood to see how a particular pale pink magnolia is doing, or whether the pure white double blossoms on a neighbour's almond tree are as lush as they were the year before, or whether the dogs who regularly pee at the base of a larch tree at the end of my cul-de-sac have finally killed it off.

And so it is with this forest, and indeed all the native forests in New Zealand. When you ask a young New Zealander living abroad what they miss most about New Zealand, they usually say 'the beaches', or in the case of my daughters, 'our holiday bach'. No one ever says 'the trees and the forests'. Perhaps it's a sign of maturity to love and value trees; I certainly don't talk to them, and I think that anyone who mentions hugging trees is barking mad, but I do love revisiting them. Old trees give me a comforting sense of place.

So you can understand from all this why I never miss a chance to drive through the Waipoua Forest and enjoy, again, the majestic awe of really huge kauri trees, many centuries old, and likely to live for a few more. It's such a pity that kauri trees, which once grew in the South Island, are now usually just found here, in the north of the North Island.

New Zealand is lucky that its isolation from other landmasses for about 100 million years saved it from being overrun by browsing and grazing animals, for it enabled dense and luxuriant forests to establish over the greater part of the country. Nearly all the land below the timber line of 1,000-1,300 metres bore forest, which developed a rich and unique floor that was not destroyed until penetrated by humans and introduced animals, but there are still plenty of places where the former glory of the land can be seen, and enjoyed mightily. The native trees of New Zealand are easily identified, famous ones to watch out for being the ubiquitous coastal pohutukawa, *Metrosideros excelsa*, the totara, *Podocarpus totara*, and the rimu, *Dacrydium cupressinum.*

We turned left onto Waipoua River Road and drove along a kilometre of unsealed road to the Visitor Centre, past a pretty, stony stream, a swimming hole, and a well-manicured picnic area. The centre was full of photographs and excellent commentaries on the early history of the area's logging and gumdigging past, but the photos which interested me the most were the ones of men hacking their way through impenetrable bush and forest below the timber line to form the roads we were driving on. An enormous effort was required to settle and survive in this part of the country, and it all happened within the living memory of our parents; no early Roman roads to use as markers here, and no vast, flat plains ready for agricultural and industrial use – everything had to be started afresh. It's a wonder the pioneers didn't give up and sail to Australia.

Ponga ferns and nikau palms lined the next stretch of winding road, and the driving was slow. But you wouldn't want to hurry it, anyway; every turn provided a fresh and beautiful vista. 'Tane Mahuta', said a sign on the left, and we pulled up alongside the walking track into the forest. A roadside caravan stall was doing a brisk trade in lunch snacks, ice cream and drinks, so we ordered cheese and onion toasted sandwiches and French fries, or hot chips as they are known in this country, and perched on a rock wall in the shade to eat them. The State Highway, for that's what it is although it doesn't look like one here, was lined on both sides for several hundred yards with sightseeing tour buses, motorhomes and campervans, and cars. We nipped in ahead of a slow-moving group of English tourists and walked in the damp shade, damp even though this was high summer, along the forest track to see Tane Mahuta, lord of the forest, the largest known kauri tree, and approximately 1,250 years old, over 51 metres high, and 4.4 metres in diameter, with its lowest branches 20 metres from the ground. *Nothing* prepares the first-time tourist for the shock of seeing it. I knew what to expect, so I stood at the side of the viewing area and enjoyed the gasps and the oh my goodnesses and the wide-eyed astonishment of everyone else. Kodak and Fuji make a fortune from this tree! We joined the queue to take our own photos, which, as always, were disappointing because it's quite impossible to get the whole tree into the frame. The clicking of the cameras almost drowned out the soft singing of *Hine e Hine*, a favourite tune, by a small group of Maori sitting nearby. The tall, extremely straight trunks of the surrounding kauri trees in the forest offer adequate explanation as to why large areas of kauri were felled for use as masts and spars in sailing ships.

There's a wonderful view of the Hokianga Harbour and its heads from the lookout at the top of the hill as you approach Omapere. The road falls away sharply and unexpectedly to the bay and the settlement below, but the glory of the view is in the massive golden sand dunes of the North Head, on which you can try sand surfing. Today the harbour was tranquil, and the water a deep turquoise blue, but the bar at the entrance is notoriously dangerous and the Coastguard requires to be notified of any intention to cross it. The Hokianga Harbour had a fairly turbulent history in the early nineteenth century, being settled initially by runaway sailors and convicts, but by 1831 the district was prospering thanks to the establishment of timber yards for the manufacture of spars, and a flax rope-making industry, a reminder of the important part the shipbuilding industry played in the economic life and development of this newly-settled country.

The Omapere Tourist Hotel and Motel (details in Appendix) is a well-loved and patronised icon of the area, and a very relaxing holiday spot, situated directly on the harbour with sheltered swimming, very safe for children, and a jetty to jump off. We have stayed there twice before in the motel accommodation, and enjoyed memorable crayfish dinners and rousing evenings in the bar afterwards. I love the place. It's a very good overnight camping spot, has both power and tent sites, and this afternoon I counted nearly a dozen motorhomes lined up.

A 10 minute drive along the edge of the harbour past small sandy-bottomed beaches which made me wish I had packed my swimsuit, took us to Opononi, home in the 1950s of Opo the famous dolphin who played in the harbour with the local residents and inspired a popular song. There is a local Information Centre, and if you want to know about the attractions of the Hokianga you will find everything here.

We decided to take the car ferry from Rawene to Kohukohu and eliminate approximately 50 kilometres of travelling through the regional centre of Kaikohe. The ferry sails every half hour from Rawene, and returns from the other side of the harbour on the hour throughout the day. The charge is $14 for vehicle and driver, and $2 for each extra passenger. We had 20 minutes to wait before our 3.30 p.m. sailing, so we parked at our place in the boarding lane, and took a short stroll to admire the colonial buildings.

Today the upper Hokianga was calm. I left the van and leaned against the side of a life raft, admiring the isolation yet wondering what drives people to live in such out-of-the-way places. The ride was uneventful, but hugely enjoyable, and we drove to Kohukohu (pron. co-hoo-co-hoo) which used to be a thriving social and cultural centre, thanks to the timber trade, but now gives the appearance of a charming town in decline, although some of the early historic buildings are still standing and the town maintains a reputation as an art and crafts centre.

At Mohuiti we turned right and headed for Mangamuka on State Highway 1, foregoing the opportunity to take the Scenic Route left to Awaroa and Ninety Mile Beach. We thought this part of the journey disappointing. The isolated land had a poor look to it, as though it could be better farmed or looked after. Murray was thankful to be on State Highway 1 and heading for Kaitaia, 35 kilometres away, and the northernmost town in New Zealand. Kaitaia is not exciting, and neither does it need to be. It is a hub town, linking State Highways 1 and 10, and sooner or later all travellers in the Far North pass through it. It was briefly famous a few years ago when an enterprising woman set up a classy brothel; and because it is easy to park in the wide main street, it's a good place to pull over and buy your weekly Lotto ticket.

But first we had to reach the summit of the Mangamuka Gorge Scenic Reserve, an attractive drive through native bush and forest, but nothing to rival that through the Waipoua Forest. The highway ground slowly upwards, and again we had the irritation of travelling on a narrow and winding road. It was late in the afternoon and perhaps we were feeling weary.

We drove through Awanui and turned off to Waipapakauri on State Highway 1A, and The Park Top 10 Ninety Mile Beach campground. Thank goodness! Some of the driving had been arduous for M. We checked in at the office and asked for more information about Top 10 Holiday Parks (rather a long name – in future I will just call them Top 10s). It appeared that there was a card for campers, which could be produced at any of the 51 Top 10s to obtain a 10 per cent discount on accommodation charges. The receptionist issued M. with a card and said we could claim the discount immediately, charged us $25.20 for the night, and provided a large fold-out map of both islands with all the Top 10 locations listed, giving addresses and freephone reservation numbers, a photograph of each camp, and a very useful small map giving the exact street locations in the various towns, cities and holiday spots. The next day I idly opened up the travel wallet given to us on departure from the Maui Motorhome depot, and inside was a similar map. We wondered if Maui had any financial interest in the Top 10 camps, but have been told they don't. The Top 10 organisation is a franchised operation, and offers excellent camps in all the best locations. As we were to find out, once you have stayed in one it is difficult to accept lesser standards unless there is an overwhelming reason to do so.

M. booked in for dinner, and peeped into the restaurant to see if the lamb-on-the-spit mentioned in the camping guidebook was on offer tonight. It was, and so was a whole roast pig, turning around nicely on the adjacent spit. We were in heaven! We showered at length in the spotlessly clean and modern ablution block, washing away two days of grime, and felt like new people.

We had been directed to a large plot of thickly grassed lawn surrounded by hedges to give some privacy and separation from other areas of this very large camp. It was still a source of wonder that all we had to do to set up the campervan was to plug in the power cable, without the elaborate ritual required of a caravan, like getting it absolutely level on the pitch before unclamping from the towbar, winding down the steadies, filling up the water container, checking the amperage before starting up the electricals, and straightening up the interior. Caravans sway when being towed, and severe motion will often force open overhead lockers and the doors of under-bench storage cupboards which disgorge their contents everywhere. This area of the park was well-provided with aluminium outdoor tables and chairs, so we poured out some drinks, plonked ourselves down to enjoy the sunshine, and chatted to our next door neighbours.

He introduced himself as Brian from Invercargill, and said he and his wife had owned their campervan, which was almost exactly like ours, for 15 years and in that time had made a hobby of camping in every town, city, country area and seaside resort in New Zealand. That day, they had driven up to Cape Reinga and back, a journey they had undertaken again eagerly because they considered it deserved its reputation as one of the finest scenic drives in the world. When you are lucky enough to talk to someone like Brian, with his wealth of knowledge and experience, you listen to what he has to say. He was emphatic that we must not leave the Far North without visiting Matauri Bay on the east coast, the resting place of the Greenpeace ship *Rainbow Warrior*. They had travelled right around the coastline of both islands, and voted Matauri Bay as the best and loveliest beach. The only drawback to the beauty of the bay was that on entering it, one was confronted with a row of disgraceful caravan dwellings, which were an indictment of the electorate, and, he thought, showed an unwillingness of local Maori leaders to confront the difficult social and financial situation of many of their people. Strong words, and they weren't put as politely as I have.

The restaurant was very full with parties of local residents. Murray voted the spit lamb and accompanying salads as the best meal he had on the trip. My best dinner was to come much later, in Kaikoura. We drank a bottle of Montana Gisborne Chardonnay 2004, costing $26; 'lolly water', I called it, but it was the best from a poor selection of whites. Stick to beer and spirits here.

We were still very tired. Although we had travelled only 210 kilometres that day, it had taken us about six hours of concentrated driving because of the winding forest roads. What we needed was a bracing after-dinner walk along the Ninety Mile Beach, just three minutes away. You can drive along the expansive, wide flat sands, providing you do not do so two hours either side of high tide. There were several cars on the beach, once a favourite spot to dig at low tide for toheroas, considered the king of shellfish, but the beds have been over-exploited and the toheroas are no more. It is hoped they will regenerate. The speed limit along the beach is that of an open highway, 100 kilometres per hour, and I know M. would dearly have loved to drive the campervan along it, but our insurance would lapse if he did. By now I had read the fine print in our Rental Agreement and discovered that motorhomes can only be driven on sealed/bitumen or well-maintained roads, and that no vehicle can be driven on Skippers Road, Queenstown, Ninety Mile Beach, Northland, Ball Hut Road, Mt. Cook, or north of Colville township or on the Tapu-Coroglen Road on the Coromandel Peninsula. For some reason, driving along the length of the Ninety Mile Beach is a legendary, macho thing to do, but I remember very clearly being told by the tour bus driver all those years ago that at the northern end, unless you knew exactly where to go, you were doomed to get caught in the Te Paki quicksands.

The long return day trip from Paihia to Cape Reinga is worthwhile and very memorable, but best undertaken with a skilled tour operator such as Fullers whose buses drive in safety along the beach. Cape Reinga is 110 kilometres from Kaitaia, and Brian told us that the last 21 kilometres are unsealed, although it doesn't appear so on my map. It is a very popular tourist attraction, and 12 years ago when we took our all-day sightseeing trip I bought postcards at the lighthouse and sent them off from there. It's quite uncanny to walk to the edge of the cliff and see the Pacific Ocean and the Tasman Sea creating enormous waves as they meet each other. The area is of intense spiritual and cultural significance to Maori, who believe that the spirits of their dead travel from there to return to their ancestral home of Hawaiiki.

The latest information brochure from Fullers states that the all day trip leaves Paihia at 7.30 a.m. and returns at 6.30 p.m., the cost for adults being $110 with lunch provided, and for children with lunch $63. Reservation details are given at the end of the book.

The walk along the breezy beach in the company of other after-dinner strollers had cleared our heads, and we again slept like logs until 8.30 a.m. the next morning. I don't want to make you envious with all this talk of wonderful sleep, so I shan't mention it again, you can just take it for granted!

CHAPTER 6

MANGONUI, MATAURI BAY, WAITANGI, PAIHIA, AND ON TO WHANGAREI

We walked over to the restaurant at 9 a.m. the next morning for the advertised cooked breakfast, but were met with a grumpy look from the manager. We soon saw why. Two full tour buses with about 90 tourists altogether had pulled up outside for a tea break on their way north to Cape Reinga. Two people against 90 have no chance, so we took off for Awanui and breakfast at the Ancient Kauri Kingdom and Café. Thank goodness we had the recommendation from our Funky Fish Café fellow diner at Baylys Beach because otherwise we wouldn't have stopped there; this is the sort of place that looks overly hyped up as you drive past so you decide to avoid it. It was a lesson well learned that morning that in New Zealand the better presented a tourist place is, the better it actually *is*.

'Everything made on the premises', said a sign on the café counter, and I was moved to try what I never eat, *a bought pie*. Indeed the only bought pies I had eaten in the last 20 years were those from the pie shop in Arrowtown, near Queenstown in the South Island, located on the right hand corner as you come down the slight incline into the main street. Their pies, I had been told by a former local, are the very best and although he himself never ate bought pies he always stopped there for one when in Arrowtown. He said that the pies are so delicious and full of good fillings that people buy them by the dozen to park in the freezer at home. When I asked the woman serving us with a lunch pie each if she did sell pies in quantity, she said, matter-of-factly, oh yes, they had just packed up 40 pies for an American customer who was taking them back that day to the USA! I promptly bought two more and carried them in the plane myself for dinner at home in Auckland the next night.

I can tell you that the steak and cheese pie from the Ancient Kauri Kingdom café has no equal on earth. The pastry was buttery, feathery and fairy light, and the filling a well-flavoured rich brown casserole of good quality beef topped with a thick layer of tasty cheese which melted nicely under its pastry lid. When I'd finished I gave a sigh of pleasure and wondered if I had room for another. M., who had decided to stick to what he doesn't get at home, namely sultana scones, strawberry jam and clotted cream *a la* Harrods, went back to the counter at my urging to eat something a little more sustaining, and demolished his pie quickly – wolfed, actually – and said if there was one thing he loved it was a good pie. I bought some thick sandwiches to eat later on for lunch, 'thick' because the fillings were piled so high, and we crossed to the other side of the kingdom to look at the kauri on display.

Now there is kauri, and kauri. The finest kauri furniture is that made around the end of the nineteenth century, hallstands, tables and chairs, and sofas, all delicately wrought, turned and carved because the hard, smooth timber lends itself to fine treatment. A curved and buttoned kauri sofa and matching side chairs, with unmistakeable Victorian styling, sits as comfortably in an old New Zealand wooden villa as the finest Georgian furniture does in an interior by Robert Adam.

In contrast to that, the most hideous kauri object you will ever see is on display at the Ancient Kauri Kingdom! It is a sofa, carved out of a solid length of trunk. It took 80 hours to chainsaw out, 300 hours to carve, and two and a half years to dry out. While I admire the dedication of the craftsman who made it, I cannot possibly guess its final destination – it is for sale – unless it is a Canadian backwoods lodge where, mercifully, only a few people will see it.

Ancient kauri is a rare resource, and comes from the trees left buried in prehistoric forests that grew more than 50 thousand years ago. The lack of air preserved the timber in perfect condition, and the brochure from the Ancient Kauri Kingdom states that it is known to be the oldest workable timber in the world. I have a bowl of stones and rocks collected from places I want to remember, so I bought a wooden kauri egg and received a certificate of authenticity saying it was carved from timber between 30 and 50 thousand years old. If you want to take home a kauri souvenir of New Zealand, you are best to buy a salad bowl, to my mind the very best wooden salad bowls in the world, which improve with age and will last a lot longer than you or your descendants. I have taken several overseas to give as gifts.

An enormous tree trunk stands slightly to the rear of the shop, with its surprise entrance concealed at the back. It is difficult to imagine a tree trunk so wide that it could be hollowed out and carved into a wide flight of steps with a curved banister leading round and up to I know not what, because I didn't venture beyond the first five steps, but it is there, it is authentic, and advertised as the World Famous 45-thousand-year-old staircase. All the children in the café ended up there!

What with the excellent café, and the uniqueness of and the long history behind its products, it comes as no surprise to learn that the Ancient Kauri Kingdom has won numerous New Zealand Tourism Awards. It is well worth a visit, has clean restrooms, and plenty of motorhome parking. Even at this comparatively early hour, 9.30 a.m., the place was busy. After the steady diet yesterday of kauri in its natural form, it was pleasantly educational to visit the Ancient Kauri Kingdom and see the end use of this magnificent timber.

We turned left onto State Highway 10, which would take us around the east coast, and on to State Highway 1 and Whangarei (pron. funga-ray), perhaps our destination for the night. If you are a dedicated map reader, this stretch of road should make you drool with delight, covering as it does the wide bays and beaches, inlets, small harbours and offshore islands, and, with detours, the sites of the earliest settlements in New Zealand. For us, the area is steeped in history and meaning, and one day is not long enough for the first-time visitor to enjoy it. I recommend at least three days.

This part of State Highway 10 provided smooth, easy driving. M. commented on the number of motorhomes in our camping ground the previous night, and said he wished we had hired one. I agreed. We were already getting tired of having to make way for each other in the narrow space between the bench and the stove top in our 2+1 campervan, and would have liked the extra width of a 4-berth motorhome. I still hadn't sorted out some of our belongings, and the extra top space above the cab would have been handy to throw a few things into.

We passed Lake Ohia and came upon Doubtless Bay curving around to the north, the beautiful stretch of beach sheltered by the Karikari (pron. carry-carry) Peninsula. Whatuwhiwhi (pron. fottoo-fee-fee), Maitai Bay, and Tokerau Beach are popular holiday destinations and perfect for swimming and fishing. The seaside communities at Taipa and Cable Bay have grown very quickly. During the New Year holiday break of 1973, when the children were small, we towed a caravan from Auckland as a dummy run before caravanning in Europe later in the year to the idyllic and late-lamented Coopers Beach, and had a memorable fortnight in the sun, swimming, building sandcastles, and exploring the rather unpopulated adjacent bays. All that has changed. The land at Coopers Beach Camping Ground, such prime real estate on the water's edge, eventually became too expensive to warrant holding as a camping site and was sold for residential development. This, unfortunately, is happening to many prime coastal camping grounds throughout New Zealand. With a lot of 'remember whens' we drove through the new and imposing gateway, past a large sign saying Northland's Premier Seafront Subdivision. The boulevard-style entry road was lined with palms, the lawns were wide and perfect, and the homes were mansions that would have graced any city. The only landmarks that hadn't changed were the ancient pohutukawa trees, left overhanging and fringing the white sand.

We needed Mangonui to cheer us up. The first time I saw Mangonui, I decided this was a place I would like to retire to. Many people have thought the same, for houses now climb the hillside behind the harbour. It is impossible to feel lonely here, even though you might look at the map and gulp at the apparent isolation, because this part of New Zealand is actually well-populated. The influx of summer visitors adds spice to the area, of course, but the over-riding impression of this quaint town is that 'well they come, but then they go…'

Anyone contemplating an overnight stop would do well to book into the old Mangonui Hotel on the waterfront for dinner, then spend the afternoon walking or driving the Heritage Trail, just three kilometres long, and stay the night at the nearest campground at Hihi Beach on the other side of the Mangonui Harbour, five kilometres off State Highway 10 and well signposted.

There's always something rather nice about parking on a quayside just a few feet above the lapping waters of a harbour. Mangonui Harbour was an early whaling station and one of the oldest ports in New Zealand, and many colonial buildings are still standing, among them the courthouse, the wharf store, whose middle section is built of heart kauri, St. Andrew's Church built in 1860, Windermere, an original homestead built in 1870 and now restored, and the War Memorial Hall built in 1894.

These days, fishing trawlers and small pleasure craft anchor in the tranquil harbour. Because New Zealand's settled history is so recent, it is easy to imagine a sailing ship finding this sheltered anchorage, the passengers thinking 'This is it!' (as I did) and stepping ashore to build their dream town.

If you want a somewhat unnerving experience, I can recommend using the toilets in the War Memorial Hall opposite the wharf. They are open at eye level onto the footpath outside, one's privacy protected only by an old grating which anyone could peep through. The boutique shops along the waterfront stock handcrafts, and the soap store is worth a visit. The hand-made soap is excellent and I have a large cake at home.

Back on State Highway 10 we passed a pine forest with a sign exhorting travellers to 'Picnic in the Pines' and, adjacent, a lonely blue Portaloo!

Whangaroa Harbour is long with many inlets, was the site of the first Wesleyan Mission in 1822, and today is a renowned base for big game fishing. Kingfish Lodge, situated at the headland of the harbour in Kingfish Cove, is the oldest coastal fishing lodge in New Zealand, accessible either by helicopter or water taxi, with 12 waterside guest rooms, a restaurant and bar. Mangrove swamps border the highway at the head of the harbour, and we passed a sign advertising houseboats for rent on the Whangaroa River.

We stopped at Kaeo to fill up with diesel, the first time in about 500 kilometres of travel, where 51 litres cost $45.33. We were to find as we continued around New Zealand that the price of fuel could vary considerably. The local lad at the petrol pump told me that the second turnoff to Matauri Bay was well signposted, and the best route to take, so off we drove, high with the anticipation of seeing the best beach in New Zealand.

The drive from the turnoff down to the bay takes 15 minutes, along a sealed road with an excellent surface. I'm always a little bit nervous about taking a road that shows as just a white line in my map book, but we drove along many of them on our tour and never struck a dud.

The bay lies at the bottom of a four kilometre drive down a winding hill road, and the impact of the clear turquoise water breaking with a small wave onto the white sand, the protective headlands enclosing the beach, and the offshore islands which contained the view, was ravishing, like a story book illustration, New Zealand at its very best.

The squalid caravans lining the sand at the entrance were as dreadful as we'd been told, an impact of a different kind, giving rise to sadness that people either want to live like this, or have to. The caravans were undoubtedly occupied for there was washing fluttering on makeshift clothes lines, dilapidated awnings and sheds had been erected to take the overflow of people or possessions, and rusting cars that belonged in the wrecker's yard were parked alongside. Yet at the top of the road we had just descended lies Kauri Cliffs, a world famous golf course and one to which dedicated golfers fly from all over the world, landing at Auckland International Airport and taking a helicopter for a scenic flight up to the luxurious resort. I wonder if they ever visit the beach.

At the far end of the bay is an attractive campground, Matauri Bay Holiday Park which, unusually for New Zealand, has a barrier arm entry system, and card access for campers to the amenities. The camp is very busy at peak season and the management has taken account of the isolated location by providing a seven day on-site store, and a liquor licence. The camp can also arrange dive charters. This is the sort of camp you would bring your young family to for their summer holiday. The beach is superb, sheltered, and very safe.

The bay is a diver's paradise, particularly in the waters surrounding the offshore Cavalli Islands where the Greenpeace anti-nuclear protest ship, *Rainbow Warrior*, rests. The ship was blown up while berthed in Auckland harbour in 1986 by French Secret Service agents, killing a photographer on board, and lay listing at the wharf for weeks before being towed and scuttled on the seabed here. The wreck has become a recreational diving attraction and a haven for all kinds of marine life. M.'s 88-year-old father, who had served in the 1st Otago Infantry Battalion and marched into Etaples, France, in 1918, and from there up through Belgium and Germany with the Germans on the run in the final stages of World War I, was staying with us at the time, and every morning I drove him to the waterfront so he could see again what he called The Travesty. He was lucky to survive the trenches. Two of his best friends were killed alongside him by enemy gunfire as they came over the top, and, although patriotic to the core like all old soldiers, he wondered whether the sacrifice had been worth it when State-sponsored terrorism such as we were looking at had reached a friendly country at the bottom of the world, and made it less safe.

We parked the campervan off the unsealed road which runs alongside the beach, sat on a grassy verge, dangling our feet above the clean sand to eat our sandwiches and enjoy the glorious view, and discussed what we should do about the electrics in the van. M. had plugged his phone recharger into the supply that morning and found he couldn't get a response, and on checking further we found the microwave wasn't working, either. We thought there must be a fault with the electric cable. We could do without toast for breakfast, and not bother with the microwave, but we had to be able to recharge our mobile phones. The only recourse to the dilemma was to use my phone, which worked, to phone the Maui Helpline for instructions.

We left the beautiful bay reluctantly, and headed down State Highway 10 for Kerikeri, Waitangi and Paihia in the Bay of Islands, Kawakawa, and Whangarei, a distance of 100 kilometres. As soon as we got back onto the main road, M. phoned Maui and was given the name and location of an auto garage in Whangarei which would carry out the necessary testing and repairs.

I had wondered whether we should stop at Kerikeri for the night, and spend the late afternoon enjoying the attractions of the area. There were five camps listed in the guidebook, one of them the Kerikeri Top 10 Holiday Park, with superb facilities including a barbecue complex with a roll-back roof and two log-burning fireplaces, one for cooking, and open spas. Of more interest to me, to be truthful, was the fact that the camp was a short walk from the Kerikeri township and restaurants. However, we needed electric power, so Whangarei and the garage it would have to be. A pity, as Kerikeri is steeped in Maori and early European history. The oldest building in New Zealand, Kemp House, built in 1822, and the second mission station established in the Bay of Islands, is located down on the inlet, together with the Stone Store of 1836, and St. Johns Anglican Church. Nearby is Rewa's Village, a replica of the pre-European village that stood on the site.

Kerikeri enjoys a sub-tropical climate and is renowned for its citrus orchards. I rate Kerikeri oranges as the finest in the world, with a vivid orange, dense flesh of superb texture and flavour. It is also a craft centre producing pottery, glassware, jewellery, woodware, and art. Unfortunately we had no option, because of the lateness of the afternoon, but to bypass Kerikeri, and instead took the turnoff at Puketona for Paihia and Waitangi in the Bay of Islands, celebrated today as the birthplace of New Zealand. Reaching the seafront, we turned left to pass the waterfront Maori marae, cross the estuary bridge, and drive up the hill to Waitangi.

I never tire of visiting the Treaty House and the beautiful grounds of the National Reserve. In the 1960s and 70s we used to stay with the children at the nearby Waitangi Hotel, and take the five minute walk up the hill to tour the house and grounds, visit the waka or Maori war canoe, and admire the view across the bay.

The Treaty Grounds have since changed beyond recognition, with the installation of a very large car park filled with tour buses, a café, a Visitor Centre with Treaty displays, an audio-visual theatre, and a souvenir gallery. We used to be able to just stroll onto the Treaty Grounds without any fuss; now one must pass through the Visitor Centre and pay $10 to venture further. One-hour guided tours of the Treaty House, the Maori meeting house, the waka, the flagstaff, and Captain Hobson's historic landing site are available daily for $20 per adult including admission, with no charge for children under 15 years of age. It's very worthwhile, for an hour here passes quickly and it is important to know the history of what you're looking at. The beautiful flagstaff halfway down the lawn marks the site where the Treaty of Waitangi was signed in February 1840 by the local Maori chiefs, and Captain Hobson on behalf of the British Crown. Copies of the Treaty were then taken around the country for all the chiefs to sign, and in May 1840 Captain Hobson proclaimed British sovereignty over New Zealand.

The articles of the Treaty of Waitangi and their fine shades of meaning are argued over today, and it is almost impossible to read a daily newspaper without coming across a reference to the Treaty, so central is it to the governance of New Zealand. The peace, tranquillity and beauty of the attractive Treaty House, which was the original British Residency, the extensive grounds, and the panoramic view across the bay, are at odds with the passions aroused over the Treaty's interpretation.

The splendid lawn in front of the Treaty House is one of my favourite places in New Zealand. I like to walk down to the very bottom and sit on the sheltered rocks and look out over the water. One memorable year we were there shortly after the annual 6 February Waitangi Day celebrations, and naval ships were anchored in the bay, a stirring sight. Stirring, too, is the beautifully carved dark red Maori waka, on view under its protective shelter. It is huge, and over 70 paddlers are required to propel it safely in the water. If you look up into the rafters of the shelter you will see the white paddles stored there, about 80 altogether. These are the huge canoes that carried Maori explorers across the Pacific Ocean to settle in New Zealand. This waka is cradled on wheels, and steel tramlines are set into the ground so that it can be launched easily into the waters of Hobson Bay, a very small cove only about 50 metres wide where Captain Hobson first came ashore. I have always believed that one of the finest sights in the world is that of a giant waka being paddled by Maori in their native dress, and if, as a visitor to New Zealand, you get a chance to see this, it is not to be missed. If you can't get to the Treaty Grounds on your tour of New Zealand, you can see waka at the Auckland War Memorial Museum and Wellington's Te Papa Museum.

The afternoon was unbearably hot, so we stopped off at the old Waitangi Hotel, now the Copthorne and almost unrecognisable after extensive upgrades, for a beer and a glass of Church Road sauvignon blanc, a fairly safe choice if you just want one glass, and feeling refreshed we drove back along the waterfront to Paihia, a big-time tourist centre full of motels and backpackers lodges. It's typical of the genre, with a Woolworths supermarket open seven days until 10 p.m., another Ancient Kauri Kingdom, scenic flights, gyms, swim with the dolphin discoveries, beach bars, cafés and Super Liquor stores. Fullers on the seafront runs the famous Cream Trip, a full-day cruise around the Bay of Islands, visiting the Hole in the Rock and just managing to squeeze through it if conditions are right, and Otehei Bay on Urapukapuka Island for lunch, a swim, and an explore. This was the island where the American author Zane Grey lived and wrote. The Cream Trip is a 'working' trip, for the Fullers boat calls at some of the islands to deliver stores and mail, and is the best way to see the bay if you have two days here. The second day can be spent at Waitangi, and at Russell, a short ferry ride across the bay.

The Bay of Islands was New Zealand's main port in the late eighteenth and early nineteenth centuries, with Kororareka, now Russell, the principal European settlement. Whalers, seal, flax and timber traders, former convicts, and ships deserters all made the settlement with its safe anchorage a refreshment stop, and it became known as 'the hell-hole of the Pacific'. In due course the bay was the focus of missionary attention, middle class settlers and their families began to arrive regularly from England, it was the undoubted centre of population, and in 1840 Russell was declared the capital of New Zealand, with the former Captain Hobson, now Lieutenant-Governor, occupying one of the settlement's substantial residences to be known as the first Government House. Unfortunately the bad state of the roads at Russell made life too difficult, so in 1841 the seat of government was moved to Auckland.

Russell is full of historic buildings, has an excellent museum, and a fine example of French architecture can be seen in Pompallier House, an early French Catholic Mission. Russell is a world-renowned port for game fishing, marlin being the specialty. If a fisherman offers you a chunk of smoked marlin, keep it all to yourself to eat. It is fine textured, truly delicious, a gourmet delight, and I've never seen it for sale in the shops. The old Duke of

Marlborough Hotel on the waterfront was New Zealand's first licensed hotel, and the veranda is a great place to sit and drink and watch the sun setting over the bay.

If you decide to take your vehicle to Russell, the car ferry at Opua saves a long journey around the peninsula.

We pushed on to Kawakawa, famous because a railway line runs through the main street and, to the Dunn family, famous because it was the first time we ever saw blue ice cream. I had to buy the girls a cone each, of course, and although the sight of it made me feel sick, they enjoyed it and said it tasted of orange.

Kawakawa has become world famous for another reason, its public toilets, designed by Freidrich Hundertwasser when he lived there. He didn't see why public toilets shouldn't be things of beauty. His are roomy, have brick floors, wondrously tiled walls and decorative, brightly painted knobbly pillars at the entrance, and are an art object in their own right, as different from the usual dank concrete bunkers you find in a main street as it is possible to be. The pillars have inspired retailers in the main street to take up the theme, and in parts the street is extremely colourful.

I directed M. onto the wrong road out of Kawakawa and we found ourselves in Moerewa, the most depressing, run-down town I have ever seen. The sign on the Social Welfare office said, in large painted letters, 'WINZ QUOTES'. How on earth could Work and Income welfare benefits be subject to '*quotes*', I wondered. Benefit rates are set, and either one qualifies or one doesn't!

The Affco meat processing plant is the major local employer in this very poor town where no one has any money and the residents live in small, unkempt bungalows, with weeds and old rattletrap cars everywhere. It was a relief to turn back to Kawakawa, which looked positively plush compared with Moerewa, and find the correct turning to Whangarei.

It was nearly 6 p.m. and we still had about 40 kilometres to travel to Whangarei. Fortunately, the road was perfect, easy driving with plenty of passing lanes. I rang the Whangarei Top 10 Holiday

Park to see if they had a power site we could reserve, got the usual answer 'Don't worry, plenty of space,' and that was the last time on the tour I bothered to phone ahead to any camp. We got in everywhere.

This is a splendid camp, set among mature trees, well-hedged and sheltered, and close to town. It advertises itself on its brochure as The Gateway to Subtropical Northland. The kitchen and laundry facilities are excellent; there are barbecues, and spotlessly clean ablutions. There is a charge of 20 cents per seven minute shower, not, I think, to raise revenue but to economise on the amount of hot water used. It has a paraplegic suite, and like all the other Top 10s, a TV room, a car wash, and the usual dump station. The tariff at $12 per person minus the 10 per cent discount should have been $21.60, but the next day when we had departed and it was too late to do anything about it, I checked the Amex stub and found we had been charged $43.40 for two nights. Must have been a major communication error somewhere!

Whangarei is about half an hour's drive from the seaside resort of Ngunguru and the deep-sea fishing town of Tutukaka. Offshore, the Poor Knights Islands and the Marine Reserve are a mecca for divers, and ranked in the top 10 dive spots in the world. Tutukaka is a base for diving trips to the islands and dive wrecks *Tui* and *Waikato*, and the home of the famous Whangarei Deep Sea Anglers Club which holds many world records for offshore catches. There is a new holiday park at Tutukaka, details of which are given in the Appendix.

We set up camp and took a taxi into town for dinner. We had no idea where to go, so the elderly driver dropped us off at the Town Basin and said we would be happy with Reva's Café. We were shown to a table on the veranda overlooking the Hatea River yacht anchorage, and passed an entertaining evening watching the water traffic. A yacht marina is a busy place, and here people were disgorging from their boats to dine on shore. One yachtie, evidently staying on board, had a row of fresh herbs growing in pots in the stern of his boat and emerged to pick a few sprigs of basil and some parsley. I suspect he was cooking pasta.

We ordered a bottle of Cottle Estate Chardonnay 2002 for $28, from a Kerikeri vineyard. We had passed it that afternoon and I thought it would be a fitting end to a satisfying day to drink a local wine. The bottle looked promising when it came, with a label saying it was a bronze medal winner at an international wine show, but the wine was disappointingly thin and flavourless. For dinner I had two pork sirloin steaks (they're fairly small) wrapped in bacon and grilled, with a fruit sauce to cut the richness of the meat, pumpkin and kumara mash, and a mixed salad, and enjoyed every mouthful. M. ordered a wing rib steak and found it gristly and underdone, and almost inedible. It did indeed look awful, it should never have been served, and it put him off the rest of his food. He wished later that night that he had returned it.

By chance, the taxi we caught back to the camp was the one we had arrived in. That's the nice thing about smaller centres; you soon get to know people!

M. checked the odometer before retiring and said we had travelled 267 kilometres that day. I thought it was a pity we had had to rush through to Whangarei and bypass so many places of great beauty and interest, but it was imperative to have the campervan's electrics fixed as soon as possible. We can always revisit this superb part of New Zealand another time.

CHAPTER 7

CAMPERVAN TROUBLES

At 8.30 a.m. the next morning we arrived at Auto Care in Lower Dent Street, Whangarei, where a mechanic gave the all clear to the power cable and decided there must be a fault both in the three-pin electric plugs and the microwave. The garage phoned Maui Motorhomes at Mangere, Auckland, who asked us to bring the campervan in to their workshop for repair that day if we could manage it. Whangarei-Auckland is about 175 kilometres, a drive of three hours for us, so we decided to dawdle back to Auckland via some of the coastal resorts.

But first, breakfast. By good luck the garage was one minute's drive away from the yacht basin of the night before, so we sat in the sun at a café and had one full English breakfast and one three-egg omelette stuffed with mushrooms and smoked salmon, coffee, tea and toast, for $31.00. M. needed to recharge his mobile phone and asked the owner if he could plug it in behind the counter. She said 'Yes, that will be $1 thank you!' I bought some club sandwiches and bottles of Charlie's orange juice to have for lunch on a beach somewhere, and we hit the road to Ruakaka Beach, one of those places you see signposted from the main road but never quite manage to visit. Today, we would.

State Highway 1 had plenty of passing lanes and since our top speed was rarely above 90 kilometres per hour it was a relief to know we weren't holding up the traffic. Every driver hates being caught behind a campervan. A road sign pointed the way to Marsden Point, New Zealand's only oil refinery, which has become a tourist destination with its own Visitor Centre and a free sound and light show.

Ruakaka Beach in Bream Bay is just a three minute drive along the turnoff from State Highway 1. The beach is long, white sanded, an attractive place to swim, and evidently a good spot for surfcasting too, for as we watched a chap walked down to the water, cast his line, unfolded a canvas chair and sat down to pass a peaceful hour or two. Much of the flat land behind the beachfront has met the same fate as other prime coastal areas in New Zealand and succumbed to a new residential development of mansion-style houses. The understated houses and cottages which remain are redolent of a time when life was simple, kids went to school in bare feet, neighbours talked to and helped each other, and everyone had a vegetable garden. The Hen and Chicken Islands out in the bay, a favourite scuba diving spot, were an attractive repetition of the many islands for which the Northland and Auckland eastern coastlines are famous. A view out over the ocean is so much more interesting if there are offshore islands to provide focus and scale.

We turned back to State Highway 1 for a 10 kilometre drive past Uretiti Beach to Waipu, intending to follow the waterfront to Waipu Cove, Langs Beach, and Mangawai Heads. I knew that the beach at Waipu Cove was a holiday hangout for teenagers and surfies, and, ever the ageing hippie, I wanted to see it. But first, Waipu.

I can't imagine why anyone would want to live here. The tiny township was practically deserted this fine Monday morning. I noticed a real estate agency, but they line the main road of every coastal town in New Zealand now, such is the attraction of the land to overseas buyers and, increasingly, to young New Zealanders who can see their dream of a beach house slipping away if they don't buy now. We passed huge cornfields, a surprise to me, and I wondered why they were there. I also noticed Scottish names in the town and surrounding area, such as Braemar Lane, and McInnes Manufacturing. We passed an old cemetery near the beachfront and I guessed this must have been an early Scottish settlement.

I had always thought that Dunedin in the South Island was the home of Scottish settlement in New Zealand, and at the end of our trip I was intrigued enough to do some research. I found that this stretch of coast was settled between 1853 and 1860 with the arrival of 883 settlers representing 19 clans from the north of Scotland. They had come to New Zealand via Nova Scotia where, after 20 years, the harsh winters had forced them to find a kinder climate. This part of the world with its sunshine and gentle water must have seemed like paradise, and they set about breaking in the bush land for farming. They brought with them their Gaelic music and customs, including eating corn porridge (hence the cornfields, still planted today). They were led by the preacher Norman McLeod, who attained reputation as a colonial leader, by all accounts a bully and a tyrant, but a man dedicated to his vision of a moral and self-supporting community. His legacy is here in this most Scottish of towns which celebrates its Caledonian Games every New Year. If you like the skirl of the bagpipes as much as I do, 1 January is The Day. Documents, photographs and memorabilia have been preserved from those early times and are on display at the Waipu Heritage Centre and Caledonian Park.

The early and mid-nineteenth century was a time of mass migration from Scotland to New Zealand and other countries in the Commonwealth. M.'s forbears on his father's side arrived in Christchurch from Auchterarder in 1855 and, like the settlers at Waipu, were farmers with a strong work ethic. Dunedin, which we were to visit later on, was the stronghold of fine Scottish settlers who turned a southern hell-hole into a noble city.

The calm water and sheltered bay of Waipu Cove a short distance away was a surprise; I couldn't see how it lived up to its rather loutish surfie image, unless there were hints of past misdemeanours in the signs on the expansive, grassy public reserve on the beachfront – no overnight camping allowed, and an alcohol ban on the reserve, with both beach and reserve closed to the public at 10 p.m. I thought it was an idyllic backwater, treed well with large pohutukawas, and a superb place for a picnic with plenty of modern seating and open wood-fired barbecues. We bought *The*

New Zealand Herald and some bottled water at the beach store, and continued on to Langs Beach just around the point.

Pohutukawa trees lean over the white sand of this small, sheltered beach, unspoilt by commercial development and one of the most exclusive places to own a holiday home. The vegetation lining the roadside, and on the surrounding hills, is typically New Zealand, with manuka, cabbage trees, ferns and flax, and there is a new elevated subdivision with good views across Bream Bay to the Hen and Chicken Islands. A gravelled road at the southern end of the delightful beach gives access to the sand for tourists. If you want to stop for a swim, this is my pick of the places.

We had heard a lot over the years about Mangawhai, its harbour and heads, and had built up expectations as to its excellence. The winding road from Langs Beach through a pretty scenic reserve, where a sign said 'All Plants Protected' boded well, we thought.

We called first at Mangawhai Heads, obviously a popular surfing spot because there were plenty of blokish cars disgorging wet-suited young men clutching surfboards. High cliffs line the ocean here, with a walking track signposted along the top, but the wind was strong, and the beach utterly uninteresting, so we drove back past the nondescript beach settlement and on to the harbour and township.

Mangawhai Heads and Mangawhai shelter behind an unusually long sand dune, which turns the harbour into an estuary, giving a cosy, lagoon-like appearance to the water. It was obvious that the magnificent sand dune, a spit, really, running parallel to the shore and home to protected birds, is the feature of Mangawhai. The Department of Conservation sanctuary here is where you can spot small shore birds, including the New Zealand dotterel and the rare fairy tern. For information on New Zealand birds, the Ornithological Society of New Zealand (Inc.), which has a world-wide membership, screens a very full website, www.osnz.org.nz.

Unfortunately there appeared to be no handy road access to what I am sure would have proved to be a fine beach on the seaward side of the dune. Small boats were anchored in the sheltered water, and the shopping centre sells bait, fishing tackle, and dive and surfing equipment, so water sports are obviously a major activity. This is the old settlement and harbour to which the residents of Port Arthur on the Kaipara Harbour tramped 150 years ago to buy essential supplies, but it has none of the charm and the colonial atmosphere of Mangonui Harbour further north. I looked in the Harcourts Real Estate Agency window to see what house prices are like, and it is impossible to buy even a very modest holiday home for under $400,000. This was one of the very few places to disappoint us in our 30 days of travelling, and as M. remarked as we drove out past the obligatory golf course, 'You can't win 'em all.'

The winding secondary road inland to Kaiwaka and State Highway 1 offered splendid, elevated pastoral views across rich green countryside and cattle farms, and the drive cheered us up. We passed a sign on leaving Kaiwaka which said, 'It's never too late to Shop New Zealand', a sentiment, when it comes to food and wine, with which I totally agree.

M. signalled with the indicator that he was turning left onto State Highway 1, and the indicator ticked, but the green light didn't come on. We pulled up and I went to the rear of the campervan while M. pressed the lever again. No indication at all. This needed immediate attention, because a warrant of vehicle fitness demands that the indicators work. Thank goodness we were on our way to Maui Motorhomes to have the electrics inspected!

The Topuni pine forest had evidence of recent logging on some hillsides, a terrible blight on the landscape, but mercifully re-planting had been undertaken on others. Pine forests are a renewable resource, a 25-30 year investment, and spend about 20 years of their life in green glory, then majesty. The trick is to drive through them at maturity, before they are harvested, to catch the scent on the wind and appreciate their simple and orderly beauty en masse. One lone pine tree is nothing, but 100,000 are a *sight*.

Wellsford welcomed us on the outskirts with a signboard for motorists which sported three logos – an information *i* and the stylised outline of a petrol pump, and a golden arched *M.* Since when did McDonald's restaurants reach such status? And did they pay for the privilege?

The Pacific and Hauraki Gulf coastline from here down to Auckland is one of the best in New Zealand. Aucklanders flock here in their thousands to retire, or to build stunning beach homes, or own lifestyle blocks of a few acres on which sumptuous country retreats are built. Commuting time from Auckland on the ever-lengthening motorway and State Highway 1 is about one hour, but in that hour you are a world away from city life and its routines. I believe that any country with an abundance of easily accessible recreational coastline cannot be said to know the true meaning of living in a 'rat race'. Just drive to Pakiri, to Leigh to dive and snorkel, to Omaha Beach, the Mahurangi Peninsula and harbours, to Sandspit, or take the ferry to Kawau Island, and see what we enjoy. It might be enough to make you want to emigrate! Warkworth, the district town, is an arts and crafts centre, has good cafés, and excellent boutique wineries, and at a recent visit to the plush native bush retreat of friends for a long Sunday lunch, we drank a very fine local barrique fermented chardonnay 2002 from Heron's Flight Vineyard, Matakana.

If you are a cheese lover, it is worth detouring to the village of Puhoi to visit the local cheese factory. The first settlers there were Bavarians from the German-Czech border, enticed to make their way to New Zealand in 1863 with the promise of free 40 acre (16 hectare) land grants. The idea was appealing, because their European homeland was already too closely cultivated. But Puhoi, when the 83 immigrants arrived, was nothing more than a small clearing in a densely-bushed valley, which had to be further cleared before farming could begin. It was a bad start for they had few tools and possessions, and in a countryside such as this, 40 acres, on which they could subsist in Germany, was barely sufficient to provide an adequate living. The settlers faced starvation and resorted to eating the edible part of nikau palms, not unlike cabbage in taste and texture, caught eels and crabs in the river, collected wild honey, and later when they had acquired guns shot wild pork and birds. Maori in the area were friendly and gave fruit and vegetables, but it was years before cropping provided adequate wheat and potatoes and the threat of extreme poverty and starvation subsided. When cleared, the free grants of land gave security to the settlers and they remained a hard-working, tight-knit Bavarian community. Today, Puhoi is renowned for its colonial buildings and excellent cheeses – the Puhoi Valley Cheese Camembert won the 2005 Champion Favourite Cheese Award. I often buy a Puhoi feta and basil cheese, made from cows' milk because I detest goats' cheese, at my local supermarket. I cube it over a salad of tomatoes, red onions, cucumber, radishes and black olives, add my own basil leaves, and it makes a fresh and substantial lunch.

The days of believing that the best cheeses come from overseas have long gone in New Zealand. I can remember the times when I bought a large high round of Stilton, carefully cut out a large hollow in the centre, replaced the cubed cheese and poured in port wine, and served it after dinner with warmed plain crackers on a buffet table. Wheels of Brie cheese from France were another favourite, and if I wanted some colour on a cheeseboard I chose the red-rinded Dutch Edam or Gouda cheeses. Parmesan always came from Italy, and occasionally I would buy a wedge of Gorgonzola for M. as a treat. I now rate New Zealand blue cheeses top for variety and excellence, particularly Kapiti Kikorangi which has had some of the pungency taken out of it with the addition of cream, and if I see a foreign blue cheese on a board I think it pretentious. The range of soft cheeses in a good supermarket is phenomenal, and I am a fan of Whitestone cheeses made in the South Island. It is only the fear of becoming tubby that stops me indulging in them daily. The sole foreign cheese I buy now, strictly for my own consumption, is Dutch Edam, because it is an excellent snacking cheese and I have not found a local equivalent. I buy the local Ferndale Parmesan cheese, which has a savoury, biting flavour and shaves well, at one third of the price of the imported Gran Padano or Parmigiana Reggiano, and I grate it happily into sauces and use it lavishly as toppings without reverence or price consciousness. Only a true gourmet would know the difference. I hope I've convinced you to Shop New Zealand, as the sign at Kaiwaka said!

It was a question of where we ate our lunchtime sandwiches, bought in what seemed a lifetime ago, but was actually only that morning at the breakfast cafe in Whangarei. Should we pull into the Wenderholm Regional Park, home to many memorable family picnics in the 1970s, or carry on past Waiwera and its thermal pools to Orewa Beach? I told M. it was a no-brainer, an easy win to Orewa.

Orewa Beach is a vast stretch of flat, hard sand, lined with beach houses, motels, open public spaces, and good camping grounds at both ends. In 1961, returning to Wellington after a caravan holiday in Paihia, we got a flat tyre and stopped on the main highway at Orewa opposite the service station to get it repaired. I saw the beach, tested the water, leapt back to the caravan to pull on my bathing suit, and swam in what I swear was lukewarm water for half an hour.

Warm coastal water is a rarity. The following year we drove up to Orewa, took a motel, and swam for two weeks in the balmy ocean. Orewa Beach in those days was undeveloped; there was no housing hinterland, no traffic jams, just two cafés, a grocer, and a fish and chip shop. Idyllic. We returned several times over the next six years, each time with another small child, and had the best seafront holidays imaginable on the wide sands. Orewa now has a Town Centre, some highrise apartment buildings, and other unattractive features of rapid growth, but The Beach remains. If

Orewa was situated on the west coast, this wide bay would be wild, windswept and wavy; here it is sheltered, warm, and the water is calm.

We sped past Hatfields Beach and drove up the hill to Orewa, slowing down on the descent to enjoy the view of the beach to the left. Orewa is kind to passers-by. There is plenty of off-road parking on the beachfront, and we walked across to the well-kept grassy reserve and perched on some large flat rocks just above the beach to have our sandwiches and orange juice. The outlook was tranquil, with large old pohutukawa trees above us on the grass, and flat, calm blue water breaking gently on the sand. This beach is wonderful for swimmers because it has a gently-sloping, smooth sandy bottom and you never feel as though you are going to step on anything sharp, or squishy.

A new motorway has put Orewa within easy commuting distance from Auckland, and the beachfront properties are in the millionaire price bracket now. There are two large camping grounds, Puriri Park Holiday Complex at the northern end of the township, and the old and very popular Orewa Beach Holiday Park at the southern end of the beachfront. Details are given in the Appendix.

We turned back onto State Highway 1A which bypasses the Orewa township, and again, as always, were disappointed by the awful cheek-by-jowl suburbia which has mushroomed on the hillside above the town. In 30 years' time people will be able to say 'Oh yes, those houses were built between 2002 and 2005', so uniform is the design and colour of the dwellings. It is not a style of architecture that grew out of the necessity to cope with the local climate, or to use building materials to hand, it is imitative Italian. I can't envisage an Italian landscape dotted with New Zealand villas, which may be an indication of how absurd the opposite is here.

An hour under the shade of a pohutukawa tree had refreshed us. We were just 50 minutes from Maui Motorhomes so we drove quickly on. Sometimes, driving on a main national highway can be an unexciting experience particularly if, for the sake of getting from A to B quickly, the road deliberately bypasses interesting towns. This will never happen to you on your journey around New Zealand, and it is one of the things that make road travel here unique. There is relatively little truly flat land in New Zealand, and nineteenth and early twentieth century roads were often pushed through the most difficult and savage terrain imaginable in order to make transport possible between existing settlements. Those settlements, some languishing, some large towns, are still there, served by the same roads. The neighbouring topography is often in its original state, particularly on the west coast of the South Island, and you can see why main highways in parts of the country are no wider than is absolutely necessary for the safe carriage of traffic and why further roads are unlikely to be built. Thus the main highways here are not merely a convenient way to reach a destination, they are a scenic journey in their own right and bring you in touch with the real New Zealand. You will never be bored.

In New Zealand we have no terrifying ring roads, where to cross a lane to exit is almost to invite death; there are no mind-numbing autobahns where you are jerked out of your stupor by a loud roar, as a metallic blur passes you so quickly in the outer lane that you cannot distinguish the make of car; there are no sad reminders of a green and pleasant, and now over-populated land carved up for mass transportation; and best of all, the motorways in and out of the main cities reinforce the pleasant nature of the development that has taken place as New Zealand has grown. I can remember clearly recoiling in shock as we drove into Prague in 1997 from the east, and saw unbearably ugly grey concrete apartment blocks which had been built during the Russian Occupation, I suppose, rising against the sky like a huge mouthful of dirty jagged teeth. Auckland, New Zealand's most populous city with over one million inhabitants, is making a valiant effort to contain urban sprawl by investing in inner-city apartment dwellings. Suburban office parks are becoming a very popular alternative to central city office blocks, and land is designated specifically for new industrial use. It is unlikely that industrial sprawl will gobble up the countryside, particularly since this is a country whose wealth depends on its farms. Some people bemoan the rise and rise of suburban shopping malls and large format retail stores contained within designated 'super centres', but the end result is that the rest of the neighbourhood is freed for more attractive use. Clever public planting along motorways, particularly in South Auckland, shields the dingy back yards of low cost housing from view, and if you are journeying south in summer you will be beguiled by the mass plantings of wildflowers fringing the edges of the motorway. They are now self-sown and a pretty and welcome sight for travellers.

I felt my usual quiet contentment when we rounded the approach to the Auckland harbour bridge and the wonderful harbour was laid out in front, in all its glory. The dominating feature is the graceful Sky Tower, a note of punctuation against the backdrop of downtown buildings and suburban villas on the slopes above the city centre. To the right are the reaches of the upper harbour, to the left is the Westhaven yacht marina, the largest in the southern hemisphere, and all around you are the bays and small beaches which line the shore. The shift from country to city is dramatic, and if you have taken the journey described so far in these chapters and bypassed the centre of Auckland on your way north, you will be unaware of Spaghetti Junction which rivals that of any other city in its motorway complexities. If you wish to bypass Auckland (a great pity because it is an interesting city to visit) just follow the signs to Hamilton.

We had to get to Mangere again, to have the campervan repaired. It was already four o'clock in the afternoon so we sped quickly along Pah Road in Epsom, over the Manukau Harbour Bridge, and turned right into Scotts Road and Richard Pearse Drive. It was incredible to be back here again, just three days after leaving Auckland. We had travelled so far, and seen so much, that we felt we had been in another country.

The workshop at Maui was expecting our arrival and we were directed by a cheerful supervisor to a side bay while an auto electrician from another company, a requirement of New Zealand law, was called to test the electrics. It took him 20 seconds to prove that our electrical troubles had been caused by a fault in the power cable connection on the outside of the van, which in turn had burned through a wire in the connecting cable plug. M. mentioned that the left hand indicator light didn't flash, although it ticked, and a check confirmed that indeed it was faulty and the van, which was new and under guarantee, would have to be returned to the agent for repair. Another, even newer, campervan of the same sort was produced and we transferred all our belongings over and packed them away, which, in the 32 degree heat on the concrete tarmac was a heavy task taking over half an hour, and were given, again, a full tank of diesel, plus a big bag of toilet chemical sachets, and a very good bottle of red wine for the trouble and inconvenience to our trip the van had caused. We drove away feeling we had been well looked after, and very happy with the unhesitating, correct response of the Maui personnel.

What to do now? It was 5 p.m. and we were at a loose end. I consulted the camping guide and discovered the Manukau Top 10 Holiday Park listed at Manurewa, 15 minutes away. M. shook his head in disbelief. He has owned a pharmacy in Manukau City for 30 years, but had no idea a camping ground existed so close by. He phoned his manager when we had booked in and said, 'Conrad, you won't believe this, but I'm camping just five minutes' drive away!' Experienced campers will agree that if you want to know a country well, then you've got to camp, but never in his wildest dreams had my husband thought he would end up doing it so close to work.

Our original plan had been to have stops at Kerikeri and Orewa, leaving Orewa early to drive to Coromandel township for the next night, but the trouble with the campervan had cancelled all that. We hadn't actually lost a night – the timetable was just arranged differently.

It felt slightly odd to camp in our own city. We could have, I suppose, driven back into Auckland, parked in the driveway and spent the night in our own apartment, but somehow it didn't tempt us. We were actually having too much fun to want to return, even for 12 hours, to what we had been rather keen to leave.

The Manukau Top 10 was typical of the other Top 10s, spotlessly clean with the best showers so far, well-kept amenities, and the added bonus of a 'village green' fringed with willows and laurel magnolias in the centre of the camp, which was exceedingly pleasant to walk across. We were charged $27 for the night, and to our pleasure found our pitch had a concrete stand.

I booked in at the Happy Days Restaurant next door for dinner and it was just as well that I had, because when we arrived at 7.30 p.m. the huge dining room was completely full, except for our table for two by the door. What a restaurant! Buffet style, eat as much as you like, for $24.90 each. The food was excellent; we had roast pork and lamb, with accompanying vegetables, but we could have enjoyed wonderful seafood, or Asian cuisine, and chosen from a vast array of desserts to follow. There were dozens of Asian families dining, so I had a prowl around the Asian section afterwards to see what was being offered and realised I had made a mistake in choosing a roast dinner. Murray had a bottle of Stella Artois, and I ordered a glass of Longridge chardonnay, a bog-standard supermarket wine, and it was far better than the rubbish of the previous two nights, at just $5.50 a glass. I had another.

We strolled back to the camp to find that the most marvellous event had occurred – a Das Rollende Hotel tour had arrived. Unfortunately the tourists had all had dinner so we didn't have the pleasure of watching the planning and efficiency that went into giving about 40 people a quick meal under the trees. Travellers in Europe will be well-acquainted with the phenomenon I am describing – a tourist sightseeing bus towing a huge, high trailer which is compartmentalised into sleeping quarters for all the passengers. The conditions under which they sleep seem so horrible that everyone in a camp watches covertly to catch a glimpse of the arrangements. Judging by the tiny windows along the right hand side of the trailer, it seems that the tourists lie in three layers in coffin-like compartments, reached by a ladder. The left hand side of the bus unclips to form a platform along which one's bunk is reached, and in all the times I have encountered a Das Rollende Hotel I have never ever been able to see what the interior arrangements are like because a stout tarpaulin drops down immediately the corridor is lowered to protect the privacy of the tourists. We can only conjecture. What happens if you have a nightmare and sit up suddenly? Would you crack your head? What say nature calls during the night? What if you are surrounded by snorers? And how do you dress and undress in privacy? These mysteries have never been solved.

In 1997, in Strasbourg, two similar outfits pulled into our camp ground, the Camping Montagne Verte, for an overnight stop. Immediately everyone went on high alert. This might be a chance to examine the inner sanctum. But so skilful were the tour operators that nothing was revealed except 60 or 70 elderly, exhausted travellers who helped set up the folding dining tables, ate a one-dish dinner, and drove off in the buses to tour the beautiful city. They departed very early the next morning after a hasty bread roll and mug of coffee, taken standing outside, for another day on the road. We never saw them smile, or relax into animated conversation; they just followed orders and did smartly as they were told. The tour was run like an army exercise. The only compensation was that these were people who couldn't afford to tour in any other way, and had the gumption to do it. Although everyone is always avid to see more, like most caravanners M. and I find the event distressing to watch. It goes against the grain, somehow.

True to form, this bus had just departed to take the tourists into Auckland for a night on the town. We were too tired to wait up to spy on their return, so went to bed.

CHAPTER 8

AUCKLAND

In the last chapter I gave details of the Manukau Top 10 Holiday Park where we stayed overnight because of its proximity to Maui Motorhomes at Mangere, and its location on the way south out of Auckland. If you are planning to bypass Auckland city altogether, then this is the camp for you.

However, The Top 10 Auckland North Shore Motel and Holiday Park at Takapuna on the North Shore (details in Appendix) is Auckland's only five star holiday park, is on a public transport route, and is the closest to town. It might suit you better if you plan to stay for a few days in the Auckland region. *The New Zealand Camping Guide, North Island,* gives it a rave review, describing it as 'more a resort centre' with splendid facilities. Although not a beach camp, you are within a short drive of the wonderful North Shore bays and beaches, which stretch from Long Bay in the north to Cheltenham and Devonport beaches at the southern end of the peninsula.

On your way out of Auckland Airport, stop at the brochure stand in the Arrivals Hall and select those which interest you. Jasons has an exceptionally informative visitor guide listing all the attractions, with their locations numbered on very good maps at the back of the booklet. This publication, which has won a tourism award and fits snugly into a handbag, should be the mainstay of your local sightseeing. Its excellence is indicative of the importance that New Zealand places on tourism, and I wish we could have found this sort of information booklet on our travels in other countries.

The Auckland i-Site Visitor Centre (ph. (09) 979 2333, www.aucklandnz.com) is located in the Atrium at Sky City, on the corner of Federal and Victoria Streets, and there is also an Auckland

Visitors Centre at 287 Queen Street (ph. (09) 302 9336, website as above), which you may find is more conveniently located.

Unfortunately, Auckland is not an easy city in which to drive. Road traffic is gridlocked during busy times, and delays occur on the motorways. If you are based at the Manukau Top 10 and wish to drive into Auckland, I recommend parking your vehicle at Mission Bay, one of the popular eastern beaches, and taking a local bus for the pleasant 10 minute ride along the waterfront into the Britomart Bus Station in the central city, from where you can start your sightseeing. There is plenty of unlimited free parking one street back from the beachfront and, as a bonus, you can have dinner at one of the excellent restaurants or cafés before returning to your camp for the night. The Maxx Contact Centre (ph. (09) 366 6400, www.maxx.co.nz) situated at the Britomart Information Kiosk in Downtown Auckland provides free information on public transport by bus, train, or ferry in the Auckland region.

The main shopping precincts in the city are High Street and Chancery, Newmarket's Broadway, Parnell Road, and Ponsonby Road. The convenient Link bus service calls at scheduled bus stops, many of them directly outside tourist attractions, every 10 minutes on its loop around the central city. The charge is $1.30 per ride, and you can do the full loop for this amount. The drivers are helpful and will make sure you get off where you want to. Easily identifiable bright red city circuit buses leave every 10 minutes from the Britomart bus station at the bottom of Queen Street and go to The Edge entertainment area, Auckland University, the Viaduct Harbour, and Queen Street. The service is free.

Although there are many open-air car parks in the central city, the cost is prohibitive for an all-day stay, and your money would be better spent on taking the Explorer Bus (ph. 0800 439 756, www.explorerbus.co.nz) which operates a hop-on-hop-off all-day general sightseeing tour, every day of the year, from 9 a.m. to 4 p.m. This marvellous service costs just $30 per adult for the all-day pass, or $45 per adult for a two-day pass, and includes Auckland's

14 major attractions. The principal departure and ticket point is the Ferry Building on Quay Street at Queen Elizabeth Square, but you can initiate your tour at any of the 14 pick-up points and pay the driver for your pass.

Auckland is the country's largest region with 1.3 million people, approximately 30 per cent of the total population of New Zealand. The 'city' that I refer to loosely is just one of four cities which make up the region, the others being the North Shore, Waitakere, and Manukau cities. Each city has its own identity and governance, embraces European, Polynesian and Asian cultures, and the combination of urban and natural environments creates a lifestyle which is ranked one of the best in the world.

The region's natural environment is varied, with rainforest to the west in the Waitakere Ranges and the Hunua Ranges in the south-east, the Hauraki Gulf with its splendid islands, over 40 dormant or extinct volcanos, and many beautiful beaches. It is said that no one is further away from a beach than 30 minutes! The German geologist, Dr Ferdinand von Hochstetter, arrived in Auckland in December 1858 to examine the province's local coalfields. He was a gifted, hard-working scientist, and in the 10 months he was in New Zealand he managed to establish the country's geological structure. He mapped and examined Auckland's isthmus, collected many botanical and zoological specimens, and described it as one of the most remarkable volcanic districts of the earth. We've all heard of the Seven Hills of Rome, which I have always found hard to locate when there; everywhere you look in Auckland you will see the cone of a volcano, some of them almost side by side.

Auckland City is located on an isthmus separating two large and lovely harbours – the Waitemata Harbour on the Pacific Ocean side, and Manukau Harbour which exits into the Tasman Sea on the west coast. It was founded in 1841 by Captain William Hobson R.N., the Lieutenant-Governor of New Zealand, in anticipation of it being the future seat of government. Errol Brathwaite in *The*

Companion Guide to New Zealand, North Island records that 3,000 acres (1,200 hectares) of land for the settlement was bought from local Maori for 50 blankets, £50 in cash, 20 pairs of trousers, 20 shirts, 10 waistcoats, 10 caps, 4 casks of tobacco, 1 box of pipes, 100 yards of gown pieces, 10 iron pots, 1 bag of sugar, 1 bag of flour, and 20 hatchets, less than that paid for Wellington. The main thoroughfare, Queen Street, was then merely a narrow, swampy gully which had to be crossed by footbridge. New Zealand's first Parliament was opened here in 1854, but transferred to the more central Wellington in 1856. Brathwaite continues: 'Auckland had a good beginning, with its tariff-free port, its position as an administrative centre, the fertility of the surrounding countryside, and its warm climate. It is not especially surprising, therefore, that it was proclaimed a city in 1871.'

The principal attractions of Auckland, in no particular order, are the Auckland Zoo, the Auckland Museum, the Auckland Art Gallery, Kelly Tarlton's Antarctic Encounter and Underwater World, the New Zealand National Maritime Museum, the Sky Tower, and the sparkling Waitemata Harbour and Hauraki Gulf.

It might surprise you to know that I consider Auckland's restaurants to be a principal tourist attraction, too. Other world cities and towns fronting a small patch of water turn 'wharfside' or 'sea front' restaurant strips into major excitements. Aucklanders tend to take their expansive waterfront for granted, as a pleasant bonus for living here, but it is 10 kilometres long, and is lined with several dozen restaurants from the Viaduct Harbour, to Mission Bay and St. Heliers; you could spend a day breakfasting at the Viaduct, having a swim and lunch at Mission Bay, and dinner at St. Heliers. I rate our local restaurants highly, and you will eat better, more reasonably priced food in Auckland than in almost any other city in the world.

It's time to get you around! Being the map-reader on our travels, I always like to orientate myself in a new city or region. The central part of Auckland is not large, but the environs are, and the panoramic view from the Sky Tower, at 328 metres the tallest tower in the Southern Hemisphere, and taller than the Eiffel Tower, is the best there is. The observation levels, which are located well above the Sky City Casino, are reached very quickly by an internal elevator, and the 360 degree views are breathtaking. The cost is a moderate $18 per adult. On a clear day you can see over 82 kilometres, from Leigh in the north, to the Coromandel Peninsula in the east, the Waitakere Ranges to the west, and the Bombay Hills which separate Auckland from the rest of New Zealand, to the south. It's a mighty view, and is worth a visit. Make sure you get a copy of the brochure *Put Auckland into Perspective* which numbers the attractions beneath you and indicates exactly what you are seeing. You might like to book in at the revolving restaurant, which has an excellent menu and quick service, and your lunch (for that is the best time to go) will be finished in the one hour the restaurant takes to complete the full circuit. It is a relaxing experience if you are jet-lagged.

If you don't have a head for heights, orientation can be gained easily by taking the Explorer Bus service to the top of Mt. Eden. The panorama is enticing, and you will have the added benefit of being at the top of one of Auckland's volcanos.

Now that you've got your bearings, let's go calling.

If you have decided to visit only one museum in New Zealand, then it should be the Auckland War Memorial Museum (ph. Infoline (09) 306 7067, www.aucklandmuseum.com), New Zealand's oldest, situated pleasantly on a knoll in the grounds of the Auckland Domain with extensive views over the city and harbour. The museum is the repository of the most significant collection of Maori and Pacific artefacts in the world, essential viewing for a tourist hoping to explore the Polynesian heritage of this part of the world. On your tour of the museum you will become acquainted with the flora and fauna of New Zealand, some displayed in renditions of their natural surroundings which will invoke instant recognition as you tour the relevant parts of the country. The Discovery Centre is aimed primarily at children, but for me is worthwhile for the several dozen specimen drawers containing pinned displays of the insects of New Zealand. The country's war history is recorded on the top floor, and the museum store on the ground floor stocks a range of New Zealand-made handcrafts and gifts.

Don't be tempted to drive your campervan to the museum; it is almost impossible to park in the Domain grounds, extensive though they are, unless you are there by 10 a.m. on a Sunday morning. Auckland City does not have botanic gardens – you will have to travel to Manurewa in South Auckland for that – but the fernery and winter gardens adjacent to the museum are pleasant to visit, as is the Parnell Rose Garden which is on the Explorer Bus route. The best months to visit the rose garden are from November to March, and you might like to look also at the small copy of a colonial garden border, which I know is accurate, because I can remember almost all the plants being in my grandmother's garden in Christchurch; some I hadn't seen since then until I stumbled across this local 'find' a few months ago.

Even if you are not particularly fond of marine life, a visit to Kelly Tarlton's Antarctic Encounter and Underwater World (ph. information 0800 805 050, www.kellytarltons.co.nz) at 23 Tamaki Drive, Orakei, is a worthwhile experience. This is one of the few attractions where you can be reasonably sure of getting a place in the free car park. Kelly Tarlton was a renowned diver who had the vision to excavate under Tamaki Drive and form tunnels in the harbour from which sea life could be viewed. The aquarium is a world-class attraction; visitors are carried around slowly on a moving walkway while the sharks, stingrays, eels and fish swim above and alongside them. You will have a view of underwater life usually reserved for divers, without needing to get wet. A prime attraction, too, is the Antarctic Encounter, which takes you in a heated snow cat around a sub-Antarctic landscape of ice and snow to view colonies of King and Gentoo penguins. A life-size replica of Captain Robert Falcon Scott's historic Antarctic hut is on display, furnished and equipped like the original hut which still stands today.

You will also find free parking space at the Auckland Zoo (ph. Information 360 3819, www.aucklandzoo.co.nz) situated in Motions Road, Western Springs, a 15 minute drive from the city centre. If you are travelling with children, be assured that this is a family-friendly zoo. My grandsons love the splendid giraffe enclosure, the elephant house, and the underwater sea-lion tank. A morning at the zoo and a quiet time in the Auckland Museum's Discovery Centre in the afternoon are the two best places to take tired children recovering from a long air journey. If you are in Manukau City, then Butterfly Creek (ph. (09) 275 8880, www.butterflycreek.co.nz) located on Tom Pearce Drive, one minute's drive from Auckland International Airport, is highly recommended. The attraction is geared towards children with an adventure playground, pony rides, a farmyard where children can cuddle rabbits and guinea pigs, and a small choo-choo train which circles an outlying wetland area. The tropical butterfly house offers a magical experience, particularly for adults, for thousands of brightly-coloured butterflies flutter around as you walk through it.

The Auckland Art Gallery (ph. (09) 379 1349, www.aucklandartgallery.govt.nz) is located within two buildings, the Main Gallery on the corner of Wellesley and Kitchener Streets in the central city, and the New Gallery 50 yards away on the corner of Wellesley and Lorne Streets. Between them, the buildings house the most extensive collection of art in the country, comprising historic, modern and contemporary art works by New Zealand, Maori and Pacific Island artists, and European painting, sculpture and print collections from the fourteenth century to the present day. There are over 12,500 works in the collection. The gallery hosts excellent touring exhibitions, and the extensive website is worth checking out before visiting. It is interesting to view the landscapes painted by nineteenth century artists to see how much has been achieved, in such a short time, in setting up New Zealand.

Now for Auckland's jewel in the crown, the Waitemata Harbour and the Hauraki Gulf. As I reiterate throughout this book, if you live inland, then you must take every opportunity while touring New Zealand to enjoy the coastal waters. Here in Auckland, they are varied, sheltered, utterly scenic, and very memorable. The harbour is small enough to be travelled across quickly by ferry, and the gulf has wonderful islands to visit. There are boat trips to suit every traveller's time frame, from the 10 minute ride to the harbourside village of Devonport, or across to Rangitoto Island, Auckland's dormant volcano and significant landmark, the 30 minute ride to Waiheke Island, or cruises to the outer islands of Great Barrier Island and Kawau Island. If you want to visit just one destination, then make it Waiheke Island.

Fullers Cruises and Tours (ph. Information and Bookings (09) 367 9111, email: enquiries@fullers.co.nz, www.fullers.co.nz) is located in the Ferry Building on Quay Street, and operates frequent daily sailings to Waiheke Island for a cost of $26 per adult return. An all-day pass on the local bus service, which meets all sailings, costs $10 per adult. Try to take a crossing which stops at the Devonport wharf on the way – it will add only 10 minutes to the half hour ride to Waiheke – and enquire, also, whether your sailing is one which calls at Rangitoto Island. You might as well see as much as you can, if this is to be your only jaunt on the sea.

The Fullers Explorer Tour ferry departs from Auckland daily at 10 a.m. and 12 noon, and offers a one and a half hour fully commentated bus tour of Waiheke Island on arrival. The cost for ferry and bus is $42 per adult, and bookings are essential for this popular service. If your mission in New Zealand is to tour the wine regions, then a Fullers ferry departs at 11 a.m. daily for the Waiheke Island Vineyard Tour. The four-hour commentated island bus tour includes a visit to three award-winning vineyards, a light lunch and tastings, and the total cost is $85 per adult.

If time is your enemy but you wish to get out on the water, I recommend Fullers' one and a half hour harbour cruise. The fully commentated cruise goes to the Viaduct Harbour, which was home to most America's Cup syndicates during the regattas, to the harbour bridge (over the top of which, incidentally, you can take a guided walk), the Naval Base, and Devonport. The cost is $30 per adult and light refreshments are served.

Sealink (ph. Reservations (09) 300 5900, www.sealink.co.nz) operates a car ferry service from Half Moon Bay, Pakuranga, in east Auckland, to Waiheke and Great Barrier Islands. There are 12 return trips daily to Waiheke Island, and the return trip for a campervan like ours costs $113, plus $33 for each adult. This is an expensive way to visit Waiheke Island, unless you plan to camp for a day or two. Unfortunately *The New Zealand Camping Guide, North Island* has only two listings for Waiheke Island, and neither reads well, but I will give them to you. Luxurious they ain't.

Fossil Bay Farm at 58 Korora Road, Oneroa, (ph. (09) 372 7569) is an organic farm in sheltered grounds with orchards, hens, beehives, and a plant nursery. There is a kitchen, and ablutions are in the form of a multi-purpose laundry, toilet and shower. Tent sites cost $10 per person and there is no mention of motorhomes. The Whakanewha Regional Park off Gordons Road, Half Moon Bay, has 'reasonably level' camping areas, and borders a shallow beach. There are no facilities; the toilets are composting, and there is only cold water. A permit to stay must be obtained from the Waiheke Visitor Information Centre, at 2 Korora Road, Oneroa, (ph. (09) 372 1234) or the ranger at the park. You will truly be back to nature here. The camping charge is $6 per adult and, again, no mention is made of motorhomes.

Having visited Waiheke Island many times, my advice is to have a day out at the vineyards. The cost is reasonable, you will see a lot of the island, talk to the local people, and you can take some bottles of nice wine back to your campervan to enjoy as you tour the rest of New Zealand.

You will have a hands-on, authentic sailing experience on the Waitemata Harbour and Hauraki Gulf if you become one of the crew on board NZL 40, or NZL 41, former America's Cup yachts. The America's Cup Sailing Experience takes two hours, and if you don't wish to be actively involved you can just sit back and enjoy your outing in the superb boat. The cost is $135 per adult and $110 per child over 10 years. You can also book a three-hour Match Race cruise for $195 per adult, and $175 per child over 10 years. The cruises are extremely popular, and offer a thrilling experience and a great memory to take home with you, if you've never sailed on a yacht before. I believe that although it's lovely to *look at* attractions, it is so much better to *participate* in one. Here, you'll be doing just that! The company to contact is SailNZ (Ph: (09) 359 5987, email: info@sailnz.co.nz, www.sailnz.co.nz), which won the 2003/04 Adventure Activity Tourist Award.

The company also offers the chance to crew the maxi yacht of the late Sir Peter Blake's 1985 Whitbread Round the World challenge on a two night cruise from Auckland to the Bay of Islands or return. Accommodation is in the original racing conditions, no sailing experience is necessary, and the cost for adults is $595.

If you are travelling with a large party of tourists, you might like to charter a skippered yacht for a day's leisurely sailing around the harbour and gulf. Chieftain Cruises (ph. (09) 528 0052, email: info@chieftaincruises.co.nz, www.chieftaincruises.co.nz) arranges boat charter and hire. We have used their services twice in the last 10 years, and have had memorable days on the water. Arrangements will need to be made well in advance, as the company requires full payment two weeks before the booked date. Prices vary according to the type of yacht.

Before you bid farewell to Auckland's waterfront, visit the acclaimed New Zealand National Maritime Museum situated on the corner of Quay and Hobson Streets at the Viaduct Harbour (ph. 0800 725 897, www.nzmaritime.org) which gives a solid account of New Zealand's maritime past, from the early Polynesian voyages of navigation to European settlement and coastal trade, and its current pre-eminence in yachting achievements. The museum houses an impressive collection of models, boats, and life-sized exhibits, and has a heritage fleet moored outside at the marina.

In 1973, when caravanning in England, we took the children to see *Gypsy Moth IV*, the yacht that Sir Francis Chichester had sailed single-handedly around the world. I had read his thrilling account of the voyage, and this was supposed to be just an educational trip for the girls, but when I stepped on board and visited his cabin, and saw his tiny quarters, his cramped bunk still with the bedding on it, forlorn leftover tins of salmon, and his slender library, I was overcome with the feeling that this was a privileged, private place, and that I was very fortunate to have seen it. I looked at his books. One, entitled *An Island to Oneself* by Tom Neale, stayed in my mind, and when I returned to New Zealand I bought it. Chichester took no chances, which is probably why he survived that arduous journey; the book is the autobiography of a recluse who deliberately chose to retire to the uninhabited island of Suwarrow in the Cook Islands Group in the South Pacific. It is an unputdownable account of Neale's efforts to get there, what he took in the way of tools and supplies, and how he fought the elements to live on the tiny, remote island for six years until he returned to Rarotonga, the principal island in the Cooks Group, for the sake of his health. I can only suppose that Sir Francis Chichester had his own survival in mind if he was marooned similarly. It is a handbook for aspiring island hermits, and is one of my most prized possessions for the memories it invokes of that intimate day at Greenwich. The moral of the story is that if, in Auckland, you get a chance to go aboard a renowned boat, then *do*.

There are sure to be howls of rage from Aucklanders reading this chapter. 'But what about the Waitakere Ranges?' 'What about the cathedral?' 'How could you leave out Motat, and Victoria Park Market!' The attractions that I have listed are the ones that *I myself* would get off the Explorer Bus to visit. On the way, you will have the chance to see the other places.

The truth, as every committed traveller knows, is that time is always short and one can't see everything. The places and attractions I have suggested are either those whose quality cannot be matched elsewhere in New Zealand, or those which exist only here, in Auckland.

CHAPTER 9

TO THE COROMANDEL PENINSULA

After having swapped our campervan over for a new one at the Maui headquarters in Mangere, the following morning we walked next door to the Happy Days Restaurant for the cooked buffet breakfast, priced at $10.90, and found we were the only people there. After a good stoke-up on scrambled eggs, bacon, tomatoes and sausages we arrived back at the camp in time to see the Das Rollende Hotel rig pull out. I hoped that they were going in our direction, to the Coromandel Peninsula, because I wouldn't have minded another try at solving the mystery of the sleeping arrangements. However, Rotorua was the more likely destination – those sorts of tours favour the famous sightseeing highlights. If you are wondering why I don't just go up to the tour guide and ask to see inside the trailer, the reason is very simple; a feature of these bus-hotel tours is that the travellers and their minders keep very much to themselves and there is an unwillingness among regular campers to consciously invade their privacy, no matter how curious we might be.

The motorway heading south from Auckland is a delight to travel on. Before it was constructed in the 1960s, all traffic had to use the Great South Road, and progress through the towns of Otahuhu, Papatoetoe, Manurewa and further south was often arduous. This day we turned left onto the Great South Road at the camp exit and drove through the Manurewa shopping centre, its busy road reminiscent of an English high street with small stores jammed together and the parking spaces already full even though it was barely 9.30 a.m., and followed the motorway signs to Hamilton.

New Zealand does not specialise in motorway rest stops and shopping and service centres, and tourists are well-advised to fill up with fuel, food and supplies at the many small centres and towns they will pass through. However, there is a fairly new and very good BP Information and Service Centre pull-in on the motorway a few kilometres south of Manurewa which has garage services, sells fuel and food, has a McDonald's restaurant, and a tourist shop. We turned off the motorway to buy the morning newspaper, a Moro chocolate bar for M. and fresh pump action bottles of water to drink on the journey, and continued on.

A few years ago someone had the brilliant idea of sowing the seeds of wild flowers along the sides and down the centre strip of the southern motorway and every summer a thick burst of glorious pinks, reds, blues and purples lights up what are normally rather predictable grassy verges. I thought the display a little disappointing this time; perhaps self-sowing only lasts for a short while and a few fresh packets of seeds need to be sprinkled next spring. I noticed a sign which read 'Pacific Seeds Field Test Trial Site', so perhaps things are in hand already. I will await developments with interest.

The land on either side of the motorway is rich and fertile, with tidy paddocks, huge glasshouses, and potato fields. At Bombay the road configuration changes into that of an expressway with a concrete safety barrier down the centre. This stretch of road, which now seems so harmless, was a notorious traffic accident black spot. At the foot of the steep Bombay Hill, the overbridge and underpasses and well-signposted turnoff left to Thames and the Coromandel Peninsula along State Highway 2 give no indication of the driving chaos that used to exist at this busy intersection. However, some good things never change, and the huge cornfields at the start of State Highway 2, and another landmark, the bizarre Castle Café and Store which looks exactly like its name, will probably go on forever.

The stretch of State Highway 2 between Mangatawhiri (pron. munga-tar-firry) and Maramarua (pron. marra-ma-ruer) has perhaps the worst accident record in New Zealand. The surface is smooth, well-marked and graded, and many improvements in the interests of safety have been made over the years, but the road is a main arterial route to State Highway 25 and the Coromandel Peninsula and to State Highway 27 and the Bay of Plenty and Rotorua, used by logging and long-haulage trucks and trailers, milk and petrol tankers, and farm vehicles, as well as hordes of holiday-makers in peak summer times, and needs to be accorded great respect and attention. This last summer had seen some ghastly multi-death accidents, and although I used to drive along the road with impunity 30 years ago, my car loaded with children on the way to our holiday home at Pauanui, I now felt quite nervous and asked M. to drive slowly. He said it was too nice a day to hurry, and anyway we had plenty of time to get to Coromandel township and our camp for the night.

There is an alternative route to the Coromandel Peninsula from Auckland, taken by turning off the southern motorway at Mt. Wellington, just south of Auckland city, and following signs to Pakuranga, Howick, Whitford and Clevedon, and passing Kawakawa Bay and Orere; you can stop for a soak in the hot springs at Miranda, visit the shorebird centre, and join up with State Highway 25 at Waitakaruru. This is a recommended drive through rich farmlands and lifestyle blocks, and along a coastal road which skirts the Hunua Ranges and offers splendid views across the Firth of Thames. If you are keen to stay off state highways this is an attractive choice and will put you more in touch with the real New Zealand than a motorway ever can.

It was, fortunately, too early in the day for much traffic on this stretch of State Highway 2. We had a clear road in front of us, and I relaxed and enjoyed the pastoral vistas. Summer had been late in coming, and land, which at this time of the year is usually dried out, was a lush, bright green. Here the hay was rolled into large rounds, and not bagged. Those bright plastic bags spoil the countryside.

I have been passing the Pink Pig Café, a well-known truck stop, for 30 years and have never pulled up to see what it offers inside. If we hadn't had such a huge Happy Days breakfast I would have but, again, we whizzed past and that delight will have to wait for another time. We came to the Red Fox Tavern, the famous local watering hole. It is a good place to break your journey if you want a beer and a pie, a round of snooker, or a play on the pokies.

In 30 minutes we reached the turnoff to the left onto State Highway 25, and met the flat, straight road which traverses the northern reaches of the Hauraki Plains. Ahead of us the long, jagged and forested spine of the Coromandel Range was clearly visible. The highway is narrow and the road surface undulating, with deep ditches on either side into which, over the years, many speeding cars have nose-dived. Old-fashioned pink roses still ramble over front hedges and fences of the bungalows and small cottages which line parts of the road, but to my disappointment I didn't see any plump goats tethered to the fences, 'mowing' the long grass. Grazing goats used to be a practical maintenance feature of the New Zealand roadsides, but on this holiday I didn't see any, so I presume their animal rights have been considered and the increasingly busy and fume-filled highways are now a danger to their health!

These flat, broad plains border the Firth of Thames, and today give no indication of the travails the nineteenth century pioneers faced in carving out productive farms. The first routes were nothing more than slushy, muddy tracks over the low-lying land, pushed through very high, dense bush, and sledges were a favoured form of transport used by the early farmers and their families. A sledge was easily transformed into a 'carriage' by nailing on a large box to contain goods, or passengers. Eventually the swampy plains were drained and reclaimed, the Piako and Waitoa Rivers dredged and cleared, small wharves were built, and what look like muddy creeks today as you drive past were the canals of the pioneers. The land was soon settled, and by the twentieth century people could journey to Auckland by vessel via the many little waterways and the Firth of Thames.

The district is famous for its large flounder and if you see a sign up at Piako Pete's advertising a fresh catch, and you fancy fish for your dinner, this is the place to buy it. You will need either a very large frying pan to cook them one at a time, or a barbecue facility at your campground.

The Piako Ostrich Farm has meat sales, and since ostrich is not readily available in supermarkets and is usually only seen on the menus of the better restaurants in New Zealand, this might be the time to buy some steaks and satisfy your curiosity if you haven't already tried it. I'm not able to comment on its taste; when it comes to birds, duck and turkey are the highest I go, and I really prefer roast chicken with a herb, lemon and breadcrumb stuffing, and lots of gravy, to anything else.

I sincerely hope you do not have to queue to use the one-way bridge across the Waihou River to Kopu. It is a nightmare in summer, with cars often banked back for over a kilometre waiting for the traffic lights which control entry onto the bridge to turn green. The local council and community have been *talking* about the need for a new bridge for several years… need I say more? Transit New Zealand now recommends continuing on State Highway 2 to Paeroa, and turning left there onto State Highway 25, rather than waiting for up to an hour to cross the bridge in the peak December-January holiday period. This route adds an extra 36 kilometres onto the journey, but saves significant time, and lots of frustration.

The waterways of this region are steeped in early New Zealand history. Captain James Cook sailed H.M.S. *Endeavour* in 1769 into what was then the southern Hauraki Gulf, and was rowed by boat up the Waihou River. He named it the Thames River, and called the deep gulf where he had anchored the Firth of Thames. Today the river is called by its Maori name of Waihou. Before the close of the eighteenth century the Firth of Thames and the Waihou River were centres of much maritime activity. Ships sailed up the river in search of flax for rope-making and timber with which to effect repairs, and it is often said that Captain Cook used the tall, straight trunks of kauri trees from this area to replace his masts. The broad, flat reaches of the river were well-suited to passenger and cargo transport, and by the 1880s it was possible to take a steamer upriver to Matamata. The river and its trade were vital to the development of the townships of the northern Waikato region for supplies could come directly from Auckland, and the local butter, cheese, timber, flax and meat sent back by return journey.

As you cross the bridge to Kopu, and turn left there to follow the coast road to Thames, the commercial centre of the Coromandel and the largest town with a population of 10,000 people, you will enter a region unlike any other in New Zealand. The Coromandel Peninsula is one large coast-to-coast forest park, ringed in its entirety by stunningly beautiful bays and offshore islands. This juxtaposition of dark, rugged, native tree and bush-clad hills and marvellous coastal scenery, all within a fairly small area, is a perfect example of what this amazing country has to offer the tourist in the way of natural and unspoilt beauty. The Coromandel Peninsula is called, with justification, the playground of Auckland, for the popular beaches are within two to three hours' driving time. Yet in spite of all the frenzied holiday activity, the Coromandel has a sense of apartness from the rest of the North Island, probably because residential and recreational development can take place only around the coastline, and the dark, sharp-sided range will stay as it is.

The road approaching Thames is low-lying and the land on either side is subject to fearful flooding in a deluge, yet I saw new housing springing up where I would have thought the flood danger still existed. A little part of history had disappeared here, with the demolition of the old vineyard and garden formerly owned by a Chinese viticulturalist who made excellent wine and apricot brandy and sold it from his roadside shop. In the 1970s and early '80s I made many stops to purchase wines, and I kept a bottle of his apricot brandy for many years, having a little tot now and then to see how it was getting on. I refused to share it with anyone else. After 10 years there was still some left, true nectar of the gods, and irreplaceable now.

Thames itself shows little of its early life as the roaring goldmining settlement it was in the 1860s, but if you drive around the centre there is still architectural evidence of those times in a number of buildings, including the old library and the police station, not used nowadays. Thames was officially proclaimed a goldfield in 1867 and mining continued in the area until the early 1920s. The biggest strikes were made at depths of less than 100 feet, for water seepage prevented much low level mining. Eventually the shafts were left to fill with water, scrub overgrew the workings, and today there is little to be seen of the glory days. Unbelievably, there were over 100 hotels serving the miners during the heyday of this frontier-type town.

We needed some food supplies, and found the Goldfields Shopping Centre off to the left of the main street, with a large Pak 'n Save supermarket and plenty of parking for the campervan. I was going to have to cook dinner that night, so I bought some excellent ham carved freshly off the leg, ingredients for a salad, a few potatoes, some cheese, and the obligatory bottle of wine, and we pressed on. If you wish to stay overnight in Thames, the Dickson Holiday Park in Victoria Street, a short distance from the town centre, has the attraction of a Tropical Butterfly and Orchid Garden located within its grounds. Details are given in the Appendix.

The drive along the Firth of Thames is spectacular, and very winding, with the road lying just a few feet above the level of the water and the shore rocks, and lined with ancient, gnarled pohutukawa trees, New Zealand's own Christmas trees, which frequently overhang the road. This is a drive to take in high summer when the large, pom-pom shaped red flowers cover the trees, and contrast in a burst of dazzling colour with the dark green foliage, the blues of the sea and sky, and the grey of the road. Even though this was February, there were still plenty of blossoms to see. A few years ago there was a dastardly move afoot by the roading authorities to fell the pohutukawas, which, they said, were too old and tired and constituted a danger to traffic. Howls of rage stopped the vandalism, and the trees are still there. This is not a stretch of road to hurry along. It is narrow in parts and I fear it would be all too easy to take a corner too wide and end up in the drink. Although the road is only 55 kilometres long, one hour's travel time should be allowed for a motorhome.

We were on our way to Coromandel town. The peninsula is a stronghold of the parliamentary Green Party which wishes, of course, to preserve the natural heritage of this idyllic part of New Zealand. I am in complete agreement with the party (for the only time in my life) that nothing should change. The small clustered settlements which line the road are nostalgic reminders of old-style New Zealand, places where you can row a dinghy out into the firth to fish for your dinner, cultivate a vegetable patch and grow marvellous dahlias along the front fence, and put down a home brew of beer in the wash-house out the back. It would be a pity to spoil it. If you want to stop for a picnic, there is a good pull-in on a grassy reserve at Tapu.

The road climbed steeply over a bluff at Wilsons Bay, and M. was able to do only 40 kilometres per hour in places, a good thing, as the view overlooking Manaia Harbour and the outlying islands was one which revised our former opinion that the best coastal scenery in the world is in the Far North, so satisfying and outrageously beautiful was the panorama here in front of us – vivid golden sand in the coves rimming water of a rich turquoise not ever seen elsewhere, the bush on the hillsides a kaleidoscope of brightest greens. A former Governor-General of New Zealand, Viscount Cobham, had remarked many times during his tenure that the quality of our southern hemisphere light is unique. Here, today, I realised what he meant. Oceans, sand and trees are fundamentally the same colours everywhere, yet we have astonishing intensity of hue in the natural landscape, and others don't.

These were the early days; as we travelled down the length of the North and South Islands we encountered many places where nature surpassed itself with its glorious palette. I had always been suspicious of the colours used in paintings of the South Island landscape. No pasture could be *that* green, the sky *that* blue and the clouds so pearly, the tussockland *that* yellow, the lake *that* ultramarine. How wrong. I was to find that the scenery of New Zealand outdoes itself with an abundance of scrumptious colour and lushness, and flawless form. Our travel posters don't lie.

We continued in reverent silence. I was impatient to get to Coromandel. It had long been a place I wanted to visit, and I marvel that at my time of life I had never got into my car, and just *gone*! As we skirted the Coromandel Harbour on our way into the outskirts of the town, there was a sign I rather liked, 'Oysters, mussels, prawns, whitebait, large fat eels', at a roadside fish shop. We drove further in, and the next great sign, above the Smoked Fish Shop, read 'You catch 'em, we'll smoke 'em'. I felt this was my kind of place.

The town has a population of about 1,500 people, of whom 17 per cent are aged over 65 years. Whether the locals like it so much that they never want to leave, or whether it is a conscious life-style choice for retirees from other centres, is not known. The local mussel factory is the town's biggest employer. This is a delightful, quirky little town, formerly a goldmining and timber centre, now home to artists and craftspeople, and with a village feel to the atmosphere. Like any other old town, the corner as we turned into the main street was dominated by the wooden building of the former National Bank, now called Assay House, built in 1873 and occupied by the bank until 1900. Banks, churches, and pubs are always on the most prominent corner sites in the early New Zealand settlements, and it must have been a comfort when you struggled into town a century or more ago to know that in one small area everything important could be taken care of!

At the Admiral's Arms, a Coromandel landmark, we ordered a beer and a glass of Corbans pinot gris, and sat in the sunny, sheltered and colourful back garden to enjoy them. M. wasn't sure he would like the Monteith's Black the barlady recommended; she obligingly poured him a good-sized tot to sample, but he settled for his favourite Monteith's Gold instead.

We drifted along the main street to find a lunch café, feeling that we were in another world; it was very hard to believe that we had quit the environs of Auckland barely three hours ago. Lunch for me, eaten outdoors at a pavement table, was a steak sandwich, with a large slice of hot, freshly-cooked steak, sautéed onions, lettuce and tomato, slopped with mayo and barbecue sauce, piled on a grilled panini and washed down with a pot of Earl Grey tea – my first proper pot of tea for four days. I'd never eaten a steak sandwich before. It was filling, and delicious, and several times on our journey, when faced with a large blackboard of choices, I found it a very safe and predictable food to order.

These days, modernity always prevails in what seem the most out-of-the-way places when you look at the map. Opposite our café was an Internet outlet, so M. went inside and caught up with his mail, while I had a loss-making session at the pokies in the den next door. Although we stopped only for a drink and some lunch, I had the feeling I was missing out on some excellent food. This, after all, was a seaside town on a peninsula renowned for the abundant seafood along its coastline. I dragged my feet as we walked past the Peppertree Restaurant to read their posted menu. They offered a fish platter, always my favourite, of crayfish terrine, marinated snapper, seared scallops, and oysters. If I hadn't already bought food for our dinner in the van I would have come here for a feast.

M. wanted to put his feet up and read the newspaper, and I had some laundry to do, so we drove the van along Colville Road for a few kilometres and came to our camp for the night, the Shelly Beach Top 10 Holiday Park. This was a very nice-looking camp, well-treed, with closely mown lawns leading down to an aptly-named shelly beach. If the tide had been in it would have been a super place for a cooling paddle. This is a very good camp for an overnight stop, with tap water on site, and an excellent kitchen and all the usual amenities provided by Top 10 camps. The showers are slow, but quite adequate, and I thought the toilet bowls needed a good dose of bleach to whiten them, but the buildings are not new and I presume that at some stage soon everything will be given a face-lift. Our site cost $24.30 for the night.

Fifteen motorhomes and several tent parties pulled in for the night. The tenters were the lucky ones, for if they wished they could have driven their cars up to Port Jackson and Cape Colville at the tip of the peninsula. After the small settlement of Colville, 18 km north of Coromandel, the road is unsealed and, like the Ninety Mile Beach, specifically forbidden in the Agreement to drivers of Maui Motorhomes and Rental Cars. If you look at the map of the peninsula and are tempted to take a short cut along the unsealed road from Tapu to Coroglen on the eastern side, don't, for a road restriction applies here also. I have done the journey several times by car, and I hate it. It is a narrow, sick-making, winding drive with badly-graded corners, slow and difficult by car, and would be nerve-wracking in a large van. It's a pity, as you are up close to magnificent forest, and some fine kauri.

Although this is a book on motorhoming, it is worthwhile to digress a little and tell you about the return journeys which can be undertaken by car from Coromandel to Port Jackson, and from Coromandel to Port Charles. Because of the driving difficulty, this is a part of New Zealand rarely seen by overseas tourists. The road from Colville to Port Jackson, described on my map as an unsealed narrow scenic route (shorthand for beautiful scenery but damned difficult driving) skirts pretty bays, but I believe the best place to visit is Port Charles, to be undertaken as a separate trip, which lies at the head of an isolated, beautiful bay where it is possible to lie on the sand and believe you have left the planet, so remote and peaceful is the area.

There is a beach campsite at Port Jackson run by the Department of Conservation, with water, toilets, a shower, barbecue, and rubbish disposal, but intending campers are advised to contact the Department of Conservation in Coromandel for availability of sites during the peak holiday fortnight of 24 December to 7 January.

You cannot, disappointingly, do a round trip by car. From Fletcher Bay to Stony Bay, the only access is by the Coromandel Walkway, a walk of at least four hours. The Department of Conservation campground at Fletcher Bay 'allows access to the spectacular Coromandel Walkway, which is the only link with Stony Bay'. The facilities available are the same as at Port Jackson, and the price per adult is the same, $7.

At Stony Bay the Department of Conservation runs what is described in my camping guide as 'relaxed, comfortable camping in a 5 hectare setting'. The fishing and diving is excellent, as is the four-hour walk across to Fletcher Bay. The facilities are as already described, but the camp lacks showers. The price again is $7 per adult.

It is possible to do a full day guided tour of the Coromandel coastal walkway, without having to use your own car, from Fletcher Bay to Stony Bay. The cost is $85, and you will need to take your sandwiches, sunscreen, and suitable footwear. Details are given in the Appendix.

The journey from South Auckland to Coromandel looks long on the map, but for the most part the highway is very straight and the distance for us from camp to camp had only been 170 kilometres. It was an enjoyable drive through well-known territory, with the excitement of getting to Coromandel and exploring a part of the country we'd never visited. This day, and the one that followed, confirmed my desire to return to the peninsula before long for a few hedonistic days on the beaches and in the seafood restaurants.

CHAPTER 10

WE INSPECT A BEACHFRONT HOUSE AT MATARANGI, HAVE LUNCH AT WHITIANGA, DRIVE THROUGH WHANGAMATA, AND SLEEP AT WAIHI BEACH

We both felt energised on arising, and were experienced enough in touring to know that the breakthrough – the mental cut-off from our normal life in Auckland – had at last been achieved. It can be difficult to detach oneself from a busy, rather structured life and embark on a departure from everyday realities and disciplines. And motorcaravanning (and indeed all camping) *is* a total departure. Except that you eat and sleep at roughly the same times, nothing you do resembles your correct suburban life. You live differently, and very publicly, in surroundings which have few of your normal home comforts. It takes a while to get used to putting on clothing in the morning which is dampish if there has been a heavy dew overnight, or stiff and cold if it's frosty; to not being able to have that crucial first cup of tea without going outside, dressed, even if it's pouring with rain, to turn on the gas cylinder so that you can light the stove and put the kettle on; to coping with a tiny fridge and realising, very quickly, that all that really matters is cold milk, beer, wine and tonic water when you want it; and to shifting the fruit bowl from the bench top, to the toaster bay, then in desperation to the top of the dashboard as you make room for very basic meal preparations in the small space. Of course there were times on the journey when I longed for my spacious Auckland kitchen, renovated to my own requirements, for my marble bathroom and tidy wardrobe. But, somehow, these became unimportant luxuries because the basic truth is that if you *have* to cope, you *do*. It took me just five days.

Wednesday, 16 February was another perfect, very hot day. We had our usual caravan breakfast of fruit and yoghurt, with the welcome luxury, today, of toast. The joy of being able to use the toaster now that we had properly working electrics was exhilarating; when one is living in a style which is confined in every way, small comforts really matter. The short drive from the camp back through the residential area of Colville Road, attractive with old-style houses set in large gardens which overflowed with late summer flowers, reinforced yesterday's impression that this is a relaxed and delightful 'Goldilocks' town to visit, not too big and not too small, with a warm coastal climate, excessive natural beauty, and high community standards, all of which have made it a first choice for the retired population.

M. was looking forward to the day, because our route along State Highway 25 passed places he had often wanted to visit. I thought the road over the ranges, visible from the town, looked frighteningly steep, but when I called into the newsagent to buy the morning paper the girl behind the counter assured me that it was a new road, sealed and upgraded about two years ago, and easy to drive on.

The high road over the range heading ultimately towards the east coast of the Coromandel Peninsula gives wonderful views to either side of the west and east coasts at the summit scenic outlook. It is wide, well safety-barriered, with an excellent driving surface, but it is also a perfect road on which to feel carsick. I was relieved to be on flat land at the bottom of the eastern descent, and to turn left at Te Rerenga to Whangapoua, situated at the entrance to the harbour of the same name. Scenery and topography changes so quickly in New Zealand. In the blink of an eye, it seemed, we had driven from high, forested ranges to the marshy, mangrove-clad mud flats bordering the causeway across the harbour.

The old baches (pron. batches) or holiday cottages on the beachfront, now worth a small fortune, are gradually being replaced by substantial houses. The bay is wide, with golden, perfect, dazzling sand. The water was a tranquil blue, little waves lapping the shore. The beach vies with Matauri Bay in beauty, but this one is inhabited, and even has a relic of the past by the beach, a small general store where everyone would be known, a safe place to send children for an ice cream. This was the closest place to a liveable paradise I had seen. M. took a walk along the beach to inspect the houses, and said on return that some of them were shacks and that a million dollars would be a lot to pay for one. I prefer to think of them as being icons of New Zealand's coastal development, and in my experience there's not much that a fresh coat of paint and new plumbing can't fix.

We drove back to the state highway and skirted the harbour until we saw the turnoff to Matarangi. We had always been curious about this beach. Twenty-five years ago a friend had stunned everyone by buying some land here. We all thought he was mad, that the area was too remote, and required, on the roads then, almost four hours' travelling from Auckland. What was the point in pioneering if there was no one there to share it with? Well, he has had the last laugh. Today, this is a millionaire's paradise.

'Matarangi Beach Estates and Golf Course. O'Mara's Restaurant and Bar' read a billboard at the entrance to the access road. Further on, handsome stone walls with 'Matarangi' in dull gold lettering announced our arrival in the purpose-built resort. The red chip sealed roads, well treed with lots of pines, and an abundance of Lockwood houses, were reminiscent of Pauanui, further down the coast, in its glorious early days. We came to a small centre with a café, real estate agency, and a liquor store. 'Avoid water shortages, conserve water, every drop counts' said a prominent sign.

Matarangi is situated on a sandy spit that runs parallel to the shore, and projects west into the Whangapoua Harbour. The further west we drove, the plusher it became. We passed the Matarangi Golf Links, ringed in part with new villas, many for sale, overlooking the golf course and the adjacent bowling green. M., a regular tennis player, slowed down to look at The Pines private tennis courts. At the end of the beach road we arrived at Matarangi Manor, a grand residence on one and a half acres, with six bedrooms, three lounges, a pool and spa, and a manager's house, which was for sale by open tender.

We parked in the cul-de-sac and strolled through the pine trees to the beach. Matarangi has become a popular, upmarket holiday destination only in the last few years, and the beachfront homes offer, almost without exception, a stunning line-up of the latest in architectural trends. They blend perfectly with the grassy front reserve separating building from beach, the tussock foreshore, the majesty of the surrounding trees, and the distant backdrop of the ranges. The beach itself is wide and smooth with snowy white soft, fine sand, and views to the Mercury Islands. Take a picnic lunch down to the sand, and sunbathe and swim! The eastern end of the beach lacks the pine tree belt, but many trees have been planted and in 10 years the area will look entirely different.

M. was so enamoured with the beach that we called in to the real estate agency to see what was for sale, and were shown a very modest three-bedroom dwelling of no particular merit which we were assured could be ours if we tendered upwards of $950,000. It seemed a bargain, for waterfront land is now priced at $1.1-$1.3 million. I was not in favour of buying it. Matarangi is about three hours' drive from Auckland, even though the land agent said it only took two and a half hours; too far for me to dash down to on the spur of the moment for a weekend away.

If you wish to explore more of the coastline, the Black Jack Road from Kurotunu takes you to Opito Bay, past weekend holiday homes which have been in some families for generations. Such places are handed on down and rarely come on the open market, and you will have to pay well over $1 million for any dwelling near the water. It is worth making the drive to see what New Zealanders love and cherish, and return to year after year after year. None of my camping and accommodation guides mention a camping ground in the area, but you may be able to free camp.

Whitianga and a seafood lunch beckoned me. We drove for 23 kilometres, over the bluff which offers panoramic views of the town and Mercury Bay. Whitianga, the main town in Mercury Bay, was first discovered in about 950 A.D. by the Maori explorer Kupe, and settled by some members of his expedition whom he left behind. The next person of note to arrive, Captain James Cook, anchored in the bay in 1769 to observe the transit of Mercury, hence the name. The bay and its environs have an enviable climate, and Captain Cook noted that Maori seemed to have no homes or fixed habitation and were able to sleep comfortably in the open air.

A busy ship building industry established itself in Whitianga in the 1830s. Coastal vessels were becoming essential for transport in a new country without roads or railways. There was plenty of timber, and labour, to cater to the growing demand for ships, and the auxiliary services of chandlers and sailmakers established themselves in the burgeoning town.

We were staggered at the extent of the residential development along Buffalo Beach. Where once comfortable old houses had fitted in well with the relaxed coastal atmosphere, now we saw apartment blocks, presumably for retirees.

Apart from dining out in the many excellent seafood restaurants, there is plenty to do in Whitianga. The Wharf, as you would expect, is the centre of the boating and fishing activity. A passenger ferry plies between the harbour and Ferry Landing Wharf across the bay, the oldest stone jetty in New Zealand, just a short walk from Flaxmill Bay. A bus from the wharf will take you to Cooks Beach, Hahei, and Hot Water Beach; but I know that Hot Water Beach is best visited two hours either side of low tide, in your bathing suit, so that you can dig your own 'bath' in the volcanic sand and wallow in the hot mineral water. A local shop sells spades. It's best to go there on your own as a separate journey. It is a unique experience and, needless to say, children love it.

The well-known Mercury Bay Seafaris (ph. (07) 867 1962, www.glassbottomboatwhitianga.co.nz) runs cruises in a glass-bottomed boat out to the Te Whanganui a Hei Marine Reserve. If you wish to snorkel, the company supplies snorkelling equipment, and has wetsuits for hire. The sheltered ocean waters here, as in the Bay of Islands, are part of New Zealand's glory, and, as I have written before, if you live a land-locked existence in your home country, every opportunity should be grasped to enjoy time offshore while you are here, where water tours and activities are easily accessible, and not overly expensive.

Big game fishing is the famous pastime here, but you will be very unlucky indeed if you go out in a smaller boat and drop your line, and don't catch a fish for dinner. Blue Boat Cruises, at 15 Robinson Road, Whitianga (ph. (07) 866 4904, mobile 025 398 819) has a two-hour coastal and island cruise on a 40-foot launch, costing $35 per adult. Fishing and customised cruises can be arranged, and bookings can be made at the Whitianga i-Site Visitor Centre, phone (07) 866 5555.

Whitianga is the headquarters of Kauri 2000, a charitable trust set up to recreate the kauri forests of the Coromandel Peninsula. The trust relies on volunteers to plant the seedlings, which are grown from seeds collected on the peninsula. It has planting days during the year, and so far has planted 14,000 new trees in 33 sites, with a further 3,000 plantings planned for 2005. The tender trees need to be visited and maintained regularly to give them the best possible chance of survival. If a planting day occurs while you are there, and you wish to participate and enjoy firsthand experience of the splendid forest and bush, all you need is stout shoes and a pair of gardening gloves. Details of Kauri 2000 are given in the Appendix.

I would like to revisit Whitianga to *eat*. The town has a reputation for its excellent cafés and seafood restaurants, and picking a place in the main street to stop for lunch was a difficult exercise. I wanted seafood, preferably deep fried (because I don't cook it at home), with hot chips, and M. fancied a grill and a beer.

We found the combination we wanted at Smitty's Sports Bar and Grill, where the beer was Stella Artois and the cooking done to order by a small team at the back of the bar. We sat on the front verandah and watched the world go by, me with my glass of Stoneleigh sauvignon blanc, M. with his Stella. My seafood basket cost $13.30 and had scallops, squid, mussels, oysters and gurnard with both orange-coloured and creamy dressings, potato fries, and a big pot of Earl Grey tea – made with *two* teabags, nothing stingy here – because fried food is even better when washed down with a good brew. Coffee just doesn't rate after a fry-up! M.'s mixed grill was a large slab of steak, two sausages, two eggs, two large tomato halves, and bacon, all for $17.50. We were fortified for the long afternoon's drive ahead of us to Waihi Beach. The bar had Internet access, $2 for 18 minutes, which M. made a bee-line for after lunch as there was a share price on the New Zealand Stock Exchange that he was following closely.

Whitianga is moving ahead. We drove around a new canal subdivision, reminiscent of those at Pauanui and on Queensland's Gold and Sunshine Coasts in Australia, where it is possible to have one's own jetty and boat at the bottom of the back lawn and sail down the dredged waterway to the open sea. The land here is very flat and well suited to this type of residential development.

We stopped at a New World supermarket to stock up on a few necessities (I knew I would be cooking dinner in the van on arrival at the beach) and found that the air-conditioning in this very new store was a welcome relief from the sweltering heat outside. We left Whitianga at 3 p.m. for the final leg of the day's journey, to Waihi Beach where we hoped to camp for the night, 102 kilometres away and a drive of at least three hours in the van on the winding roads.

We turned out of town onto State Highway 25, heading for Tairua, knowing that the drive would be full of interest. The road to Tairua is tortuous in parts, and hilly, but the countryside is beautiful, and the journey exhilarating. The road was dotted with signs advertising the local produce for sale – sweet plums, tangelos, zucchini, sweet corn, tomatoes, beetroot and cucumber. If you wonder what a tangelo is, it is a cross between a New Zealand grapefruit, or poorman's orange as we used to call them as children, and a mandarin. It has the fresh flavour of the grapefruit, but the sweetness and easy-peel qualities of the mandarin. Tangelos are cheaper than other citrus fruits to buy when in season, and much-beloved by mothers for inclusion in school lunch boxes. The local kiwifruit orchards had fully-laden vines, and there were beehives everywhere. I often wonder at the curious colours beehives are painted. A collection of hives might have five or six different colours, and I have always supposed that they are painted in whatever bit of paint the beekeeper has left over at the bottom of a tin, purely to protect the timber from rotting. I wonder, too, if bees can distinguish between colours and like to return home to the pale blue or the burgundy-painted hive at the end of the day where they will meet their friends and family.

Tall ponga ferns lined the road as we descended to Tairua, and saw the twin peaks of Vista Paku, which guard the ocean beach and the difficult entrance to the Tairua Harbour. The narrow bar is prone to weather conditions, ocean current movements, and the tidal outflow from the Tairua River. I've seen quite a few small vessels come to grief. Pauanui, the holiday resort centre, is just across the river, and accessible by ferry in summer. Tairua has become very built up on the hillsides, with large holiday homes and permanent residences. The township is small, pleasant, and like the rest of the Coromandel Peninsula is home to potters, artists, and crafts people.

It used to be the place to come to, to buy freshly caught crayfish. In the 1970s and '80s, I would telephone one of the local fishermen's wives from Pauanui, ask whether any were available, and always the answer was 'Yes,' or 'My husband is out looking at the crayfish pots now – he'll be back at noon, so come at 12.30 and I'll have some ready-cooked for you.' I would drive my elderly father-in-law, who always spent the summer at the beach with us, across the hill from Pauanui to Tairua, and we would go down to the wharf to watch the catch being landed, and wait for our crayfish to be cooked for us. There was a hot bread bakery across the road from the fisherman's house where I would buy a fresh loaf, and that, well-buttered and still warm from the oven, and the not-quite-cooled crayfish, dobbed with a light mayonnaise, would be our lunch at one o'clock, washed down with a glass of lager. I once saw the amusing sight of a dozen crayfish, freshly caught and cooked, and still steaming slightly, pegged up by their tails on the clothesline outside a small cottage to drain and cool! A backpackers' lodge, motels, and artists' studios line the main road now, and to my delight the hot bread bakery is still there.

The road out of Tairua follows the mangrove-lined river estuary on the left. There is a sawmill at the side of the road, and a double-trailered logging truck laden with freshly-felled trunks that we had been following for some distance pulled in, much to our relief. I wouldn't say that our campervan was the fastest vehicle on the road, but compared with a logging truck it was a Ferrari.

We were in dairy country on the flat land here, and passed a huge herd walking sedately at the side of the road to the milking sheds. Just past Hikuai we turned left to stay on State Highway 25 and headed over the steep, native bush and pine-clad hill, to Whangamata. The Tairua Forest is extensive, with mature pines, and evidence of pine replanting after logging. For the first time in our travels we passed a fire danger sign. You will see many of these signs as you travel around New Zealand, particularly in the centre of the North Island where the man-made forests abound. The fire danger sign consists of a fan-shaped graphic divided into colour segments of green to yellow, orange and red, with an arrow pointing to the relevant degree of fire risk. Today the fire risk was low, but it was the only time I saw that, and for the remainder of our journey, in this very hot Indian summer, the fire risk was almost always high, or very high. One would not throw a cigarette butt out of the car window.

Whangamata is a well-favoured seaside resort, with an attractive estuary harbour full of small craft, launches and yachts, and extensive, protected sand dunes lining the beach. There is a sign saying 'Dunes growing. Please use access ways provided.' Actually, this part of the North Island is one long beach, extending from Pauanui down to Waihi, Mt. Maunganui, and Whakatane to Opotiki. The main street has traffic lights, the first we encountered on the Coromandel! Whangamata's reputation rests on its super surf beach – there is a public reserve and parking lot on Esplanade Drive by the Surf Life Saving Club – and on the wild New Year's Eve parties attended by all the teenage rabble-rousers the area can muster. Fifty to sixty thousand party-goers descend on the town, which has a normal population of just 4,000, and the local constabulary of four policemen has to be beefed up to one hundred men; even so, they are not enough.

Whangamata has an eclectic mix of architectural styles. I thought the large new houses and low-rise apartment blocks spoiled the beach frontage, probably because there is no cohesion of first class architecture like there is at Matarangi. Nothing ruins a fine coastline more quickly than piecemeal development. But back from the beach, the humble houses and the old, old baches are what Whangamata and every other beach resort used to be like, and worth seeing.

We were getting tired, but there were still another 25 kilometres to travel to Waihi, and another 10 kilometres further on to Waihi Beach. This next stretch of road, on the outskirts of the Coromandel Forest Park, and still State Highway 25, is steep, lined with native bush in large part, and climbs steadily to 236 metres' elevation with views to splendid stands of pine forest on the hills. There were sleek, shining herds of cattle everywhere. We passed some roadside cattle yards, very well designed, I thought, to get the beasts into the pen, up the ramp, and onto the truck to take them to the abattoir before they had too much time to figure out their future. Cattle always know when the outlook is bleak, and I was told by a butcher, in the days when we shared some land and a few cows with a friend, that their meat always toughens with the stress of waiting around if they're not loaded quickly, and slaughtered immediately on arrival at the freezing works.

We took State Highway 2 south of Waihi, and looked for signs to Waihi Beach and our camp for the night. It was 6 p.m. and we had had a long and active, but fulfilling day. The Waihi Beach Top 10 Holiday Park, on the beach, charged us $28.20 for the night, including discount. There was a large school party celebrating the start of the new academic year in residence on the upper levels, so we were directed across the road to the beach frontage and a small, intimate, and closely-mown ground which held about 12 vehicles.

This camp, a large one with 154 sites, issues all arrivals with a colourful and easy to follow site map of the park. On the back, as well as the usual opening and closing hours, and camp rules, were helpful lists with addresses of essential supply stores like the butchery, pharmacy, supermarket, a list of recommended restaurants with phone numbers, and the location of Hot Pipi Takeways and the local fish and chip shop, and a suggestion of things to do and see. Judging by the comprehensive list of do's and don't's, the camp is a magnet for campers with children; the TV room is locked and is for adults only, no skateboards are permitted, bike helmets must be worn, and there must be no water fights in any form, i.e., bombs, pistols, etc!

I was so dehydrated and exhausted that I needed to drink half a litre of water before I could begin to think about pouring a gin and tonic. We had travelled only 214 kilometres, but the driving had been slow and difficult in parts.

A friendly, interesting couple came over when we had settled in, and introduced themselves. She was a hairdresser by profession, but concentrated now on doing locum work, her main activity being that of a Justice of the Peace, a marriage celebrant, a funeral conductor, and now that the Civil Union Act permitting recognised union between homosexuals and others who wanted to formalise their partnership status without the final step of marriage had been passed, she was about to undergo training to perform these ceremonies also. She was so busy that if she wanted to camp with her husband, who had variable days of work, she had to block out her diary otherwise she would never enjoy a break. They had camped everywhere in New Zealand, driving an old station wagon kept expressly for the purpose of towing a trailer, which converted into a nice little tent and sleeping area, with awning, when they pulled at a few ropes. All they did to set up camp was to put up the barbecue, pull out the folding lounging chairs, and plonk their drinks on the table!

M. mentioned we had been thwarted in our plans to drive around the East Cape to Gisborne, and would have to do it another time. They knew all about it, having taken that same trip, on State Highway 35, once before and vowing never to do it again. They had stopped in the Bay of Plenty to visit an old friend, a policeman of Maori descent, who advised them to fill up their car with petrol at Opotiki and not to stop driving until they reached Gisborne. They did as he said, but to their consternation, halfway through the journey, were chased by Fisheries officers who thought, because of the make and age of their car, that they were there to poach paua shellfish. They were forced off the road, ordered out, and made to stand facing against their car while the boot and the trailer were searched thoroughly. It was a fascinating story and I immediately decided not ever to put a toe on State Highway 35, and that when we did travel to Gisborne we would take the more direct route from Opotiki overland to Gisborne along State Highway 2. It was disturbing to think that these eminently respectable people were subject to such an indignity; but what needs to be considered, of course, is whether one would meet interference of any description, from anyone, if driving an easily recognisable Maui van. M., who is still hankering to do the journey, says 'No'.

The distance from Opotiki to Gisborne on State Highway 35 is about 330 kilometres, and needs to be done in two stages for the driving is slow and there is much of historic importance to see. The road follows the coastline to Whangaparaoa and then cuts inland to Hicks Bay. Twelve kilometres further on is Te Araroa, about half way on the journey, and probably the best overnight stopping place. The most important thing is to find a good camp, and my *Camping Guide, North Island* describes the Te Araroa Holiday Park well. This will be my pick if we ever do the trip ourselves. I quote from the guidebook:

'Midway between Gisborne and Opotiki… The grounds are lavish with many trees. A walk over the bridged stream, through the paddock and you are down to the beach. Sites are level with plenty of taps. In this remote area you will find a full cinema. The on-site store is well stocked, open from 7 a.m. – 7 p.m. There are 80 tent sites, 38 with power… The amenities are great, but outdoor lighting is minimal. In the kitchen you will find individual preparation areas, microwave and conventional cooking. The ablutions also have individual vanity areas and excellent showers… Laundry with automatic equipment… everything is well kept. Choose your TV programme from two separate rooms (one for TV1, and one for TV2). There is a fish smokehouse and a car wash. Drinking water must be boiled. Powered sites $11 per person.'

I must mention that some far areas of New Zealand do not enjoy full television coverage. The camp advertises itself on its website (see Appendix) as '…the most easterly holiday park and cinema in the world'. It will arrange horse riding, and sea kayaks and mountain bikes are available for hire.

The East Cape drive, famous in New Zealand, is the best one to undertake if you wish to meet Maori communities in their traditional, dignified surroundings, and enjoy the distinctive architecture of their many meeting houses and villages. It is a cultural offence to enter a marae uninvited, and you will need to gain permission before doing so. The New Zealand film *Whale Rider*, whose 12-year-old star Keisha Castle-Hughes was nominated for Best Actress in a Leading Role in the 2004 Academy Awards, was filmed along this coastline in and around the small beach township of Whangara, north of Gisborne.

I had better warn you that *Driving New Zealand* mentions that for the passing traveller petrol is expensive, tearoom food is produced from pie warmers and vats of fat, and no one has cracked the art of making good coffee.

I consulted my *Camping Guide, North Island* to see what campsites are available in Gisborne, and my pick of the several listed is the Waikanae Beach Holiday Park, situated just a few minutes from the Gisborne commercial centre. The Gisborne District Council allows 'freedom camping' along the East Coast at Waipiro, Tokomaru and Tolaga Bays, at Kaiaua, Waihau, Pouawa and Turihana Beaches, and at Donneraille Park. Camping permits are required by law but are free on application to the Council, and campers must provide their own chemical toilets and drinking water. Contact details for the Holiday Park, and for the Gisborne District Council, are in the Appendix.

CHAPTER 11

THE BEAUTIFUL BAY OF PLENTY AND ROTORUA FOR THE NIGHT

We were a little slow leaving Waihi Beach on Thursday. Eight hours' driving the day before had proved tiring, and we needed an early walk along the expansive beach to restore some energy. By 9 a.m. the sun was very hot, and promised another scorcher of a day.

Over the years the newspapers had run articles on the environmental controversies surrounding the opencast goldmining activities at Martha Mine in Waihi, the latest one being the recent collapse of a tunnel, which carried with it several homes in the town and threatened more. I had never seen an opencast mine and was curious to know what it looked like. Our knowledgeable friends at the camp had told us not to follow the sign to the mine at the roundabout in the main street, but to carry on up the hill a few hundred yards to the signposted lookout point. We parked at the side of the road and set off for the short walk up the path to the lookout, scarcely believing that the mining site was so accessible. A motorcycle rally group (i.e. bikies) had just pulled in, 20 of them in their leathers, their appearance and the roar of the engines making us start nervously. When they removed their helmets they were, to the surprise of everyone, well past 50 years old, and their bikes looked middle-aged, too! Sighs of relief all round. You never know what will be revealed when a bikie removes his/her helmet. I say 'her', because a few years ago, in France, a large gang of bikies roared into the car park of the Mont St. Michel in Normandy, where the tourists, including us, gave them a very wide berth until they removed their helmets and revealed they were all women!

I hadn't expected to see anything as grand as Martha Mine. It is a huge, awesome, open oval, reminiscent of a giant's sunken colosseum, with the curving ledges and roads taking the place of hewn seating. The scale is enormous, and the huge trucks, laden with fill, look like Matchbox toys as they labour up and along the 'aisles' between the 'rows'. Martha Mine produces more than $1 million worth of gold and silver each week, about 80 per cent of the total revenue remains in New Zealand (thank goodness), and $18 million is spent annually with New Zealand businesses that supply goods and services. On completion of mining the open pit will be developed into a lake with adjacent parklands.

An information board at the lookout point states that the tailings storage areas will be rehabilitated to form wetlands. Already 120,000 native trees and shrubs have been planted on and adjacent to the tailings storage facilities, and 29 hectares of productive pasture have been sown. The outcry over the mine's establishment would seem to have come to nothing. It is possible to take a guided tour which goes about 70 metres underground. More details on the operation are available on the website, www.waihigold.co.nz.

We took State Highway 2 and headed for the Bay of Plenty. The road was superb, level for a change, and followed the coastline of the Tauranga Harbour. We reached Katikati (pron. katty-katty), 24 kilometres away, very quickly. If you need to stock up with food, there is a large Woolworths supermarket in the main street, with easy parking. I've always found shopping for supplies very much easier in a small town where there is only one highly visible supermarket.

Katikati *bustled.* This is the start of serious kiwi fruit country. If you have never seen this brown oval fruit with the distinctive hairy skin growing before, you will know an orchard by the very tall shelter belts planted around the perimeter. Kiwi fruit vines do not like the wind. The countryside was very green, a tribute to the wet early summer, and the highway ran pleasantly through the Athenree pine forest. Lushness abounded in the orchards of Nashi pears, avocadoes, oranges, lemons and mandarins, and I saw several honey producers. There seemed to be no end to the roadside blackboards advertising onions, courgettes, spring onions, cabbages, and fresh watercress for sale. We passed a lavender farm, many cornfields, even bird gardens, the Rolling Cloud Pottery, and Titles Book Gallery. Roadside cafés included the Flippin' Bear Pancake Den, the Twickenham Café which reportedly has very good coffee, and a Devonshire Tea stop. The well-known Morton Estate Winery, set up on a slight rise to the right of the road, and built in an attractive, cream-painted Spanish style, offers tastings and door sales. If you want a bottle to accompany your dinner, choose one of their reliable chardonnays.

Katikati was founded in 1873 by George Vesey Stewart, a farmer from County Tyrone in Northern Ireland, who had travelled to New Zealand with the express purpose of establishing a settlement for Irish families with adequate capital to farm and improve the land. The site was carefully chosen, for the extremely fertile land was covered in easy-to-clear fern, and in close proximity to the town of Tauranga and the burgeoning goldfields on the Coromandel Peninsula which would provide markets for the farmed produce. The somewhat idealistic project got off to a good start with the arrival of the first settlers from Ulster, and crops of corn, wheat, oats, potatoes and turnips all flourished. The cattle fed on newly-sown pastures and young fern, and English shelter trees were planted and orchards established. But farming, even in this perfect setting, was not without its difficulties. The first settlers ignored the need to maintain soil fertility, production fell, and subsequent settlers struggled to break in newer, poorer land. However, by the end of the nineteenth century the early promise of the area had been realised, and Katikati and its dairy and agricultural farms prospered. Today, as you will realise when you drive through the countryside, it is one giant foodbasket, and the Bay of Plenty does indeed live up to its name.

A New Zealand Police road sign warned 'Keep Left High Crash Rate', and it was easy to see why. The other side of the road was difficult driving for any vehicle, being full of heavily laden trucks and trailers roaring through to Auckland, presumably. Yet our side, going east, was almost completely clear and we bowled along the Pacific Coast at a steady 90 kilometres per hour, thankful for the much easier driving after the rigorous, mostly hilly journey of the day before. At Bethlehem, where the Mills Reef Winery is signposted at a turnoff to the right, we were astonished to see mushrooming housing subdivisions on either side of the road. This region of New Zealand is booming big-time, and the population and commercial increases are not all due to the desirability of owning a coastal property, but to the dramatic growth of the Port of Tauranga, now New Zealand's second largest port after the Port of Auckland. On the outskirts of Tauranga we took the expressway which bypasses the city, and exited in the left lane following the sign for the Mount, the Port, and the City Centre. The Mount, a famous and favourite holiday resort, was clearly visible across the harbour.

M. wanted to visit a colleague's pharmacy in Devonport Road, and after some searching for a suitable off-street park for the van we found one down on The Strand, on the water's edge, underneath an old wooden harbour bridge. We had plenty of space and two hours' free parking, and the main shopping street was just a short climb up wooden stairs to the to the top of the cliff. M. went to the pharmacy, and I made a bee-line for the smart Café Mediterraneo opposite to have my morning fix, a double shot large flat white, for $3.50, and so utterly delicious and body-building that I ordered another, then moved on to a Greek frittata, well-made with egg, feta cheese, spinach, pine nuts, red pepper and black olives. M. joined me later for a bacon and egg pie (a treat for him because I never make them now) which he pronounced truly excellent and close to my best.

We drove slowly along the waterfront, lined with trendy cafés, and to my delight passed the berthed *Kestrel*, an early twentieth century wooden passenger ferry which used to ply the Auckland harbour, and on which, as a teenager, I travelled to college in the early 1950s. Memories! Mt. Maunganui, or The Mount, as it is known, loomed at the end of the peninsula as we crossed the harbour bridge, passed the extensive yacht marina, and drove along

Marine Parade. It is a fashionable address, and is lined with new apartment blocks and cafés. The Mount is a former Maori fortress, still with traces of its earthworks, and guards the entrance to Tauranga Harbour. There are easy paths which take you to the 250 metre summit, and from there you will have a good view of the coastal islands, and White Island, an active volcano situated about 80 kilometres offshore. The long stretch of beach at the foot of The Mount is stunning, and famous for the good surf and the surfies who invade it, but on this still, baking-hot day in late summer the coastal water was bright blue and unrippled. The Mount Beach, engagingly enclosed at its eastern end by a small promontory, and the adjacent Mt. Maunganui Beach are blessed with wide white sands, views to the outer islands, and are lined with a boardwalk, grass, and shady trees which give a proper resort atmosphere. Parking is easy, and it's a good place to stop for a swim or a picnic.

We continued on the coastal road to Papamoa Beach, once considered the poor relation of Tauranga and The Mount, but now coming into its own as an increasingly expensive, fast-growing seaside town. The old 'beachy' look is disappearing and the road is lined with substantial houses. On the left, on the absolute beachfront, was an attractive camping ground full of motorhomes and expensive caravans. A quick check of the North Island edition of my *Camping Guide* proved this to be the Papamoa Beach Top 10 Holiday Resort, a large ground with 260 sites, 220 of them with power. There are the usual high-grade facilities you would expect to find at a Top 10, including private spa pools and an adventure playground, with the added bonus of adjacent shopping, a restaurant, takeaways, a bank and a service station. Once there, you need never leave! The *Guide* states that sites, which cost $14 per adult, should be pre-booked between Christmas and February. Contact details are given in the Appendix. We turned inland to Papamoa township, self-described as 'Sunshine Paradise', and rejoined State Highway 2 to Te Puke. 'Crash Black Spot' warned another road sign.

I felt that we had rushed past Tauranga rather too quickly, for the surrounding region is rich in history. I noticed that several pa sites were shown on my map. 'Pa' is the Maori word for a fortified stockade, a place of safety for tribes to live, and often shielded by palisades from outside invasion. Commanding hill sites were favoured, and the pas built as defensive battle posts had superior fortifications and escape trenches, giving Maori their reputation as masters of defensive warfare. It was at Gate Pa, south of Tauranga, that the last Kingite battle between Army and Maori was fought, bringing to an end an era of warfare in the Waikato.

Tauranga was established as a church mission settlement in 1838, a remarkably well-endowed one with nearly 500 hectares of land, and relations between the settlers and local Maori, who were converted to Christianity, became harmonious and friendly. In 1864, some local Ngaiterangi warriors crossed to the Waikato to support the leaders of the Maori King Movement, set up to help Maori assert their identity and to act as a unified force to prevent further confiscation of their land by Europeans. This defection to what was deemed by the politicians of the time, and the Governor, Sir George Grey, to be a rival authority to the British Crown, led to the readying of the Army and Navy for battle with Tauranga Maori who responded by establishing a string of fortifications, their most famous being the pa, subsequently known as Gate Pa, just outside the mission station boundary. Affection for each other made the settlers and the majority of local Maori unwilling to fight, but on 29 April the British Army bombardment began at Gate Pa. Seventeen hundred British soldiers and their heavy artillery were no match for the ambushing tactics of 230 warriors hidden in their network of trenches inside the pa, and the army suffered heavy losses. The British Army ultimately achieved victory two months later, at nearby Te Ranga, when it killed the Ngaiterangi leader. History records the encounter as an unnecessary battle fought without the argument for it being sustained by fact, but it brought to an end hostilities between Waikato Maori and the Crown. It is commemorated today in the military cemetery on the Te Papa peninsula, and the preservation of the mission house, the home of the founder of the mission, Archdeacon Brown, where military officers, destined to die, dined with Archdeacon and Mrs Brown on the eve of the battle. Today, the Maori King Movement is still located at its birthplace in the Waikato region, and is led by the Maori King Tuheitia Paki I, and the battle is memorialised simply at the site of Gate Pa on Cameron Road to the south of Tauranga by a stone block containing a bronze relief of the plan of the pa, and a plaque commemorating the battle.

Te Puke has grown to prosperity, thanks to the kiwi fruit industry. It was the centre of the astonishing kiwi fruit boom in the 1970s, when fortunes were made, and often lost later. The flat, fertile land of the dairy and cattle farms in the region was converted into what seemed at the time like instant cash crops, syndicates were formed by entrepreneurs who knew nothing about horticulture, and the derogatory description 'Queen Street farmer' came into use. The size of the industry can be gauged from the very large cool stores and packhouses adjacent to the highway. Well-established kiwi fruit orchards are pleasant and tranquil to visit. The very high shelter belts screen out noise, and the vines lie attractively over fence posts and supports and form an overhead arbour from which the fruit hangs waiting to be picked.

The cancellation of our tour via the East Cape to Gisborne and the Hawkes Bay had thrown us into a quandary, for we were left with two nights to fill in before arriving in Pauanui for the conference. We had always intended to travel from Napier across to Rotorua before continuing down the North Island to Wellington and the Cook Strait ferry crossing on 25 February – an inviolate booking not subject to last minute alteration – so after some discussion we decided to stick to the plan to visit Rotorua, and to turn off onto State Highway 33 outside Te Puke. M. was loathe to leave the coast, for he was enjoying the drive and wanted to see Whakatane and Ohope Beach, but I felt strongly that no campervan tour of New

Zealand was complete without a stop at New Zealand's premier tourist centre of Maori culture. As a bonus, it would put us on track to stop for a night at the Waitomo Caves before driving across the rich Waikato countryside back to the Coromandel Peninsula and Pauanui on the east coast. What clinched the argument in the end was the fact that there are *three* Top 10 Holiday Parks in and around Rotorua, all in excellent locations, such is the tourist and holiday importance of the city. We just had to camp there.

The drive along State Highway 33 to Rotorua was scenic, and green, and passed through the large pine forests of the area, the Kaingaroa Timberlands. Again we were the solitary occupants of our side of the road, but care was required in the face of all the oncoming logging truck and trailer combinations laden to the very top with freshly milled pine logs, heading to the Port of Tauranga. The port exports most of the logs in New Zealand. A glimpse of Lake Rotoiti, a large, placid lake famed for its holiday homes but now the victim of heavy algal growth which is destroying the water quality, was the indication that we were entering the lake district of the North Island. Lakes are everywhere, and so is underground thermal activity, making the region one of extreme beauty and interest. It is impossible to tire of Rotorua. I have been visiting it all my life, and still rate a weekend here, with some soaks in a hot mineral pool and a tour of the natural wonders, a relaxing escape from Auckland.

So it was with a sense of homecoming that we drove past the Rotorua Airport, beautifully situated alongside Lake Rotorua, and called in at the Te Ngae shopping centre at the junction of the turn-off to the Blue and Green Lakes and Lake Tarawera. This excellent and well-located shopping centre has a supermarket, pharmacy, hardware shop, liquor store, a Lotto outlet, and a petrol station. We stopped for wine, diesel fuel, and a Lotto ticket, and drove on round the lake to the city and our camp for the night. The familiar, bracing, nostril-clearing smell of sulphurous thermal activity seeped through the closed windows of the van. This is a smell you either love or hate, but for those of you who *gag* on first encountering it in Rotorua, it may be a comfort to know that it is not all-pervading, and that after a while you do get used to it!

Oh, the perfection of our camp for the night, the Rotorua Top 10 Holiday Park in Pukuatua Street, chosen unashamedly because of its proximity to the many restaurants at the lake end of Tutanekai (pron. too-tarna-kye) Street. This was the only camp on our trip where the receptionist knew the wheelbase length of our campervan, and efficiently allocated us a paved site of the appropriate size. By the time we were ready to ask the receptionist to call a taxi to take us to Tutanekai Street (actually only about 10 minutes' walk away but we were a bit tired), our row, up against a tall hedge at the side of the camp, was full of similar-sized vehicles. Short-bodied vans were opposite, and large touring rigs and tents were elsewhere in the campground. Again, we were the only New Zealanders in our particular enclave, most of the campers being from Europe. Brand new ablution chalets fitted with superior shower rooms and toilets were just 50 yards away. The roads in the grounds were formed attractively with concrete tiles and there was plenty of closely mown lawn. Grass has now become a luxury for M. and me, since our apartment building relies for its outdoor beauty on closely-planted terraced gardens, lovely to look at but impossible to walk on.

The camp is completely geared towards short-stay tourism, and has a free booking service, pick-up and return for local tours and sightseeing. Rafting, sky-diving and trout fishing activities, bookings for a Maori concert and hangi evening, and tours to the various thermal sights, can all be arranged at the office. It is very worthwhile to have a Top 10 card, for the major tourist operators all offer 10 per cent discount to holders. There is a wet weather activities list available, high-speed Internet, swimming and spa pools, and even a petanque court, and the camp has facilities for handicapped visitors. The other two Top 10 Holiday Parks are fifteen or twenty minutes' drive from the city centre, on the lakefront at Holden's Bay, and beside the Bluc Lake, and while these are both attractive and relaxing places to stay, I do not recommend them unless you have several days in which to explore the region. Your stay in Rotorua is most likely to be quite short, your days will be completely filled with the many things to do and see, and you need to be handy to the excellent attractions in and around the city centre, and to the main roads leading to the outlying ones. The town camp in Pukuatea Street offers this.

The taxi dropped us by the Novotel Hotel and we strolled along the restaurant strip, discussing what cuisine we fancied. It's all here, casually, in café or restaurant, from Mexican, to European, Chinese, Thai, Indian or Italian. We had good memories of the Star of India Restaurant from a recent sojourn with an English guest who fancied a curry for dinner one night, so we got a table there and ordered prawns malabari, a lamb curry, an Indian salad of tomato, cucumber and onion slices arranged in a wheel shape on a flat dish, jasmine rice, and all the etceteras that come with an Indian dinner, for $53.00. The waiter recommended a bottle of Church Road Chardonnay 2003 at $36.00, widely available throughout New Zealand, and it was so pleasant and drinkable that we ordered it several more times on our journey.

The 173 kilometres travelled from Waihi Beach to Rotorua proved to be one of our shortest daily distances, and the easy driving conditions over good highways were a bonus for M. I relaxed under a superb hot shower, and climbed into my sleeping bag with the pleasant feeling that all was right with the world.

CHAPTER 12

SIGHTSEEING IN ROTORUA

I recommend a stay of three nights in Rotorua, which will give you two full and busy days to cover the main attractions. The Rotorua tourist industry is a sophisticated and well-oiled machine capable of processing large numbers of visitors at the various locations without overcrowding or spoiling the intrinsic nature of the region. The city, which attracts 18 million visitors annually, is approached on State Highway 5 from either Hamilton or Taupo, and on State Highway 33 from the Bay of Plenty. It is exceptionally easy to drive in, with the bulk of the traffic to the tourist locations being routed on wide and well-signposted roads away from the small city centre. I find it delightful to navigate in a place where it is impossible to get lost.

The i-Site Visitor Information Centre at 1167 Fenton Street (ph. (07) 348 5179, freephone 0800 768 678) is open every day and has maps, every brochure, and all the visitor information you need, and operates a booking service and currency exchange. To help you decide what to see and do, you can visit www.rotoruanz.com, a full website giving excellent information on Rotorua and all its activities and sightseeing.

If you plan your driving carefully, it is possible to include several major attractions within one general destination.

The Agrodome (ph. (07) 357 1050, freephone 0800 339 400, www.agrodome.co.nz), situated visibly in Western Road off State Highway 5 as you approach Ngongotaha and Lake Rotorua from Hamilton, brings sheep farming home to town dwellers. Unless they arrange a farm stay, it can be difficult for busy tourists to access New Zealand's sheep farming life. Usually, their encounters with animals consist of driving past the paddocks where sheep have been mustered for slaughter, or shearing. The Agrodome changes all that, three times daily, with its educational live sheep show in a purpose-built auditorium which presents 19 breeds of champion rams on stage, identifies each breed and the characteristics of its wool, and finishes with a shearing display. The audience is invited to mingle with the sheep, which are docile and securely chained. There is an outdoor demonstration of mustering with Huntaway dogs, a dog trial, a 13 hectare sheep and cattle farm to tour, the opportunity for children to pet animals and feed baby lambs, a kiwi fruit orchard to visit, a wool carding demonstration, a large sheepskin and woollen goods souvenir shop, a café, and a restaurant. Everything you need to know about sheep and sheep farming is at this splendid, unique attraction, which was started by New Zealand's champion sheep shearer and his family 35 years ago. You will leave full of interesting information, and with a valuable understanding of New Zealand rural life.

Ten minutes' drive away on Fairy Springs Road leading to the city is Rainbow Springs Nature Park (ph. (07) 350 0440, freephone 0800 724 626 (www.rainbowsprings.co.nz). This is another educational and pleasant place to visit, where you will see, first hand, the progress of rainbow, brown and tiger trout from hatching to mature adults. The sight of dozens of large trout swimming in the natural pools is quite magnificent, and if you are not an angler this will be your best experience of our world-famed trout. Bags of pellets with which to feed the fish can be bought on entry. The native ferns, trees and plants provide a sheltered haven for many protected bird species, and you can view adult and young tuatara lizards, and the iconic New Zealand kiwi in the darkened kiwi house. I mention in a later chapter the park developed by the Otorohanga Zoological Society which has a famous kiwi house and aviaries, but it involves a side tour into the South Waikato, so if this is your one chance to see native birds, you should take it. Like the Agrodome, this is a top attraction where you can tick several 'must sees' off your list.

If you continue on and turn left into Lake Road, you will pass Ohinemutu Village with its distinctive Maori architecture, and arrive at the Rotorua city lakefront. Cruises leave from here to Mokoia Island, rich in Maori legend and native bird life, situated in the middle of the lake, and Volcanic Air Safaris (ph. (07) 348 9984, www.volcanicair.co.nz) offers scenic air tours over Mt. Tarawera, Hell's Gate, and White Island. At the same time you will enjoy the splendid panorama of the 16 lakes in the Rotorua district, all of which are formed from the craters of extinct volcanoes.

The Government Gardens a few hundred yards away, unmistakable because of the Tudor-style architecture of the main building which houses the Rotorua Museum, are the site of the internationally recognised Polynesian Spa (ph. (07) 348 1328, (www.polynesianspa.co.nz), voted the seventh best medical and thermal spa in the world by the influential magazine *Conde Nast Traveller*. There are 31 hot mineral bathing pools and a wide range of spa therapies and wraps to choose from. Included in the complex are four luxury outdoor lake spa pools, and 17 private pools each with its own shower and changing area. These last pools can be hired by the half hour and you can regulate your own water temperature.

I suggest rounding off the day with a Maori hangi, or feast, and a concert. *This is not to be missed.* You will learn more about famous Maori ancestry and culture in one hour of music and visual presentation than any amount of reading will offer. We went to an excellent evening two years' ago at the Royal Lakeside Novotel Hotel (ph. (07) 346 3888, www.novotel.co.nz) on the lakefront, ate spectacularly good food from the hangi, and enjoyed the Maori concert and the poi dances, the famous haka, or war dance, performed notably by the All Blacks at the start of international rugby matches, the stick games, and the musical singing. Audience participation was encouraged, and M. got up onto the stage and acquitted himself very well in the haka.

A hangi is the traditional Maori way of cooking food. A large pit is dug in the ground and lined with hot stones, the wrapped food is placed on top, covered well with flax mats, and water is poured over to create steam. The pit is covered with soil and the food is left for several hours to cook in the retained heat. Modern shortcuts have speeded up the process, but the pit and steam principle remains the same, and pork, lamb, potato, kumara and pumpkin lifted from the hangi are tender and delicious. My favourite is pork and kumara, which I consider to be a very fine traditional hangi dinner. A wide range of salads and cooked vegetables is also served at a hangi, and M., who has a very sweet tooth, found the array of desserts the night we went to the Novotel concert rather exciting. Pavlova is the dessert of choice, because then you have added another great New Zealand experience to your day!

Early on the second day, travel south on State Highway 5 towards Taupo for 27 kilometres and follow signs to Waiotapu Thermal Wonderland (ph. (07) 366 6333, www.geyserland.co.nz) for a walk through this spectacular volcanic area. The landscape, with its hissing craters, geothermal pools, colourful lakes and boiling mud pools is just as nature made it, and walkways across which clouds of warm steam drift get visitors close to the action. A feature of the wonderland is the nearby Lady Knox Geyser which erupts daily at 10.15 a.m.

On the journey back to Rotorua, watch for signs to Waimangu Volcanic Valley (ph. (07) 366 6137, www.waimangu.com) and turn right onto Waimangu Road. Waimangu was formed on 10 June 1886 when the Tarawera volcano erupted, flooding Lake Rotomahana and destroying the renowned pink and white terraces. Large, devastating volcanic activity continued until 1917, when the valley began to establish its own plant and bird life. This scenic reserve is protected and conserved by careful management, and has won many Eco Tourism Awards. You can take the three-hour walking tour and boat cruise on Lake Rotomahana, or spend an hour wandering along the crater walkways, or just do the cruise on its own. On the way you will see Frying Pan Lake, the world's largest hot water spring, and Inferno Crater, the world's largest geyser-like feature.

As you approach Rotorua, turn right into the New Zealand Maori Arts and Crafts Centre to see craftspeople at work in the traditional carving and weaving schools, and the Rotouhine model pa, which has on its reserve buildings typical of pre-European pas, and a magnificent carved gateway. A pleasant walk down the hill past the 40,000-year-old mud pools leads you to attractive silica terraces and the Pohutu Geyser which jets to 30 metres, and is reputedly the most visited tourist attraction in New Zealand. Do not be tempted to take the lower entrance to these attractions, across the bridge at the Whakarewarewa Village, for you will find your way blocked by a fence.

It would be a pity not to round off your visit to Rotorua with a trip to some of the nearby lakes; to be honest, after the walks you will have undertaken this day, you will probably feel like a nice little drive and a sit down! Take Te Ngae Road, State Highway 30, in the direction of Tauranga and Whakatane, and turn off shortly at Lynmore to Tarawera Road on the right, and follow it as far as you like. You will pass the Blue and Green Lakes, so-called because of the difference in the colour of their water, and arrive eventually at Lake Tarawera, a favourite holiday and fishing retreat. The drive is well-treed and pleasant, and passes Te Wairoa village, buried when Mt. Tarawera erupted, and now partially excavated.

If you manage to do everything I've suggested, in two rewarding days you will have seen the major attractions that M. and I always return to with overseas visitors. You can leave Rotorua safe in the knowledge that you have 'done' Maori art and culture and the world famous thermal activities, and continue with enjoying the other delights on offer in New Zealand.

CHAPTER 13

A VISIT TO THE KING COUNTRY, THE WAITOMO CAVES, AND ACROSS THE WAIKATO FARMLANDS TO PAUANUI

It's always entertaining to watch campers walk across to have their shower, for some people find it impossible to shake off the private morning habits of home. Munching my toast before departure from Rotorua, I saw a woman emerge from her motorhome wearing a full-length white satin robe and high-heeled black satin mules with sparkly bows on the toes; astonishing items to pack for a camping trip, I thought, and so did others as heads turned to follow her progress. Later on in our trip, at Haast Village, the door of the motorhome next to ours opened and out climbed a very stout woman wearing flimsy, pink rose-patterned pyjamas, with her garments for the day draped visibly over one arm – shorts, a top, ballooning knickers, and an outsize bra – and wobbled over to the ablution block. Why make a spectacle of yourself? M. averted his eyes. In Dunedin, our elderly German neighbour ran true to national form and emerged importantly from his motorhome wearing a thick towelling robe striped in red, navy and green, and brown leather slippers; those robes are heavy and take up half a suitcase! Why clutter up the limited wardrobe space with a *robe*? As I've said before, why not quickly put on your clothes for the day, remove them in the shower, and put them on again when you've finished? Easy!

We were looking forward to seeing new country on our way from Rotorua to Te Kuiti and Waitomo and by 9 a.m. were driving along the wide, treed avenue of Fenton Street, our closest exit south to State Highway 5. Keep a close lookout for the turnoff onto State Highway 30 signposted Tokoroa and Te Kuiti; it is just a short distance from the outskirts of the city, and easily missed.

The taxi driver taking us back to the camp from dinner the previous night had said that we should allow two hours to get to Waitomo in a campervan. The scenery started off well with a splendid view of the dramatic, high Horohoro Cliffs to the right. We skirted the Kinleith Forest, perhaps the source of all the laden logging trucks we had encountered on our way to Rotorua yesterday. At Upper Atiamuri, State Highway 30 merges with State Highway 1 from Auckland and Hamilton for a short 6 kilometres, before turning right to Waitomo and Te Kuiti. We passed the Bull Ring Tavern and Accommodation, a well-known truckies' stop, and the dam of the hydro-electric Ohakuri power station, at Atiamuri, the first hydro-electric power station I saw, 45 years ago.

There is something very calming about a forest drive, particularly in the morning when the air is overnight-fresh and the scent of the trees drifts in through the window. We were in the central North Island, which when I was at school had the biggest man-made forest in the world. The ranks of pine trees stretched as far as we could see, green to the sky. State Highway 30 was wonderfully straight here, and M. belted along at 100 kilometres per hour with Ray Charles blaring on the CD player. The road skirted Lake Whakamaru on the left, a long, narrow lake bounded by tall cliffs on the other side. We entered some hilly country with a sign warning us to beware of falling rocks from the steep slope on our right, and slowed down. The pines here were so densely planted that no sunlight fell between the trees, and because the trunks were uniformly trimmed to the same height the effect was of driving through a black cave. We drove across the top of the Whakamaru hydro-electric dam, and who should be there looking at the water and the works but our bikies from Waihi the day before. Dozens more bikies had stopped for morning tea and a catch-up at the hydro village corner.

We were into flat, open country now, with cattle farming, level pastures, modest farmhouses, and beehives everywhere. There was no indication of the inhospitable territory which greeted the first settlers just 100 years ago, when bridges had to be made across creeks by felling trees over them, when horseback was for years the only means of transport on the rough tracks, and when every metre of habitable and productive ground had to be cleared by hand. We crossed the Mangakino Stream, green and still, and oops! nearly missed a sign to turn left to Te Kuiti. Nothing changes quicker than a New Zealand landscape; suddenly the ground became drier, and tall, creamy fronds of toi toi waved in the breeze. Heavily-coated sheep, the first we'd seen for a while, were gathered for shearing, and a sign read 'Welcome To Waitomo District And See What You're Missing!'

The road skirted the Pureora Forest, with unsealed side roads off to the left signposting the Totara Walk and the Pureora Field Centre. The forest is known for the enormous trees that were once the subject of a conservation battle, and the 30 minute Totara Walk passes amongst them. We came to the Benneydale meat processing plant, handily located near all the sheep and cattle farms we were passing. The animals wouldn't have time to get nervous! Benneydale is a small rural service town with its own police station, a petrol garage, and a general store. The public toilet, next to the store, is an old converted water tank painted bright blue. We stopped for the morning newspaper, and a Topsy chocolate-coated ice cream, my first for 20 years. A surprisingly cool wind was blowing, a welcome change from the sticky heat of the last week, and I stood at the side of the road to eat, enjoying the breeze, while M. read the newspaper for half an hour, saying he needed a rest. We were in the back of beyond, and it was easy to feel the isolation of rural life. Imagine driving into Benneydale and finding only three people to chat to – the grocer, the petrol pump attendant, and the local cop!

The entry to Te Kuiti, the centre of the King Country, as it is known geographically and politically, was inauspicious, with another quirky sign which said 'Welcome To Te Kuiti And See What You're Missing!' and old, old wooden stores lining the main street. However the flower beds were full of bright marigolds, impatiens and begonias, and we were able to park in the shade of a large oak tree.Te Kuiti had a moment of fame a few years ago when its local Member of Parliament, in protest at the introduction of the tax on diesel fuel which he said was an unnecessary tax on farming, drove his tractor to Wellington and up the steps of Parliament.

Lunch beckoned, and the most obvious place was the Central Café, situated as its name implied, full of locals in town for traditional Friday shopping. It looked a safe bet. M. ordered a mini pizza and a small meat pie, which he said were tough and tasteless, and he left most of them, and in desperation, after examining the rest of the food, I took some curried egg mayonnaise and chopped vegetable salads, where the vegetables had been attacked randomly by a cleaver, thrown into bowls, and dumped in the salad bar. I poured a cup of filtered coffee which turned grey when I added milk, and tasted how it looked, so I abandoned it and ordered a cappuccino like everybody else. When I parted the froth, the coffee underneath was, again, grey! How did they do it? The café badly needs some competition. The service was surly and very slow, although three people were behind the counter, and the miserable lunch cost $29, more than we had paid for the divine coffee and food in Tauranga the day before. Give this place a miss! I ventured into the public toilets on the main street, found they were clean and very spacious, and we pressed on to Waitomo, exiting State Highway 30 after about 10 kilometres onto State Highway 37. Allowing for the stop at Te Kuiti, the journey had taken two hours; the taxi driver was right.

The eight kilometre drive on State Highway 37 to Waitomo through delightful rolling countryside passes The Legendary Black Water Rafting Company (www.blackwaterrafting.co.nz) which is billed in their brochure as cave tubing at its best with the 'original and most popular black water rafting operator', where you 'weave, jump and float through the glow worm-flecked underworld…' The large parking area was almost full, with many campervans dotted around, and the attraction is open every day.

We arrived at Waitomo Caves (ph. (07) 878 8227, freephone 0800 456 922, www.waitomocaves.co.nz) and drove directly to the car park, down a steep incline to the right off the main road. We had to leave the campervan in a rather lonely spot at the bottom, and I felt uneasy until I saw a sign saying that electronic surveillance was in operation.

The last time I visited the caves was as a teenager in the 1950s. Then, we slipped and slithered along a poorly-lit narrow track, with nothing to hold onto except the guide's hand, watching every footstep. Now, the main cave is laid with slab aggregate flooring, perfectly level, and flights of well-marked steps with handrails on both sides lead easily downwards. The tours are limited in size to the numbers of people that can fit into the boats, and the organisation is efficient, friendly, and caters to tourists from all over the world with brochures in Korean, Japanese, Chinese, Spanish, German and French. We seemed to be the only New Zealanders in our group.

Our welcoming and knowledgeable Maori guide gave a brief history of the discovery of the limestone-formed caves in the late nineteenth century, which have been visited by tourists since 1889, then led us into the glorious Cathedral Cave with its high, vaulted ceiling, where the acoustics are so pure that Dame Kiri Te Kanawa, Dame Malvina Major, Sting, and UB40 among others, have given concerts in the perfect setting. The cave also hosts chamber music concerts. I can't imagine anything more glorious than listening to operatic arias being performed here. Our guide invited one of us to sing a song to test the acoustics, and when no one offered, did so herself, charmingly.

We stepped into a flat-bottomed boat, the torch went out, and in pitch-blackness the guide pulled us along on an overhead wire across the inky water. Talking, photographs and videos were forbidden. The caves are over 30 million years old, and glow because the tiny worms, properly called larvae, are able to become luminescent in the pitch-blackness to attract insects, which they then eat. You could say that every twinkle represents a mouthful! We drifted gently for 10 minutes, looking up at the myriad glow worms, then emerged blinking out into the sunshine, with a short walk ahead of us up the hill to the entrance and the inevitable souvenir shop. If you live where you are never going to get to limestone caves and glow worms again, this is as good as it gets, so do it. If, like me, you are nervous of falling in the dark, stick close to the guide and the torch.

We drove back to the little township of Waitomo and booked in for the night at the Waitomo Top 10 Holiday Park (see Appendix) at a cost of $25.20 including discount. This is a very pleasant, well-kept site on three levels, with gravel standing on level two for vans, power and water to each site, and picnic tables. There is a swimming pool, a delightful rural outlook across to the surrounding hills, sloping lawns, and, near the ablution block, a magnificent and very old spreading chestnut tree which probably dates back to the days of early settlement in the area.

I was longing for a cup of tea and went outside to turn on the gas, but couldn't budge the tap on the cylinder. Neither could M., nor Barry the camp handyman with his spanner. This was very strange, because I had used the gas that morning in Rotorua, and had locked the door to the cylinder before we set off so it could not be tampered with. M. rang the Maui Helpline, and within the hour a serviceman from Munro Caravans International in Otorohanga, 20 minutes' drive away, pulled up alongside with a full replacement cylinder and swapped them over. Munro Caravans are an established coach-building firm, and do the coach works for the Maui vans. The serviceman told us that the Maui company has 4,000 vehicles on the road, and had recently ordered another 1,000 more to meet demand! We wondered whether the forthcoming British Lions rugby tour of New Zealand had caused an increase in bookings.

At 6 p.m. we ambled across the highway (not too many cars, here,) to the Waitomo Caves Tavern, a most excellent establishment built on an incline above the road, with extensive views over the camp and the countryside. Huge tables hewn from single slabs of timber were conducive to informality, and there were three giant TV screens on the walls, so no matter where you sat you saw Judy Bailey reading the news. We hadn't seen television for a week, and it was quite a surprise to realise that the world's disasters were still occurring nightly on TV One. The house wine of the week, the bottle freshly opened for me by the obliging barman, was Allan Scott's Marlborough Sauvignon Blanc costing $7 for a very generous glassful, so I had two.

The tavern's standout feature was the local colour. It seemed that a dozen Barry Crumps were out on the verandah, leaning against the table for their end-of-day beer and a smoke, with rugged bush shirts and shorts, heavy hiking boots, battered, wide-brimmed hats, weather beaten faces, and a week's stubble. They were authentic rural men, with voices and drawled speech to match, as far removed as possible from townies in suits. The tavern was carpeted, and others who came inside for a drink thoughtfully left their muddy boots at the door and padded inside wearing the thick ribbed socks that partner hard-wearing boots.

The barman said the Morepork Café 100 yards up the hill served good food, so we had dinner on the balcony there under the clear pale sky, which had just a hint in it of a light frost to come later on. The servings of bacon-wrapped fillet steak, buttery mashed potatoes and stir-fried vegetables were generous, and cost $23 each.

Back at the camp we watched local lads practising for the winter season on a neighbouring rugby field. By now we had plenty of neighbours on the adjacent pitches, several of them Japanese, all young, in small-sized campervans, with an array of wetsuits and towels spread out to dry off. They had spent the afternoon black water rafting, a much more interesting and exciting experience for them than our sedate tour of the glow worm cave. We drifted off to sleep to the sound of morepork birds in the bush calling out (you cannot possibly call it *singing*), another experience we never have at home.

It was ghastly getting dressed into cold, dampish clothing the next morning. The windows of the campervan were dripping with condensation, and heavy dew sparkled on the grass. But the sun shone, the sky was bright blue, the air pure, and we were away by 9 a.m. to reach the Coromandel Peninsula and Pauanui in the early afternoon. We'd driven 174 kilometres the day before, and had about 225 kilometres to cover this Saturday. I was very sorry to leave the camp. It was the best we had yet stayed in, even better than the Rotorua camp, because of the magical setting, and I recommend it for an overnight stop.

We turned left onto State Highway 3 for Otorohanga, the kiwiana capital of New Zealand. The 10 kilometre drive to Otorohanga was through the prettiest and most orderly countryside we had encountered in eight days of travelling, with lush, well-kept farms and an air of prosperity which was to last, as we crossed the Waikato region, until we reached the Coromandel foothills. Hanging baskets of bright flowers gave the main street a festive look, the well-kept buildings and closely mown lawns speaking of civic pride. The town is proud of its kiwiana image, and the blank side of a building was painted with iconic New Zealand images of jandals, pavlovas, buzzy bees, ice cream cones, and so on. Otorohanga is famous for its nocturnal Kiwi House and walk-through aviary, where native birds can be seen in a natural rainforest habitat. A variety of rare and unusual birds, and tuatara lizards and geckos, are also displayed. The Otorohanga Kiwi House and Native Bird Park (ph. (07) 873 7391, www.kiwihouse.org.nz) at Alex Telfer Drive, which is run by the Otorohanga Zoological Society, is a good place to visit if you think you may not be able to view native birds and other species elsewhere in New Zealand.

We sped past Munro Caravans, our saviour of the night before, through countryside with an Englishness achieved by lavish plantings of oak trees, laurel magnolias, birches, willows, and ash trees, punctuated by belts of tall poplars which gave scale and definition to the landscape. On the outskirts of Te Awamutu we turned right off State Highway 3 onto a secondary road signed in blue, in the direction of Cambridge, and a short distance on turned right again to take the Cambridge Road. This was a very good highway, flat and better-marked, surfaced and maintained than most of the state highways we had travelled on. At 10 o'clock in the morning we were the only people using it. We were in dairy country, with large herds everywhere, reinforcing the view that New Zealand is really just one large farm, broken up by the four main cities, provincial towns, scenic reserves, lakes, and alpine ranges. Not a bad place to live in, actually.

Cambridge, 'The Town of Trees', is memorable for the manicured gardens in front of well-kept houses, and the green avenues of trees in the town centre. Any plant seems to thrive here, but you might find it difficult to live in if you don't like gardening, or mowing lawns till they are velvet-smooth. Cambridge has always had a few good antique shops, so it's worth a stop if you are on the hunt for something.

We followed State Highway 1B, signposted Taupiri, along Duke Street, past famous horse stud farms en route to State Highway 26 and Morrinsville. This is a three star drive to cleanse the soul, for I am sure that never in your life are you likely to see such wonderful pastures, such healthy, well-fed, shiny-coated dairy herds, such picture book perfection, as you can see here in the Waikato region.

Real Estate Institute figures published in *The New Zealand Herald* of 24 January 2006 show that dairy farm prices have recently risen to a median of $3.2 million. New Zealand farms of all types are more expensive in the Waikato than elsewhere, with the median price being $2,147,188, against the national median of $1.2

million. The wealth of the region is evidenced everywhere as you drive through. Morrinsville, a typical regional service town, with farming, marine, building and auto industries lining the approach on the main road, has a very good café, the Crazee Cow, full of locals enjoying brunch this Saturday morning. We ordered coffee, hot chocolate, and enormous wedges of fresh and delicious carrot cake, for $14, and read the morning paper before continuing on State Highway 26 to Te Aroha and Paeroa.

The Kaimai Range which divides the Waikato from the Bay of Plenty rose up ahead of us as we crossed the flat plain. Te Aroha, home to many racing stables (country race meetings in New Zealand are great fun), had gone trendy and the old bank building had become Café Banco. M. was relishing the straight, flat roads after driving round Northland and the Coromandel Peninsula. At Paeroa, home of the famous fizzy drink Lemon and Paeroa, we turned off the main street at Father's Tavern, a lovely name, still following State Highway 26, to the turnoff just south of Kopu. There we would turn right onto State Highway 25A to Hikuai, and on to Pauanui.

The foothills of the Coromandel Range loomed on our right, a sign of what to expect on the road ahead. The road over the range to Pauanui is steep and winding, and needs to be driven with care, but the surface is good and the native bush on the slopes is typically luxuriant, full of tall fern trees, and exquisite to behold. A landscape gardener could not have arranged it better. The fern is the national emblem of New Zealand, and deservedly so, because more than 150 species exist here, one-third of them unique to this country.

At Prescott's Garages we turned onto the side road to Pauanui and enjoyed the view over the Tairua River estuary. The Tairua State Forest had been logged drastically, and some of the tranquillity of the approach to Pauanui had been lost. Over the years we have seen the trees grow, be felled, replanted, and now felled again. The kiwi fruit orchards on the left were flourishing, and the oxidation ponds were still there. We called at the Supervalue supermarket in the Pauanui Shopping Centre to get supplies to last me through the next two days, and booked in at The Glade Holiday Park situated on the estuary in Vista Paku, one of the earliest roads in the resort. Dinner that night was at Shorty's Restaurant at the shopping centre, the only restaurant in Pauanui, where bookings are essential if you are there over a weekend. The food was excellent, although not cheap, this being Pauanui, and dinner for two plus wine cost $103.50.

CHAPTER 14

TAUPO, AND THE ROAD TO WELLINGTON

I will draw a veil over the three nights and two days spent at The Glade Holiday Park in Pauanui. Perhaps I had been spoilt by the marvellous facilities at all the other camps, or perhaps I expected too much from a camp as old-established as this one. All I will say is that to be charged $33 per night and have to put up with shower walls so badly soap-scummed that I shuddered if my elbow brushed against one; toilets where a hose was sprayed daily around the concrete floor, but no one bothered to clean the bowls and seats; a laundry where the washing machines were rusting and the one dryer swallowed money yet left everything damp, so that I had to peg the washing on a clothesline to finish off the drying; and where a tub was full of cold, stagnant, grey water for the duration of our stay, nobody from 'management' being brave enough to plunge an arm in and pull out the plug – or perhaps they hadn't set foot in the laundry for ages – and where the thinly gravelled camp roads were full of ruts and dips, was an absolute cheek. The camp suffers, I believe, from the large number of caravanners who leave their vehicles permanently on site all year round, who have been returning over many years (we have friends who have done just this for 30 years) and have not noticed any deterioration in standards. If I had known of another camp at Pauanui I would have moved immediately. I checked with my *Camping Guide North Island* and read that new owners have made considerable improvements!

M. went off to the Mercure Grand Puka Park Lodge (ph. (07) 864 8088) both mornings for breakfast and a day of conference, and returned to the van after dinner at night, and I passed the days peacefully on the surf beach, walking, and reading. We had covered a lot of territory in the preceding 10 days, and the opportunity to relax and do nothing was very welcome.

The lodge, built in the late 1970s on a steep hillside at the southern end of Pauanui, is notable for its layout. Accommodation is in 48 wooden chalets tucked under the native bush canopy, with nothing visible above the tree line except the wooden outdoor dining deck and the high gable of the lodge itself. The well-appointed and comfortable chalets are reached by winding pathways (which jeeps carrying one's luggage can, thankfully, negotiate with ease), and the atmosphere is one of privacy and solitude in the sunlight which filters through the trees. It is unspoilt and magical, with native birds singing outside one's balcony, and good food and wine just a short stroll away down the hill. I adore staying there. The Miha Restaurant and the café have excellent food, and bookings are recommended. We've had some memorable twilight dinners out on the deck in summer.

There is just one reason to brave The Glade Holiday Park for a night, and that is to go on a Johansen Guiding Adventure. Doug Johansen began taking family parties and overseas tour groups on treks into the Coromandel Range 30 years ago when Pauanui was in its infancy, and the company has grown from there. There are a variety of treks suitable for all ages and levels of fitness. I can especially recommend the nature treks, having done one myself, where all you need is a stout pair of boots, or even old trainers, and where you will penetrate the bush to learn about the habitat of the native flora and fauna, Maori medicines and foods of the forest, boil a billy for tea by the side of a stream and have a few wonderful hours believing you were Born to the Wild.

The Johansen family will arrange any activity you want, from adventure treks and tours, camping, hiking, or bush walking, which take you right into the rugged mountains. Private customised tours are easily arranged. All-year-round hunting trips can be organised, with the opportunity to stalk deer and bag wild pigs, goats, possums and rabbits. Game birds can be hunted in May, June and July. Transport to and from the hunting areas is by 4WD, accommodation and food is inclusive, or, if you prefer, you can travel by helicopter if the particular area is suitable. Bookings are essential. If you decide to take advantage of the opportunity to trek or hunt with the Johansens, you will consider it one of the best experiences you have had. I and my family have all taken treks with Doug Johansen, some several times. M. took our daughters and their English and German partners on a tour just two years ago and they had an unforgettable day. Details of Johansen Guiding Adventures are given in the Appendix.

At last it was Tuesday 22 February. M. had a morning session and lunch at the lodge and didn't arrive back at the camp until 3 p.m. We had to reach Taupo for the night, otherwise our journey to Wellington the next day would be uncomfortably long. I had the campervan ready for departure, with all loose items packed away, the electric power cord wound into a tidy circle and stowed flat on the floor, the cupboard doors all locked tightly so they wouldn't burst open and spill the contents everywhere if we took a tight corner, and the gas turned safely off. We sped over the hill road, quite deserted at this hour, back to Hikuai, and the turnoff at Kopu to Paeroa and Te Aroha, retracing our Saturday's steps to the southern Hauraki Plain. An oncoming truck and trailer threw up a stone which cracked the windscreen, low down on the driver's side. The windscreen would have to be replaced by Maui, but fortunately we had total insurance cover. We just had to hope it would see out the remainder of the journey, and it did.

If you are in any doubt about the size of the New Zealand dairy industry, just take a look at the dairy factory of Fonterra at Waitoa, and count the cows in the herds as you cross the plains. On the outskirts of Paeroa we saw a huge herd of cows walking sedately in perfect crocodile formation along a field path, towards the sheds for their late afternoon milking. It was a beautiful sight, the lowing herd winding 'slowly o'er the lea', described memorably by the poet Thomas Gray in *Elegy in a Country Churchyard*, and the lines once learned at school, never forgotten!

Our most direct route to Taupo was through Matamata, and at Tatuanui we turned onto State Highway 27, a pleasant and familiar road through excellent farmland, to Matamata.

A quick word about State Highway 27. If you travel directly from Auckland to Rotorua and/or Taupo, I recommend turning off State Highway 1 at the foot of the Bombay Hill and onto State Highway 2, then turning right onto State Highway 27 at the junction with State Highway 25 (which continues across the Hauraki Plain to the Coromandel). State Highway 27 links up with State Highway 1 to Taupo and State Highway 5 to Rotorua at Tirau.

Why this route? There is little of merit to see on the stretch of State Highway 1 from Bombay/Pokeno to Tirau. The very busy road bypasses the small town of Huntly, and Hamilton city, and although the outskirts of Cambridge are attractive the drive, overall, is not as scenic as the route through Matamata. If you must take State Highway 1, then turn off at Taupiri and onto State Highway 1B to Cambridge, and bypass the environs of Hamilton completely. This is a delightful drive, passing well-settled farmlands and old homesteads. We consider the regular route south on State Highway 1 to be the dullest of all the options available, and for years have taken State Highway 27 as the quickest and most enjoyable route to Rotorua and Taupo. As you would expect, New Zealand country roads, which run through flat farmland, are well-surfaced, straight for long distances, and the absence of heavy traffic makes them a pleasure to drive on.

A pleasant way to reach Tirau from Matamata is to drive to the end of the main shopping street and follow signs to Tauranga Te Poi and Tirau. The flat country roads are empty and the aspect is serene and pastoral.

We stopped for diesel fuel at Matamata, 56.9 litres costing $43.47. Matamata is a regional service town, the focus of rich farming and racehorse breeding industries, and worth a visit. Firstly, it boasts the famous Ronnie's Café, a main street food stop where you can gorge yourself on a huge variety of quintessentially New

Zealand sandwiches, savouries and cakes. This is the place to indulge your secret craving for buns, pies, hot dogs, fries, scones, neenish tarts, lamingtons, ginger slice, butterfly sponge cakes, anything else that is ruinous to your figure and absolutely yummy. We always take overseas guests here on our way to Rotorua and Taupo, and wait, naughtily, for the dropped jaw and the look of wonder as they see the vast array of food. It has become a favoured place for tour buses to offload passengers for a mid-journey stoke-up, and in recent years the premises next door have been taken over to absorb the crowds. Be warned, though – to reach the toilets you will have to walk through the kitchen, and the toilets themselves are dilapidated and unpleasant.

Secondly, the district is famous for its hot mineral springs, in particular the Opal Hot Springs on Okauia Springs Road, and the Okoroire Hot Springs south on the Matamata-Te Poi-Rotorua road, and the historic Firth Tower (www.matamata.info.co.nz) built by a settler in the 1880s as a place of refuge during the Waikato War. It is set in several acres of lawns and gardens, the museum and historical buildings and displays are open daily from 10 a.m. to 4 p.m., and there are overnight facilities for campervans.

But Matamata's biggest attraction, now, is the local sheep farm that was transformed by the vision of Peter Jackson and his designers into the Hobbiton movie set for the trilogy of *The Lord of the Rings*. Private visits to the farm are not allowed, but two-hour guided tours in a free courtesy van depart twice daily from the Matamata Information Centre (phone (07) 888 6368, www.hobbitontours.com) at 45 Broadway. Although some of the set was demolished before it was realised what a tourist attraction the Shire of Middle-earth would become, there are still plenty of hobbit holes to see, and you can walk up Bagshot Row to Bag End. Over 50,000 fans have made the pilgrimage since the tours began.

The little town of Tirau is a must for antiques junkies. There are several good shops on and around the main road which are worth a browse; I like Cartwells, and I usually find it impossible to pass through without stopping. However, sadly, this day, we had to press on to Putaruru and the logging town of Tokoroa, taking State Highway 1. M. said that he was quite pleased, actually, to be driving on State Highway 1 after taking the lesser roads. Yet parts of State Highway 1 are not as good as the 'lesser' roads we have driven on, due to lack of investment in upkeep and improvement. I think that State Highway 1 is a state of mind! But the road *is* wider, with plenty of lanes for overtaking provided in both directions, and the vision is good.

It was nearly 6 p.m., the road was fairly empty, and M. pushed the van along at 100 kilometres per hour. It was 11 years since I had travelled on this stretch of highway and the pine trees were noticeably taller, with a high fire danger registering on the warning board. At the turnoff to Te Kuiti and State Highway 30, at Atiamuri Dam, we realised we had come round full circle after leaving Rotorua four days ago!

At Wairakei, just a few kilometres before Taupo, we passed the notable geothermal field on our right, with gushes of steam rising into the air, and the lines of pipes giving the weird look of a science fiction movie to the landscape. The Wairakei Geothermal Power Station harnesses a vast reservoir of hot water and steam under the valley to provide electric power to the national grid. It is worth a visit, for you can drive in to the field, and if the steam is high and swirling it's an exciting experience. The Wairakei Tourist Hotel on the left of the main road is a well-known resort, much-favoured by golfers because of the excellence of the golf course across the road.

As you continue towards Taupo, it would be a pity not to take a well-signposted road on your left and spend half an hour at the Huka Falls, famous for the colossal rush of water which roars spectacularly over a ledge and into the wide Waikato River below. The thunderous falls are coloured bright aqua, and can be seen by crossing a suspension bridge over the upper rapids and taking the path to the well-fenced viewing areas. They have recently been successfully kayaked, and you will wonder at the foolhardiness of people who undertake such an adventure. Huka Falls is still free of charge, and is another scenic wonder to which we take our visitors.

We came to the turnoff to the renowned Huka Lodge, regularly voted one of the top luxury lodges in the world by *Conde Nast Traveller* and other influential publications. The ambience and design of Huka Lodge is utterly luxurious, the setting on the bank of the Waikato River superb, and unlike its rival Blanket Bay Lodge on the shore of Lake Wakatipu in Queenstown, it is happy to serve lunch to casual visitors. If you stop there, you will probably never want to leave.

We reached Taupo at last, spread out below us from the top of the gentle hill leading down to the Waikato River Bridge and the control gates which regulate the output of water from Lake Taupo. Our destination was the municipal Taupo Motor Camp in Redoubt Street, just off the main highway leading into the township. It's the only camp 'in town', and I chose it after a quick phone call to the office ((07) 377 3080) to make sure it was handy to the lakeside restaurants. Very! We were charged $26 for the night. The camp is beautifully situated in the Taupo Domain on the Waikato River bank, adjacent to the boat ramp, and the marina which gives straight onto the lake. Many caravans were lined up along a side fence, ready to be towed by the owners onto a site when required. Taupo is a favourite holiday spot and the camp would be too busy over the Christmas holiday period to be attractive to us. We found an ideal pitch to drive the campervan straight onto, and out the other side the next morning. Thoughtful town planning has made access to the water from the camp available to all, and we took a picturesque stroll around the river and lake front on our way to dinner.

Dinner at the Pub 'n Grub at an outdoor table overlooking Lake Taupo was entirely suitable for two hungry people – Steak Amsterdam for me, which turned out to be grilled sirloin garnished with fried onion rings and bacon, smothered in béarnaise sauce, and fish and chips for M., with salads. It was a busy, friendly place with a wide screen showing, to loud cheers, Australia being slaughtered by New Zealand in the cricket, several snooker tables, some pokie machines, and a long bar with menus from which we ordered our dinner. Dinner for two plus Stella Artois for M. and two glasses of wine for me cost $52.90. The lake was serene in the greyish blue evening light, but Mt. Ruapehu at the end was obscured by mist. I hoped it would clear in the morning, for it is a glorious vista and I wanted to enjoy it again.

M. passed an Internet Café open in the main street on our way back to the camp and checked his emails, and we crossed over to the domain and the camp feeling remarkably contented. Unfortunately, we were unable to use the showers because they were so dirty and poorly lit. No reasonable camper expects absolute perfection from a communal facility, but these showers, and the poor standard of cleanliness of toilets and basins which had several other campers also wrinkling up their noses in disgust, were too much to cope with, this night being one of only two in 30 days of touring where we flunked a wash because of the unhygienic conditions.

The latest information on the Taupo Motor Camp, nine months later, is that it is to close after 54 years of operation. The grounds are to be redeveloped into an arts event arena, with amphitheatre and walkways. This is a pity, because the camp is so perfectly situated by the lake and the shopping centre. For this reason I give details of an alternative camp, the Lake Taupo Top 10 Holiday Park, in the Appendix. The camp is off Spa Road opposite the Taupo Golf Club and has a rave review in my *Camping Guide North Island* handbook.

Now, a little about the lake and the attractions of the region.

Taupo is New Zealand's largest lake, formed by one of the world's most violent volcanic eruptions. A fishing guide who took us out on the lake a few years ago for a day's trolling at Turangi, at the southern end, told us that the bottom of the lake has never been established. The lake is one of the most popular holiday destinations in New Zealand and world-famous for its trout fishing; indeed Taupo is known as the Trout Fishing Capital of the World, the best time for fishing being mid-March to the end of June. Hire boats are available from the marina for trout fishing, sailing, or just cruising on the lake, and there are plenty of firms to choose from. Lake Taupo Charter Boats (ph. (07) 378 3444), with over 20 boats, is run by the Taupo Launchmen's Association and has a lakeside booking office where you can organise trout fishing and cruising on the lake. Kiwi Charters (ph. (07) 378 5596, www.kiwicharterstaupo.co.nz) specialises in trout fishing, as does Te Moana Charters (ph. (07) 378 4839, www.gusgrace.orcon.net.nz). If you wish to do river fly fishing at Taupo, Grant Bayley Outdoor Guides Limited (ph. (07) 377 6105) offers a full fishing guide service, providing equipment, pick-up from your campground, tuition, and a picnic lunch.

Waterskiing and windsurfing are popular activities on Lake Taupo, and the mighty Waikato River, New Zealand's longest, has facilities for jet boating, white water rafting, canoeing and kayaking. The Huka Jet 30 minute boat ride at 80 kilometres per hour up the Waikato River to the Huka Falls is an exciting experience. The rides operate 365 days a year, weather permitting, from the Wairakei Tourist Park, and reservations are essential (ph. (07) 374 8572, freephone 0800 48 52 538, www.hukajet.com). A courtesy coach runs on request from the Taupo Visitors Centre to the start of the ride, and life jackets, which are mandatory, are provided. You will need to wear a hat, gloves and warm clothing if you do the trip in winter. Jet boating is thrilling; we've done it several times on the Shotover River at Queenstown.

If you want a more sedate river experience, contact Canoe and Kayak (freephone 0800 529 256) or call at 38 Nukuhau Street off Spa Road to enquire about their two-hour guided kayak trips. They also run a lakefront hire shop on Lake Terrace, on the waterfront south from the town on State Highway 1, and you can paddle to your heart's content on Lake Taupo, enjoying the mountain view and perhaps dropping a line overboard.

Taupo's reputation as an adventure playground is enhanced by Skydive Taupo (freephone 0800 586 766, www.skydivetaupo.co.nz) situated at Taupo Airport, who can take you sky diving from as high as 5,000 metres, and will video you doing it! If you wish to go for a bungy jump, then Taupo Bungy (freephone 0800 888 408, www.taupobungy.co.nz) has a cantilevered bungy platform 47 metres above the Waikato River from which to take your jump.

You can pilot a helicopter around Taupo with no experience necessary, by contacting Flight Training Taupo (ph. (07) 376 9209, www.flighttrainingtaupo.co.nz) who will take you up and 'train' you. It is described as a 'hands on experience' and rated 'nothing but sensational' in the company's brochure. For an orthodox flight over Lake Taupo, the Tongariro National Park where you will see the craters of Mts. Ruapehu, Tongariro and Ngauruhoe, as well as Wairakei, and Huka Falls, contact Taupo Air Services at Taupo Airport (ph. (07) 378 5325, email: taupo.air@xtra.co.nz) to book. A flight of approximately one hour is advertised at $210, and several flight options are available.

Twenty-five minutes north of Taupo is the unspoilt geothermal area of Orakei Korako (ph. (07) 378 3131, www.orakeikorako.co.nz) which we have not visited ourselves; all I can say is that it is reputed to be one of the finest thermal areas in the world, and if you have missed out on seeing the geothermal activity in Rotorua, this is a good opportunity to cross the Waikato River by boat to explore the geysers, boiling mud pools, hot springs, and caves, and to take a bush walk through native flora and fauna. Campervans are able to park overnight, free of charge.

We left Taupo at 8 a.m. on Wednesday 23 February anticipating a long drive of at least six hours ahead of us. We'd travelled 257 kilometres in four hours the previous afternoon, and today's journey to Wellington would cover over 400 kilometres. Well, that's how it happens, sometimes, when you've got a deadline. Our plan was to get the journey behind us in one day, and spend the next day in Wellington visiting the national museum, and relaxing, before crossing in the ferry to Picton and the South Island on 25 February.

As we drove off from the camp I looked south and saw that low grey cloud obscured the mountains of the central plateau. My hoped-for view of Mt. Ruapehu was not likely to happen, it seemed. State Highway 1 around the lakefront is lined with good motels, and the road, which used to be hilly and winding once past the town, is now level and very good to drive on – perhaps too good for some, for there was a sobering road sign on the left in white lettering on black 'The Coroner Thanks You For Driving Carefully'. Fishermen in waders were casting in the lake to find their lunch or dinner, and I noticed with satisfaction that in a fast-growing town which in parts is too newly-minted and glossy to be attractive, many of the shabby old properties further around the lakeshore, which started off life as weekend fishing cottages 60 years ago, or more, and are now very valuable because of their location, are still there. Some things should never change.

If you wish to camp on the shore of Lake Taupo you should try the Motutere Bay Caravan Park (ph. (07) 386 8963) half way between Taupo and Turangi. The campground is situated on both sides of the highway, there is room for about 235 sites, 150 of which have power, but kitchen facilities are limited and the *Camping Guide North Island* mentions also that the ablution blocks are '...possibly undersupplied when the camp is busy'. This is a camp to avoid during the Christmas holiday period, I think. Today, at the end of February, it was half empty and the motorhomes parked on the lake verge had the fabulous site all to themselves.

Turangi township at the foot of the lake offers outstanding facilities for trout fishing. M. and I have come here three times to fly fish in the Tongariro River and troll on Lake Taupo. We are absolute novices, but have booked a guide for the day who has supplied us with waders and all the gear, plus lunch, and driven us to favoured pools where we have been assured of a fish, and then taken us trolling in the afternoon from an outboard motor boat on the lake. We have never caught anything, but have had the joy of learning to fly fish, and of bobbing on the lake hoping for a catch. Many people consider this the best fishing spot in the North Island, and if you want to fly fish I can recommend it. Tongariro Guides (ph. (07) 386 7946, www.tongarirolodge.co.nz) caters for both beginners and experts, and has an all-inclusive service.

The Rafting Centre at Atirua Road, Turangi (freephone 0800 10 10 24), runs whitewater rafting and kayaking trips on the Tongariro River for more adventurous tourists, and has a bike hire service so you can explore the bush. Bookings are essential.

One of my favourite drives is that from Turangi to Waiouru across the Desert Road. I have never tired of it, and this day, after an absence of at least 20 years, I was looking forward tremendously to doing it again. If you cross the Desert Road in winter, watch for the roadside noticeboard on the outskirts of Turangi which will tell you if the road is passable, or closed due to snow. If you cannot take State Highway 1 to Waiouru, then to get south you will have to take State Highway 47 from Turangi to Taurewa and on to National Park and State Highway 4, if it is open, or else the longer detour towards Taumarunui on State Highway 41 and State Highway 4 to National Park, and follow State Highway 49 to Ohakune and Waiouru. This sounds complicated, but the navigation is easy. Another warning: if you are getting low on fuel fill up at Turangi, for there are no petrol stations on the 56 kilometres from there to Waiouru.

South of the straight roads of Turangi, State Highway 1 begins a gradual ascent to the summit of 1,074 metres by means of a series of horseshoe bends where the recommended speed is 35 kilometres per hour. Fifty years ago this stretch of road used to be the benchmark for tricky driving in the North Island, and many were the tales told of icy skids, near misses, and failure to take a bend often resulting in a plunge into a stream. People talked with pride and satisfaction of having 'gone on' the Desert Road! Now the road is widened, with slow vehicle passing bays, and most of the excitement has gone out of the early part of the drive; however the road is still unpredictable in winter, and is often closed due to ice and snow. M.'s view on this part of the road is that if it were in Italy it would be one long viaduct with tunnels!

The Desert Road plateau affords sweeping views to the right of the Tongariro National Park, a World Heritage Site, and the three mountains of Ruapehu, Tongariro and Ngauruhoe. It is an area of daunting beauty. The enormous variety of the physical landscape of the central North Island, from lush pasture and pine forest to hissing geysers and boiling hot springs, from tranquil lakes and foaming rivers to snow-covered peaks which exist alongside a dry, dusty desert unique in New Zealand, and the speed at which these changes occur as you progress through the region, is miraculous. The Kaimanawa Mountains to the left frame the gently undulating, tussocky pumice land over which you can sometimes see tanks hurtling on exercise, and gunsmoke in the air, for the New Zealand Army has a training base at Waiouru. It can be surprisingly chilly on the Desert Road, even in summer; M. said his legs felt cold and turned the heater on, a welcome change from the constant air-conditioning of the previous 12 days.

The dignified and imposing Waiouru Army Museum on State Highway 1 at Waiouru is worth a visit, particularly if you wish to see realistic mock-ups of the First World War trenches; otherwise this self-styled 'Desert Oasis' is a handy place to stop for a meal at the local pub, a newspaper and a tank of fuel.

Now for some information on *The Lord of the Rings*. If, on the way south, you wish to visit the site of Mordor, take State Highway 47 from Turangi and travel about 35 kilometres to the turnoff to State Highway 48, following directions to the Grand Chateau and the Whakapapa Ski Field. The Grand Chateau hotel, built after World War I, is famous throughout New Zealand for its splendid location and its elegance. When I was young it was a destination hotel, one where you spent a week; you would hardly be happy with just one night in such surroundings. The hotel was used as the headquarters for the cast and crew of *The Lord of the Rings* for several weeks while filming went on further up Mt. Ruapehu. You will need good walking shoes to cover the volcanic rock and ash, but the Mordor location, in all its summer desolation, is quite accessible. The Pinnacle Ridge was used for a number of scenes in *The Two Towers*.

If you decide to give the Whakapapa Ski Field location a miss and head on south from Turangi, then turn off at Waiouru onto State Highway 49 for Ohakune, and stay at the Powderhorn Chateau where cast and crew stayed for the filming of Ithilien and Mordor scenes. Ithilien is reached by driving up the Turoa Ski Field road as far as the Mangawhero Falls, and climbing down to the rocky riverbed. For excellent detailed information on the film trilogy, read *The Lord of the Rings Location Guidebook* by Ian Brodie, details of which are given in the Acknowledgments at the front of this book. As well as all the detailed information for fans, the book is an excellent tourist guidebook giving succinct information and advice on much of New Zealand.

In the space of a kilometre after leaving Waiouru the landscape became pasture-clad, with treed slopes and plenty of sheep. Unfortunately, late summer, when the peak holiday rush is over and the weather is still fine, is the season for roadworks, and we began to pass heavy machinery, piles of gravel, and have our direction marked out by orange safety cones. The road surface was poor, but the road works were quite massive, and were cutting through much of the countryside.

Taihape (pron. tye-happy) and a cup of tea were 30 kilometres away, and we forged ahead to the Brown Sugar Café, recommended to us by a friend. I can safely recommend it to you, too. The food and coffee were exceptionally good, and we had a choice of eating indoors or out in the pleasant courtyard. From the counter I could see into the kitchen where young cooks were doing everything properly. The pastry looked homemade, so I ordered two sausage rolls (which I hadn't had for years) and the pastry was crisp, flaky and light. We ordered also two flat whites, mine with the usual double shot of coffee which was so good that I had another, and paninis spread liberally with butter and garlic and herb mayonnaise, filled with freshly-sliced ham off the bone, crisp lettuce, and plenty of tomato. *Scrumptious*. The country garden surrounding the courtyard is as it was before the building was converted into a café, very old-fashioned and blowsy, with clumps of globe artichokes, rhubarb, roses, honesty, columbines, rosemary and parsley all nestling together, and a spreading pear tree as a backdrop, and quite delightful to stroll in. The new outdoor toilet was the cleanest in the world.

Next door to the café, on the corner of the main street, is a sports and outdoors store whose goods in the windows tell you everything you need to know about Taihape and the surrounding region, its people and their pastimes. I even saw a camp oven with a rimmed lid designed to hold hot coals, a piece of cooking equipment from New Zealand's pioneer days I thought had vanished forever. At 11.30 a.m. we were on the road again, stoked up with food until dinnertime. Rule of the road: when you find good food, *eat it*!

A film site of *The Lord of the Rings* was nearby, and south of Taihape we turned left at Ohutu, crossed the main trunk railway line and drove to the one-way bridge across the Rangitikei (pron. runga-tickay) River Gorge. It wasn't too difficult to imagine the gorge's superb propensity for the site of the River Anduin in *The Fellowship of the Rings*. At this point the dark green water flows quickly through the long gorge enclosed by sheer, high rock walls, and my first impression was of danger, and daring. If you wish to raft this location, Rangitikei River Rafting at the township of Mangaweka 20 kilometres further south offers a tour which takes in the site. Ian Brodie mentions in *The Lord of the Rings Location Guidebook* that the tours are suitable for all ages.

We drove on to Hunterville with the high Ruahine Ranges rising on the far left, and in front of them the celebrated limestone cliffs lining the Rangitikei River. The old narrow and very winding road from Mangaweka had been replaced by a smoothed-out version, and we made good time. The vintage Argyle Hotel on the corner of Hunterville's main street had been repainted in bright apricot, with orange and black trim, and looked extremely stylish and welcoming. Why is it that old New Zealand buildings look stunning in colour combinations that you would normally consider dreadful? The road from Hunterville south can only be described as 'lovely'. As I've mentioned, just because a road is designated a State Highway, even State Highway 1, does not mean it is superb. The New Zealand terrain is quite difficult, flat land is limited in parts, and it is unrealistic to expect autoroutes/bahns/stradas of the quality one drives on in Europe. Our motorways exist only as approaches to and from the four major cities. But this stretch of road on the Rangitikei Plains was, by local standards, superb, and fortunately for us and our time schedule, it continued most of the way to Wellington.

In the days before roadside cafés were commonplace, and became big business, there used to be a prized food stop just to the south of Hunterville run by an elderly mother and her daft son from the kitchen and dining room of their old wooden cottage. There were two choices on the menu, bacon and eggs and bubble and squeak, or rump steak, fried onions and bubble and squeak, the steak tender and the onions ringed with brown and with just a touch of crispness, plus a large pot of strong tea. They kept a cow and chickens in the back garden where rows of cabbages for the bubble and squeak grew, and a goat to keep the front roadside looking tidy, and the only hint to passing travellers of their enterprise was a small hand-lettered sign which simply said 'Food'. It was a word-of-mouth dining room, beloved by commercial travellers, and we stopped there many times. The mother and son will have met their Maker, by now, but although I watched out for the cottage I couldn't find it, so I suppose it has fallen down.

We had our first sighting of the irrigation 'aeroplanes' which have horizontal rotating wings, and give the best result as the area covered is very wide. They can be moved easily on wheels to new situations in a pasture, and are a wonderful invention for flat land. We were told a year ago by a South Island farmer that the only way to survive on cattle farms today is by this form of aerial irrigation, which simulates gentle rainfall and doesn't injure the emerging blades of grass. Hill farmers, he said, can't compete because they are entirely dependent on natural rainfall. With aerial irrigation, the farmer creates his own rainfall, and because the pasture grows more quickly it can be rotated more times per year.

Bulls is a country township, famous for being near the Royal New Zealand Air Force Base at Ohakea, and the Air Force Museum located there. We could see a single wind sock, but not one plane, as the RNZAF has been reduced severely in size by the present Labour Government. It pays to slow down on the outskirts of Sanson so you don't make the mistake of forging straight ahead and missing the right hand turn to Wellington on State Highway 1, or you will end up in Palmerston North, as we nearly did. I was so busy trying to peer in the window of an exciting-looking antique shop as we flashed by that I forgot to navigate M. properly!

State Highway 1 and the flat coastal plain is divided from the equally flat Wairarapa plains by the steep Tararua Ranges, highly visible on the left, a Mecca for trampers, and snow-capped in winter. If your laptop needs attention, there is a handy computer business at Himatangi, clearly visible on the corner of State Highway 1. It seems an unlikely place to find such an enterprise, so I can only presume that passing trade is profitable.

We were now on what is known locally as the Foxton Straight. We turned right to Waitarere Beach in search of the location used for Osgiliath Wood and Trollshaw Forest in *The Lord of the Rings*. This is a very old seaside resort which hasn't changed much over the last 50 years, and the beach, part of the long open coastline from Wanganui to Wellington, is flat, quite gentle, and with low surf. We took a side road hoping to be able to drive through the Waitarere Forest, but a sign said we were on private property and vehicle access was prohibited, although pedestrians were welcome. We just didn't have the time to walk into the forest, so left disappointed; if you feel like a hike to the film location, it is there, and is an excellent opportunity to enjoy the surroundings of a pine plantation forest.

At Otaki we entered the foodbasket of Wellington, acres of silverbeet, courgettes, corn, tomatoes, pumpkin, potatoes and strawberries, some fields just harvested, others newly-planted. We were on the Kapiti Coast, and had a good view on the right of Kapiti Island, a noted native bird sanctuary. I wanted another attempt at finding a film site of *The Lord of the Rings*, so just south of Otaki we crossed the Otaki River on the left to take the Otaki Gorge Road towards the foothills of the Tararua Ranges. Ian Brodie writes in *The Lord of the Rings Location Guidebook* (p. 38) that this road '…was used to portray the young Hobbits' journey to the border of their beloved *Shire* through peaceful and productive gardens and farms, providing an interesting parallel with Otaki's real-life industries'. He warns that the 19 kilometre road soon becomes unsealed and that drivers should take care of the conditions. I was unwise enough to read that part out to M., and as soon as we left the sealed road and saw a sign that said the road ahead was not suitable for long vehicles, he refused to go any further. He did look very tired, it was after 4 p.m., and we had at least another hour's drive ahead of us, so I gave in without a single whine. However, the drive along the sealed part of the country road wasn't wasted; the area is entirely pleasant and very picturesque, a good choice for its film fame, with a long green avenue of totara trees and, I was amused to see, a Middle-earth Hideaway which had its vacancy sign up.

As we approached Wellington we were astonished at the way former beach and country resorts of Waikanae, Paraparaumu and Paekakariki have boomed into dormitory suburbs. Just south of Waikanae is the Southward Car Museum. The late Sir Leonard Southward built up his collection over many decades, and it has become the haunt of classic car buffs. The local Kapiti Cheese

Factory is famous for its range of superb blue vein cheeses and ice creams, and the Deep South Vanilla and Kapiti Fig and Honey ice cream is an award winner. New Zealand's ice creams are made from the finest ingredients as befits a country with a huge dairy industry, are wonderfully rich and luscious in texture and taste, and I hope you try some; hokey-pokey ice cream is the biggest seller, I believe, but if you look in the frozen ice cream section of any big supermarket you will have a tough time making a choice. I suggest you try them all…

McKay's Crossing, where State Highway 1 crosses the main rail track, has been the scene of many horrific accidents. It was unbelievable to approach it and find that, after more than 40 years of talking about it, there is still no overbridge! An AA road sign warned that the next 10 kilometres to Plimmerton were an 'Accident Area', and again it's hard to comprehend the lack of a median safety barrier along this notorious stretch of road which regularly claims lives. Here, State Highway 1 runs narrowly along the coast with steep hill faces on one side, and the ocean on the other, and there are no safety shoulders on either of the single lanes. You don't have much of a chance if a vehicle crosses the centre line and comes hurtling towards you. We could see Nelson and the South Island across Cook Strait; in two days' time we would be there!

Oh, we felt glad we didn't live on the outskirts of Wellington. The sun went behind a cloud and suddenly the coast, and the windswept suburbs with the houses cheek by jowl and no colourful gardens, looked grey, and grim. M. commented: 'Who on earth would want to stay here!' There was a noticeable lack of vegetation on the steep hillsides as we travelled down the Ngauranga Gorge to Wellington Harbour, and we remembered from years gone by that even on a sunny day this road always had a gaunt look to it.

Our camp for the night was to be the Top 10 Hutt Park Holiday Park (see Appendix) so we stayed in the left lane of the highway and followed signs to the Hutt Valley. It was 5 p.m. and the homeward commuter traffic was gridlocked. M. decided that though

Wellington is a 'hole', it is pleasant to come back to because it makes him glad we left, 40 years ago! Blue caravan signs directed us to Hutt Park along The Esplanade on the Petone (pron. pet-oh-nee) foreshore. There is a good view from here down the length of the harbour to the Heads and Wellington city, and a building commemorates the landing on the beach by Captain James Cook during his circumnavigation of New Zealand.

We arrived, at last, at the camp, after over eight hours on the road. We were stiff, tired, and hungry, and after parking and setting up the van took a $10 taxi ride to Jackson Street, Petone's shopping and café strip. The Indian taxi driver recommended Curry Heaven, and that's what it was, and full of locals, too, always a good sign (except in Te Kuiti). We had our usuals – lamb, and prawn malabari, and a mixed vegetable curry full of chilli and fresh coriander. The wine was predictable, the Church Road Chardonnay 2003 we had enjoyed with our curries in Rotorua, and the cost for dinner plus wine was $82.70. Petone has come up in the world. It used to be a poor working class suburb, and very down-at-heel. M. knew it well as he used to play table tennis occasionally at a club nearby, and he remarked during dinner that if anyone had told him 40 years ago that one day he would be eating a delicious curry in a smartened Jackson Street, he wouldn't have believed it!

The vastness of Baylys Beach, Northland.

Famous flagstaff and Mission House, Waitangi,
Bay of Islands.

Martha's Mine, Waihi.

In for the night – a line-up at the Rotorua Top 10 Holiday Park.

The Lord of the Rings jeweller, Nelson.

Pancake Rocks, West Coast of the South Island.

On top of the Fox Glacier, Southern Alps.

Cooking Blackball sausages in the campervan.

Whale watching at Kaikoura.

The pleasant Meadow Park, Top 10 Holiday Park, Christchurch.

CHAPTER 15

WELLINGTON

We'd covered 447 kilometres on Wednesday and it was heavenly to wake up the next morning with nothing to do except visit Te Papa Museum. We'd heard and read so much about it that we had set a whole day aside for the purpose and had booked into our campground for two nights, at a charge of $54.00 including discount. Wellington is rather badly-off for good campgrounds. This Hutt Park Top 10 camp is well-established, and set quite attractively in mature grounds. Don't be misled by the name 'Hutt Park' – there is no nearby park, and the camp is situated on the edge of an uninspiring light industrial area. There are 80 sites with power, and 40 tent sites.

At 11 kilometres from the Wellington Ferry Terminal this is not the closest campground to Wellington. A new one, the Capital Gateway Motorhome Park, advertising itself at five minutes from the Ferry Terminal, has recently opened in the suburb of Newlands off the Ngauranga Gorge (see Appendix for details). This small camp has 27 paved motorhome sites, all with power, and showers, toilets, kitchen facilities and a dump station, plus a licensed restaurant and bar, and public transport at the gate. We were happy with our Top 10 choice, however, and would stay there again.

Our pitch was grassed and protected at the rear by a tall hedge, and a nearby tree lent a bit of personality and shade. Plump ducks waddled around, but when I looked through the hedge and saw them swimming in the yellow-slimed turgid stream that the campground backed on to, I wondered how they were alive at all. Factories bordered the far bank of the stream and had obviously been discharging waste into the water for years. There is hostel-style accommodation in the grounds, and the camp has a good games room with Internet access, snooker, TV and table tennis, and large dining halls. The kitchen needs upgrading, but is very clean and practical. A little spying into the large fridge showed that tenters like to store butter or margarine, mayonnaise, tomato ketchup, orange juice and milk. I peeped into several camp fridges on this trip and the contents were always much the same, with occasionally a packet of sausages or some Vegemite and jam for variation. The shower stalls were large, and the handbasins well-equipped, as is usual, with liquid soap dispensers, hot air hand dryers, and two hair dryers. The glory of the camp, for me, was the spacious white laundry, which looked like a sales showroom with six new commercial washers and four new driers, all Maytag equipment. The charge to do a load of laundry was $4, and to dry, $2.

After breakfast we took a taxi to Woburn Station and caught the local train to Wellington, a journey of just 17 minutes, our off-peak return tickets costing $2.50 each. It was a memorable journey, for the guard cum ticket collector greeted almost every passenger by name, stopped for a chat, and asked a young man opposite and the girl in front of me how their studies at Victoria University were going. He had been on the line for over 20 years, he told us, had seen the passengers come on the trains as babies, and now they were grown up and often travelling with babies of their own. He asked where we'd come from and what we were going to do in Wellington, and, by chance, he was on our homeward train later in the day. 'Hi, how did you like Te Papa?' he said as he clipped our tickets. We felt quite special!

We took a $7 taxi ride from the Wellington Railway Station to The Museum of New Zealand, Te Papa Tongarewa, to give its official name, situated magnificently on the edge of the harbour in Cable Street. M. and I both grew up in Wellington, and it was delightful to be travelling past well-remembered places of our childhood. Memories came flooding back, some good, some bad. The Star Boating Club on the waterfront was the venue for high school dances in the early 1950s, and I remembered with a horrid twinge the Wellington College dance where I thought I was partnering the Man Of My Dreams, only to find him outside snogging a girlfriend.

Wellington is bound on all sides by its beautiful harbour and steep hills. Houses of all architectural persuasions cling to the sides of the hills and I know, from my own experience of living there, that it is almost impossible to have a good flower garden. There seems to be no shelter from the wind – it catches you from the north, and the south. February is the best month to visit Wellington; the peak holiday season is over, the weather is calm, and the harbour occasionally glassy-smooth in the early morning.

Indeed the harbour is Wellington's glory. Captain James Cook entered it in 1773 on his circumnavigation of New Zealand, but it was not until 1826 that the first Europeans arrived with the aim of settling there. After examining several sites they left, but not before naming the harbour Port Nicholson. In 1839 a land-buying expedition arrived from London on the ship *Tory*, and selected Petone at the mouth of the Hutt River, with its abundant supply of fresh water, for the first settlement. After buying the land from local Maori, the site was abandoned for one on the south side of the harbour, near where Te Papa Museum now stands. What eventually became Wellington City, named after the 1st Duke of Wellington, was purchased from Maori for muskets, gunpowder, tomahawks, spades, hoes and adzes, tobacco, clothing, writing materials and sealing wax, ladies' clothing, soap, and other barter goods brought over on the *Tory*.

The land was covered in bush, and early settlers who bought land built their first houses of ponga fern tree trunks and mud, to be replaced eventually by wooden cottages. The road known as The Terrace, which runs just above the central business district, was a cliff top, and what is now Lambton Quay was the beach; all the land from there to the harbour edge is reclaimed land. In 1865 the location of Wellington at the mid-way point of the North and South Islands made it the logical choice for the capital of the Colony of New Zealand, and the seat of central government.

It will take you two days to 'do' Wellington properly. If you plan your itinerary carefully, much can be carried out on foot in the central city, on the first day, leaving the second day free for touring further afield by campervan. If you do as we did, and camp at Hutt Park Top 10 and take the train into Wellington, you can start with a visit to Old St. Paul's Church (ph. (04) 473 6722, www.historic.org.nz) at 34 Mulgrave Street, 10 minutes' walk from the railway station, to see an outstanding example of Victorian Gothic architecture carried out in native timber. In spite of its Englishness, the church has a distinctly New Zealand appearance because of the local building materials used. It is open seven days from 10 a.m. to 5 p.m.

From there, if history is your interest, the National Library Gallery (ph. (04) 474 3000, www.natlib.govt.nz) on the corner of Molesworth and Aitken Streets houses the world-famous Alexander Turnbull Library collection of art and historical documents. This is open seven days a week, from 9 a.m. to 5 p.m., with reduced hours over the weekend.

Excellent free one-hour guided tours of the nearby Parliament Buildings and the Debating Chamber take place daily, on the hour, weekdays 10 a.m. to 4 p.m., with shortened hours at the weekend. The tour desk is situated on the ground floor of Parliament House, and I suggest you visit on a weekday when the House is in session. If you are frightened of earthquakes, the basement under this building is one of the safest places in Wellington, and the tour takes in a look at the devices used to prevent its collapse should disaster strike. It is worth mentioning that the circular structure to the left of the main building is known as The Beehive, and was designed by the English architect Sir Basil Spence who was responsible for the new Coventry Cathedral rebuilt after the Second World War.

Across the road, on Lambton Quay, is reputedly the second largest wooden building in the world, known as Government Buildings, built on land reclaimed from the harbour. Finished in 1876, it is built of New Zealand timbers, partly because there was plenty of timber available, but also because brick and stone were deemed risky at the time for such a large structure in earthquake-prone Wellington. It housed the Civil Service and Cabinet Ministers, the Executive Council Chamber, and Cabinet rooms, and cost approximately £48,000 to build, and it became the symbol of centralised government.

From there, a pleasant stroll of 15 minutes past the shops of Lambton Quay will take you to the Kelburn Cable Car and a short ride to the suburb of Kelburn for a sweeping view of the city below, and Victoria University. The central shopping area is compact, much better than Auckland's, and enjoyable to walk around.

Wellington is renowned for its excellent cafés and restaurants, and you are unlikely to have a poor dining experience. On a previous visit to Wellington, M. and I had a memorable fish dinner at one of the wharf restaurants, and there are good places in Courtenay Place and on Oriental Parade to try. Check out the old Embassy Theatre if you are in Courtenay Place; it was the venue for the Australasian premieres of *The Fellowship of the Ring* and *The Two Towers*, and the 2003 world premiere of *The Return of the King*.

Day Two is campervan day, visiting the extensive, sheltered Botanic Gardens in Kelburn, and the nearby Carter Observatory and Planetarium (ph. (04) 472 8167, email: astronomy@carterobs.ac.nz, www.carterobservatory.org), Te Papa Museum (where there is a charge for parking), then driving to the top of nearby Mt. Victoria to enjoy the splendid panorama of the harbour and Cook Strait, and, if you are a *Lord of the Rings* fan, to drive along Alexandra Road to the forested location of the Outer Shire in *The Fellowship of the Ring*. Ian Brodie's *The Lord of the Rings Location Guidebook,* gives explicit directions for getting to many of *The Lord of the Rings* sites in and around Wellington.

If you want information on Wellington, call in to the i-Site Visitor Centre (Ph. (04) 802 4860, www.wellingtonnz.com) on the corner of Victoria and Wakefield Streets adjacent to the Public Library, where a comprehensive array of services is offered.

Now for Te Papa Tongarewa, New Zealand's National Museum, known locally just as Te Papa, or Our Place, which opened to much controversy in 1998. If you expect to find glass cases full of conventional exhibits you will be disappointed, because it is designed to be an interactive museum, and many displays can be touched, and worked. The history, art and culture of New Zealand is presented informally in a contemporary atmosphere and will jolt any preconceived ideas of how a museum can best work to serve its community.

It was obvious when we arrived in the central atrium that a guided tour would be the best way to come to grips with the multi-level floors of exhibits above us. The Visitor Information Desk is on Level 2, and we booked there for a one-hour tour of the museum's highlights, which proved to be a very worthwhile orientation. The layout is bewildering, and you will need a copy of *Te Papa Explorer* to find your way around when the tour is over. M. and I separated after the tour and arranged to meet at a café on Level 4 in two hours' time. We agreed, there, over excellent quiche and coffee, that the exhibit which we really enjoyed was one entitled Passports, on Level 4, with the stories of migration to New Zealand, and photographs of pioneering days. A week later, when we drove down the West Coast of the South Island and crossed numerous bridges over rocky streams, I was reminded of the information and the descriptions of what it meant trying to settle in such inhospitable territory.

I wondered if we were too old for Te Papa. We've been brought up for nearly 70 years alongside Maori and Pacific Island cultures, we know all about sheep farming, Tiger Moth aeroplanes and vintage Holden cars (we used to drive one), household memorabilia, and we've done our fair share of native bush walks. The museum didn't offer us much information that was new. But for New Zealand school children, it's a *must*, and when our grandsons are old enough to enjoy and understand what they see, we will take them there. My comments should not put off overseas visitors from going. If you take the exhibits in a logical sequence you will learn a lot about this wonderful country, its traditions and its people, and enjoy the fresh and original way the information is relayed. I discussed our visit with a friend when we returned to Auckland at the end of the trip. He has been to Te Papa three times; his initial reaction was similar to ours, but he said each time he visits Wellington he goes back, likes it better, and now he is a *fan*.

Back at the camp in mid-afternoon – Te Papa had not tempted us for the whole day – I was lured by the wonderful facilities to catch up on our laundry, and we sank large gin and tonics while we debated dinner. I didn't want to cook, M. said he didn't want to see Jackson Street, Petone, ever again, so we took a taxi to Lower Hutt and asked the driver, from Kuala Lumpur, to drop us off at a nice restaurant. You won't be surprised to hear that he stopped outside a Malaysian restaurant near the bus station, which he said had very good food, and was cheap! Dinner at the Sungai Wang cost $62.60 with wine, was delicious and portioned largely, and we took home the remainder of the nasi goreng to have for breakfast the next morning.

CHAPTER 16

THE MARLBOROUGH WINE COUNTRY, AND NELSON

The nasi goreng, heated up in the microwave, made a tasty and substantial 5.30 a.m. breakfast before we departed from the camp to catch the ferry. I had booked our 25 February crossing of Cook Strait on the interisland catamaran the *Lynx* on the Internet (www.interislander.co.nz) six weeks in advance, and faced with a choice of departure times had chosen 8 a.m., arriving in Picton, the South Island port in Queen Charlotte Sound, at 10.16 a.m. We were required to check in at the *Lynx* terminal on Waterloo Quay at 7 a.m. at the latest. If you are approaching Wellington from the north, exit onto Aotea Quay and follow signs to the appropriate terminal.

In spite of the early hour the *Lynx* ferry was fully booked, and my heart sank when I saw the length of the queue ahead of us. However, we and the other campervans and motorhomes were quickly directed to our own lane, and we had the pleasure of being boarded last and told to make a U-turn inside the vehicle bay so that we would be first off. The website had warned that limited catering was available at the terminal prior to departure, but once in the cabin I found a full coffee bar service with light snacks, and cooked breakfasts available in small tinfoil containers which were quickly heated up. A shop sold magazines and the morning newspapers, and the trip passed quickly. Upon entering the narrow Tory Channel at the entrance to Queen Charlotte Sound, the cabin emptied rather quickly as everyone went out on deck to see and photograph the stunning scenery as the ferry slid through the calm emerald green water between steep, bush-clad hills.

The Marlborough Sounds were formed over millions of years when the area sank beneath the ocean, flooding valleys and creating the coves, islands and headlands that make up this unspoilt waterway. Captain James Cook landed in Queen Charlotte Sound at Ship Cove in early 1770, and hoisted the British Union Jack to claim the South Island for Britain. The Tory Channel and Queen Charlotte Sound got off to a rather shaky start in the late 1820s with the arrival of whalers, and their rough and lawless society, to work in the shore stations of the Marlborough whaling industry. In a few years they had transformed parts of the superb coastline into a stinking hell-hole. It was to this place that one John Guard, a schooner captain, had come in 1827 when his ship, blown off course in Cook Strait, had been picked up by raging seas and carried through the narrow opening of the Tory Channel to ultimate safety in the tranquil waters inside. He immediately saw the potential for shore whaling, returned to Sydney to sign on whalers, and came back to New Zealand with his young wife, Betty, the first white woman to land in the South Island and the only one for many years. It was a difficult life. Marauding parties of North Island Maori regularly visited the Sound to burn the whalers' huts and steal their stores, and the whalers were often forced to take to their own boats, which could outstrip the Maori canoes, to save their lives. The lack of stores meant whalers and the few settlers often had to subsist on whale meat and wild cabbage or turnip tops, and pounded fern root. Fortunately for the future of the Sound, within 10 years the whale numbers had declined due to the thoughtless extermination of both females and their calves, and so the whalers and their ships left for other places. With the whaling industry over, John Guard, ever the entrepreneur, bought Oyster Bay on the Marlborough coast from the local Maori chief, and large tracts of land from the Maori chiefs Te Rauparaha and Te Rangihaeata. For the latter purchase he paid 10 axes, 8 iron pots, a cask of tobacco worth £50, and 5 pieces of print, and became a trader, and a whaler again, at Kakapo Bay.

Picton is attractive, a little reminiscent of European lakeside towns with bright flower beds of roses and begonias and tall dark trees in the waterfront park, and white yachts berthed offshore. It started life as a thatched hut trading post for the Tory Channel settlers at the Te Awaiti whaling station, first home of the Guard family, who had to undertake a 27 kilometre row along the Sound in an open boat to buy supplies. The history of Picton is written in the street names – London Quay, Victoria, Leicester, Sussex, Suffolk, Canterbury, Oxford, Dorset and Scotland Streets, and Nelson Square. It is the sort of town where people don't need to look carefully both ways before stepping out onto the main road, and can leave their car windows down while they shop. We stocked up with provisions at a very good supermarket in the local shopping mall, refuelled at a garage opposite in High Street with 58.88 litres of diesel for $46.28, and took State Highway 1 and the hill road which leads out of town. If you want to see more of Queen Charlotte Sound, you should join a water taxi on one of its trips around the bays.

Our immediate destination was the coastal town of Blenheim, just to have a look at it, then to take the five kilometre drive back along the highway to Spring Creek and the turnoff to Rapaura Road where many of the famed Marlborough wineries are situated, before continuing on to Nelson and our camp for the night. If wine doesn't interest you, the drive west from Picton to Nelson along the 35 kilometre Queen Charlotte Scenic Drive is highly recommended; it offers very fine views of the Sound and is easily the shortest route. We were taking our detour of over 40 kilometres *more* than willingly; although the Marlborough wine industry is barely 20 years old, its fame as a first class New World wine region is already world-wide, and we had long rated it as a 'must see'.

A pleasant panorama of bush and pine-clad hillsides wearing every possible shade of green, set off by the contrasting gold of the tussocky roadside, unfolded as we drove to Blenheim, and the marshy Para Wetlands on the right managed by Nelson/Marlborough Fish and Game were a reminder that Picton was originally one large swamp. We crossed the wide, stony bed of the Wairau River and caught our first glimpse of some of the fabled Marlborough vineyards. We were immediately aware of the fact that, in Europe, growing grapes is an age-old *art*; here, in Marlborough, it is distinctly a *science*. As quickly as suitable land becomes available it is being turned into precisely planted vineyards, with nothing hit-or-miss about the planting, the technology, soil quality, climate and temperature, and market destinations.

The New Zealand Herald of 2 April 2005 reported that grape-growing land in Marlborough was selling for between $200,000 and $250,000 per hectare, and that Allied Domecq, the multinational wine company, had just paid $5.6 million for 28.2 hectares, and intended to concentrate on meeting the 'huge demand for sauvignon blanc in their international markets'.

Blenheim is a large regional town with the usual mix of light industry and building, car and boat companies on the outskirts. State Highway 1 runs through the centre of the town, and the air of busy prosperity is appealing. Like all New Zealand towns, within two minutes' drive of the centre you encounter true suburbia; what makes Blenheim attractive are the splendid front gardens which, being February, were full of roses in late summer bloom. Blenheim and northern Marlborough are sheltered by the Richmond Range to the west and the Kaikoura Ranges to the south, and the benign climatic conditions that help the grapes to grow also benefit Blenheim's pretty domestic gardens.

Having satisfied our curiosity about Blenheim, we retraced our route along State Highway 1 and turned left into Rapaura Road for three hours of pleasure visiting some of New Zealand's major wineries. I know of little sightseeing as relaxing as following a wine trail. Time slips by while you taste, debate what to buy, then move on to the next vineyard and repeat the process.

In 1997 when we last toured Europe by caravan, M. and I visited the Champagne and Alsace wine regions of France, and revisited the Mosel wine region of Germany. Except for a large glass of champagne given to visitors at the conclusion of a memorable tour around the vast and dripping wet cellars of Moet et

Chandon in Epernay, I did not sample a *single* glass of wine. I find it hard to believe I was such a good girl, but in a foreign country, navigating unfamiliar roads, I didn't dare risk a fuddled head. M., who was driving, stayed with a glass or two of beer for the same reason. In Germany I was moved to try a glass of non-alcoholic red wine with my lunch, and it was so ghastly that I quickly abandoned it. In Bernkastel-Kues, situated on the Mosel River, a serious wine shop in the main street had a fine array of gewurtztraminers, possibly my favourite wine, and I bought without tasting knowing that I was on safe ground. So I decided to be naughty in Marlborough, and do some sampling. The country was my own, I knew what to expect from the roads so navigation held no surprises, and M. could be relied upon to sip just a few wines.

Well, it's not possible to be naughty in Rapaura Road. The charming ladies at the vineyards knew how to make one bottle serve about 25 people and were adept at sorting out those who had come in hoping for a quick guzzle, and those who, like us, had come to buy. This 15 kilometre stretch of road boasts some of New Zealand's most famous wineries, including Hunter's, Cloudy Bay, Allan Scott, Lake Chalice, Villa Maria, Domaine Georges Michel, Clifford Bay, Matua and Nautilus, and other major wineries such as Whitehaven, Mount Riley, Wither Hills, Drylands, Montana and Jackson Estate can be found among the four dozen that produce wine in the flat land south of the Wairau River. Altogether the Marlborough Region has over 84 wineries, which supply approximately 60 per cent of national production. The grape-growing potential is locked into the superb soil, described as free-draining alluvial loams over gravelly subsoils. The climate offers more sunshine than any other region in New Zealand, followed by cool nights, with the benefit from that of a long growing season. The wines are fruity and intensely flavoured, and I now find it difficult to enjoy the blander Old World white wines. Perhaps that is why I favour buying gewurtztraminer when in Europe. Main varietals produced are sauvignon blanc, chardonnay, pinot noir and riesling, with pinot gris and gewurztraminer produced in smaller quantities. The area also grows grapes used in methode traditionelle sparkling wine.

The Marlborough Food and Wine Festival takes place every February. The one-day event is famous for the high quality of its food and wines, and if you are in the region the opportunity to attend should not be missed.

The Marlborough Visitor Information Centre (ph. (03) 577 8080, email: mvic@destinationmarlborough.com) will give you all the details you need.

To me, the art of enjoying a wine trail lies in wandering along it at leisure. I can't think of anything worse than going on an organised wine tour; but if you want to visit the Marlborough wineries and are not inclined to drive yourself, there are several companies offering a guided service. Tourists with a few weeks to spend in New Zealand are likely to make the Marlborough wineries an important destination, so I give guided tour options in the Appendix.

I have always had a soft spot for Hunter's wines. In the mid-1980s, the late Ernie Hunter, a true entrepreneur, raised money to start his fledgling vineyard by offering New Zealanders the opportunity to own their very own sauvignon blanc vine, with the promise of a free bottle from their vine every year. I bought a vine (I can't remember the price) and was issued a certificate of ownership of my numbered vine. My free bottle arrived a year later and I opened it immediately; sauvignon blanc was a new wine to New Zealand and I wondered what it was like. I didn't receive any more free bottles, but I ordered a case for the next few years and tried very hard to keep them cellared for a reasonable length of time! The winery, now run by Ernie's widow Jane who received an O.B.E. in 1993, and in 1997 an Honorary Doctorate of Science from Massey University for her outstanding services and contribution to the wine industry, has remained an independent, family-owned winery, building steadily on its reputation for quality.

We turned off Rapaura Road into the winery and parked the campervan in what must be the prettiest parking lot in New Zealand, where mature grape vines have been trained to form a shady arbour over the individual bays. A walk through a well-tended and interesting garden planted with the native trees, shrubs and grasses of the region, and past the studio of the artist in residence, Clarry Neame, brought us to the wine shop. A good array of two chardonnays, four sauvignon blancs, two gewurztraminers and a sparkling wine were ready for tasting, and we bought a mixed case of gewurztraminers from the 2002 and 2004 vintages, and then turned our attention to the sparkler. Hunter's Vintage Brut is a delicious, well-flavoured sparkling wine held back from sale until it is ready to drink, and I always keep a few bottles on hand for celebratory emergencies. I prefer it to other similar New Zealand wines. The beautiful blonde behind the counter mentioned that their 2001 vintage premium sparkling wine, *Miru Miru*, a Maori word which translates as 'bubbles', was now being sold, and perhaps we would like to consider it. I tried a small glass, loved it, and we ordered a case of that, too. M. flashed the Amex, and for the moderate charge of $7.95 per case the wine was couriered the next day to our business address in Auckland. This winery has an excellent restaurant with an award-winning executive chef, and uses the best of Marlborough's produce to complement the company's outstanding wines. It offers fireside dining in winter, and alfresco and verandah dining in the acclaimed garden surrounds in summer.

Our lunch was alfresco too, but in the acclaimed Maui campervan parked alongside the grape vines! I'd bought some soft bread rolls, ham and tomatoes, and a good cheese at the Picton supermarket, and we washed it all down with a nice cup of tea-bag tea before tackling the next vineyard.

M. has always liked Cloudy Bay wines, so we drove a few kilometres further on and turned left along Jackson's Road. The Cloudy Bay winery was very busy, but the wait to be served gave us time to look through albums with early photographs of the area, and view the line-up of pale oak wine barrels visible through a wide window. I liked the 2002 chardonnay so we bought a case of that, and two cases of the 2004 sauvignon blanc, and arranged for them all to be couriered to Auckland.

Time was getting on and we decided to cut short our tour of the wineries and continue to Nelson. I reminded M. that in two hours we had splurged $1,600 on *wine*, and he replied that it was a very pleasant way to part with one's cash! And he's right; I defy anyone to say they've had a bad experience, or met a nasty person, in a winery or a wine shop. There must be something about the product that brings out the best in people.

Ahead of us were the distinctive lilac and blue coloured hills of the Richmond Range depicted on the famous Cloudy Bay bottle labels. I felt quite woozy; although I sampled just six wines (and I've already mentioned how judiciously the measures are poured) I felt as though I'd drunk half a bottle. Must have been the hot sun. We took State Highway 6 to Nelson via Havelock, a distance of just under 100 kilometres, where we would stop for the night.

The road followed the Kaituna River on its way across the flat valley floor, the steep hills of Mt. Richmond Forest Park rising on either side to the upper reaches of Pelorus Sound, the largest of the sounds, and the fishing settlement of Havelock. The road was excellent, and M. called it a super drive. There are some good views of the sounds as you near Havelock, but if you wish to see them from the water then you should stay in Havelock and take the mail boat which delivers mail and supplies to the outlying settlements three days a week, on Tuesday, Thursday and Friday. The Havelock Motor Camp, 24 Inglis Street, Havelock (ph. (09) 574 2339) which is situated right by the port, will arrange mail boat bookings for you. I have been informed by the camp owner that the best trip to take is the one on Friday, a full day tour which takes you out to the Heads. The cost is $95 per person, and, being in a sound, you will never get rough seas.

Havelock is unspoilt, with plenty of old buildings to look at, calls itself the 'Greenshell Mussel Capital of the World', and the well-known Mussel Boys restaurant was packed with late lunchers as we drove past. There was a salty, briny smell to the air as we skirted the head of the sound on the way out – just like freshly-caught mussels!

If you miss out on lunch at the Mussel Boys restaurant, you will find plenty of places to stop at in Rai Valley 27 kilometres further on, for the main street is lined with taverns and cafés, and three campervans which had been travelling behind us since Rapaura Road pulled in for refreshments. The little town, which is sheltered by the encroaching hills of the Rai Forest, gets as hot as hell in summer. The road here winds steeply upwards, and a road sign promises that 'curve alignment' is to be carried out. It's slow driving in a campervan. There is a worthwhile lookout point well before the descent to Hira, with panoramic views down forested slopes, and at Wakapuaka you will find a splendid view across Tasman Bay to Nelson Port, Motueka and the Abel Tasman National Park peninsula. At Hira, a turnoff leads to the aptly-named Cable Bay from where, in 1876, the first telegraphic cables were laid to Australia.

We were pleased to be in Nelson at last; from Hutt Park very early that morning, we had driven 176 kilometres, and enjoyed a varied and extremely interesting day. Although Nelson is only a 20 minute flight from Wellington, in a campervan it takes about two and a half hours to drive there from Picton, and the time taken to cross Cook Strait has to be taken into consideration as well. If you are arriving from Wellington, as we did, it is best to allow one full day for the journey especially if you detour to the Marlborough wineries. There is plenty to see, and whether you take the Queen Charlotte Sound Scenic Route, or Rapaura Road, you will not be bored.

Trafalgar Street, the main street of Nelson, is adorned beautifully with hanging baskets resembling huge multi-coloured puffballs, so profusely do the impatiens, begonias and petunias grow. The secret lies in the automatic watering system, which links each basket and waters the plants morning and night. There is an air of new prosperity, fuelled by the recent housing boom which has seen prices skyrocket in this desirable corner of New Zealand. We booked in at the centrally-situated Nelson City Holiday Park (details in Appendix) at 4 p.m., and it proved to be a good base from which to take taxis to explore the city. The small camp was run by nice, obliging people, the facilities were OK, and by the time we departed for dinner the camp was full of touring vehicles. We, and one other couple, seemed to be the only New Zealanders.

Once we've taken up a camp site for the night, M. is always very loathe to drive out again, and I don't think he did it more than twice on the trip; so taxis are always a priority for us, and Nelson city, being small, offers very cheap rides. I was anxious to get to Jens Hansen Gold and Silversmith on Trafalgar Square, to see the One Ring he made for *The Lord of the Rings*. The shop was very busy, even in the late afternoon, and a young lady with a huge, formidable-looking camera on a tripod was photographing the display of rings. Jens Hansen made 40 rings for the trilogy, in different sizes to suit different scenes. One was a small *hoop* nearly 16 centimetres in diameter, which when tossed into the air looked perfectly in proportion to its surroundings. The rings were priced at $1,195 for one in 18 ct. gold, $895 for one in 14 ct. gold, and $695 for one in 9 ct. gold. They are handsome, would make smart wedding rings, and are deservedly popular with *The Lord of the Rings* fans.

We strolled down Trafalgar Street, enjoying the warm weather and the lack of wind after Wellington, and had the usual beer and wine at a pleasant outdoor table on the footpath before hailing a taxi to take us to Olivia's Restaurant on the Quay; it had been recommended by the lady in the camp office who had obligingly made a table reservation for us, it being a Friday night and bound to be busy, she said. The setting was nice, as waterfronts usually are, the restaurant was full, the portions were huge, and the service abysmally slow. I ordered a Greek salad topped with tomato fritters to start with, and had to leave half, and M. ordered gazpacho with prawns, and some bread. I chose the seafood platter for my main course and M. had seared scallops and bacon on salad. He pushed it around his plate, said it wasn't very nice, and became restless with the slow service. The cost plus wine was $105.50, and he didn't tip, which is rare.

When I grew up in Wellington in the 1940s and 1950s, the favourite holiday destinations within New Zealand were Taupo, Rotorua, Nelson and Queenstown. (I always holidayed in Christchurch where all my relatives lived). Listening to girlfriends and work colleagues talk about their holidays, I felt I knew those places before I ever got there. Nelson was especially favoured for its comparative closeness to Wellington, its reliable weather, its beaches and beautiful scenery. Nelson has moved on from that early beach image, and now the city is renowned for its craft galleries, its food and wine, and its culture.

The prosperity of Nelson today gives no hint of the difficulties faced in establishing it as a planned settlement. The first wave of British immigrants, largely married men who wished to carve out a decent living before sending for their wives and children, arrived in 1842 having paid in advance for smallholdings of land in the new town, and larger parcels of farmland in the countryside. Unfortunately, much of the land proved quite unsuitable for agriculture. Nelson had no sustainable industries like whaling or fishing, and although there was timber on the steep surrounding hills which could be exported, it was quickly realised that felling would cause erosion and damage any suitable farmland that did exist. At the same time, the New Zealand Company, under whose aegis the settlement had been founded, continued to send over from Britain large numbers of labourers to help establish the infrastructure of the fledgling colony, the hope being that in due course these men would earn enough to be able to afford to buy land, too.

More, and better, land was urgently needed, and a party of surveyors and influential leaders of the colony set out for the nearby Wairau Valley. They acted without wisdom or discretion, and tried to commandeer land instead of negotiating payment to local Maori as the astute John Guard had done. The would-be settlers met strong resistance from Maori, and in June 1843 the bloody Wairau Massacre occurred in which nearly all the Europeans were killed, or else badly wounded.

In 1844, to compound the land troubles in Nelson, the New Zealand Company in London became financially stretched and was unable to keep its programme of public works going. The loss of the labourers' wages, plus the fact that local farmers could barely afford to employ them, plus the non-arrival of supply ships largely owned by the New Zealand Company, brought the settlement to the point of starvation. Native leaves and roots that could be cooked were eagerly sought, and grass was boiled, although this proved to be tough and inedible. Potatoes were dug up and eaten, the eye being carefully removed for replanting, and the settlers, whose physical stamina was crucial in breaking in land and building the colony, suffered from greatly reduced strength. Relief came in 1847 when the New Zealand Company was granted financial assistance by the Colonial Office, Maori reached agreement with the Crown over the sale and disposal of their land, and the Nelson pioneers were granted the right to surrender their unproductive landholdings and take up fertile rural land in the Wairau Valley.

Nelson's popularity is well-deserved. Not only does the region have a pleasant climate and a marvellous recreational coastline, but it also attracts talented people whose interests are reflected in the Montana World of Wearable Art Awards, the October Nelson Arts Festival, and the Festival of Chamber Music held in January/February.

The Wearable Art Awards, as they were originally known, began in 1987 as a promotion for a rural art gallery in Nelson, and have increased in importance as a showcase for the creativity of New Zealand designers, and in size, each year. The Awards shows have outgrown their Nelson beginnings and in 2005, as the Montana World of Wearable Art Awards, were held in Wellington for the first time, running over two weekends in late September. Thirty thousand people can be accommodated in the Wellington Events Centre for the eight performances and the shows were sold out well in advance. Among the beautiful and sometimes bizarre creations were a garment made of 140 black umbrellas, and a gorgeous, frothy wedding dress of recycled white plastic milk bottles. Designs are submitted not only from New Zealand, but also from all over the world, and about 200 garments are selected to be shown. The event, which has assumed iconic status in New Zealand, has become an artistic extravaganza that attracts international fashion and media attention, and in 1999 it won the Supreme New Zealand Tourist Award.

Fortunately there is now a location in Nelson where many creations can be viewed. The wearable art has been cleverly combined with a classic car museum to provide an entertaining experience for everyone, whether you are a car buff or a lover of art. The World of Wearable Art and Collectible Cars Museum, or WOW, is situated at 95 Quarantine Road, off State Highway 6, at Annesbrook, Nelson (ph. (03) 547 4573, www.wowcars.co.nz).

The Nelson Annual Arts Festival held in October brings theatre, music, dance, jazz, cabaret, a readers' and writers' symposium, and a dozen art exhibitions to the city, and is opened with the Port Nelson masked parade featuring music and street performers, circus acts, and food stalls.

The New Zealand Festival of Chamber Music held in January/February is renowned for performances by the very finest New Zealand musicians, and the concerts are held in the Nelson School of Music or in the Nelson Cathedral. Should you wish to attend any of these major events, the relevant website for further information on dates, venues, programmes and ticket prices, etc., is www.nelsoncity.com, or you can telephone the Nelson Visitor Information Centre, ph. (03) 548 2304.

I wish that we had allowed ourselves more time in Nelson. We had been on the road for two weeks and this was the first place I felt I would like to revisit and tour in depth. The coast of Nelson is an outdoor paradise, and the drive up to Farewell Spit, one that friends had recommended highly, is still waiting for us to do.

State Highway 6 from the city goes to Richmond, named after Richmond, London, and a turn right onto State Highway 60 and the Appleby Highway to Mapua will take you across the Waimea Plains and past some excellent wineries and craft galleries. If you only have time to visit one winery, make it the Seifried Estate, the region's biggest. I consider their gewurtztraminer is the best in New Zealand, and have been drinking it since 1980; I have a bottle of the 2004 vintage in my fridge as I write this, and will be enjoying it tonight. There are about 20 boutique wineries producing excellent wines in the close vicinity, in particular the Neudorf Winery at Upper Moutere, which produces a noted chardonnay. Most of them lie within a 30 minute drive from the city, some south of Richmond and some to the west along the Moutere Highway. Local wines under production include pinot noir, chardonnay, sauvignon blanc, riesling and pinot gris, and the best of them are expensive. You can expect to pay nearly $50 for a top Neudorf chardonnay and pinot noir at a wine merchant, so a visit to their winery is very worthwhile. Although wine production is big business in Nelson, you will not see the relentless kilometres of cultivation which characterise the Marlborough Region. More information on the wineries can be obtained from the website www.nelsonwines.co.nz., which also gives excellent information on the dozens of art and craft studios for which Nelson is famous. The region is an art and craft lover's dream, with ceramics and pottery, jewellery, glass blowing, wrought iron work, wooden sculpture, candlemaking, fibre art, homespun knitwear, and contemporary art all on show. It is no accident that the famous Wearable Art Awards originated in Nelson!

One of M.'s business colleagues, an outdoor enthusiast, considers that the Tasman Bay coastline north of Motueka has the finest sea-kayaking in New Zealand; indeed Kaiteriteri (pron. kye-terry-terry) was voted one of the top five beaches in the world (U.K. *Guardian* 2003). There are several companies offering kayaking facilities, and you can book guided tours ranging from half a day to two or three days. Accommodation for the longer tours is at local beach or bush campsites or huts, all equipment is provided, and a picnic lunch is available on the one-day trips. The two and three-day tours are fully catered. If you don't want an organised tour, day hire, called 'Freedom Rentals', is available. You can visit seal colonies, caves, lagoons, islands and beaches, the Tonga Island marine reserve, and take short walks in the Abel Tasman National Park. Full contact numbers and websites of three kayaking companies are given in the Appendix. If you plan to travel to Kaiteriteri direct from the Picton ferry, note that the driving time is at least three hours.

The Abel Tasman National Park comprises 15,000 hectares of Crown land, and was formed after conservation concerns were raised at the prospect of logging activities ruining the beautiful coastline. The 51 kilometre walk along the Coast Track is regarded as one of New Zealand's great walks; all streams are bridged, it can be walked in three to five days, and is reputed to be the easiest long walk in the country. The Department of Conservation provides four huts, 21 campsites, and a campground as accommodation along the way. The huts have heating, bunks, toilets, mattresses and a water supply, but visitors have to provide their own portable stoves, candles and a torch. The Coast Track is accessible at Marahau, the southernmost entry, 67 kilometres from Nelson, or at Wainui, Totaranui, or Awaroa. Car parks are located at these four points of access. During the peak summer season, hut, campsite and campground passes must be purchased. Contact details are given in the Apppendix. Passes can also be obtained from some information centres, outdoor stores, campgrounds, and transport and kayak operators in the region.

Those who wish to undertake a longer walk should try the 82 kilometre Heaphy Track which takes four to six days. Entrance to the eastern end of the track is reached up the Aorere Valley from Collingwood in Golden Bay, and exit is 15 kilometres north of Karamea on the West Coast at the Kohaihai River. The track is well-formed, and accommodation is available along the way in seven huts, or at seven designated campsites. As with the Abel Tasman Coast Track, a pass, which is available from the same sources, must be purchased before entering the track. It is worth mentioning that the Kahurangi National Park, which the walk traverses through to the West Coast, is a botanist's delight, for it is home to more than half of New Zealand's native plant species, including 80 per cent of all alpine species.

The distance from the turnoff at Richmond onto State Highway 60 to Collingwood, the old gold mining town in Golden Bay, is 117 kilometres, and if you get as far as that it would be a pity not to drive 22 kilometres further on the coastal main road to Cape Farewell. The cape, named by Captain James Cook as he left New Zealand in 1770, is the northernmost tip of the South Island. The cliffs, like those at Cape Reinga at the top of the North Island, are buffeted by strong winds and the waves of the Tasman Sea, but if you are a photographer there at the end of the day, stay on, for the area is renowned for its beautiful sunsets. The adjacent Farewell Spit, which extends out to the east, is very tidal, with mud flats and swamps, but is worth visiting if you are a bird lover, or would like to see the lighthouse. It will be best to enquire in Collingwood as to the feasibility of taking a vehicle out to the sanctuary, as conditions alter according to the time of year.

In a country which has a lamentable tendency to pull down anything old and interesting, I find it heart-warming that so many lighthouses are still standing. They serve to remind that seafaring, and the establishment of New Zealand's vital sea trade, was a dangerous occupation in the nineteenth century, and although modern technology, in particular the advent of global positioning systems, has made them redundant, the lighthouses still offer visual safety on the headlands they occupy. Today they have an aura of romance, and are an example of an ancient technology which has refused to die.

You may develop an overwhelming thirst for a good beer as you head back along State Highway 60. The Mussel Inn Pub at Onekaka is the place to stop to sample the range of boutique beers sold exclusively there, in particular the Captain Cook Manuka Beer. If you wish to camp overnight in Golden Bay before returning to Nelson, the beachfront Pohara Beach Top 10 Holiday Park is situated in Takaka. A restaurant and bar are directly across the road. Details are given in the Appendix.

Another reason to stay in Takaka overnight is that, if you are following *The Lord of the Rings* filming locations as you travel through New Zealand, Takaka Hill is the site of Chetwood Forest. Ian Brodie in *The Lord of the Rings Location Guidebook* recommends heading for the summit of Takaka Hill, turning along Canaan Road on the right just past the Ngarua Caves, and crossing the cattle stop eight kilometres from the main road. You will be in the place where the Hobbits were led into the wilds after leaving Bree, and it is also the location of a scene showing the Hobbits leaving the Shire.

Mt. Olympus in the Kahurangi National Park is the site where the Fellowship hide from Saruman's crebain, and at the southern end of the park, near Murchison, is Mt. Owen and the bleak landscape that was the site of Dimrill Dale. These last two sites are best visited by helicopter, and Ian Brodie pays tribute to Nelson Helicopters, situated at the Nelson Airport at Stoke, for the logistical support the company provided while filming was undertaken in the region. Nelson Helicopters (ph. (03) 547 1177) have one, two or three-site flight options, and prices for two passengers are $1,160 for the flight to Mt. Olympus where there is a suitable site there for the helicopter to land; or $770 for the closer flight to Mt. Owen, where the helicopter remains airborne. If you wish to fly to all three sites, the price is $1,450 for the round trip, which takes two hours. The flight to Mt. Olympus (site two) and Mt. Owen (site three) takes one and a half hours. It was mentioned by the company that it is possible to drive up to Takaka Hill, site one; but if you wish to see all three sites then the round trip is the cheapest option. Flights are dependent on the weather, and it is best to book close to the day of travel.

CHAPTER 17

ARRIVAL ON THE WEST COAST

We left the Nelson camp at 10 a.m., a late start, to drive to Westport on State Highway 6 via the Buller Gorge. The day was overcast, warm and still, with the promise of a clear sky later on – perfect travelling weather.

We skirted the upper reaches of the harbour at Richmond, a dull, industrial township which is growing very quickly judging by the amount of new housing. Richmond specialises in engineering firms, building supplies, car, truck and farm machinery outlets, and all manner of small trades and light industry, and M. remarked as we drove through that Nelson stays pretty, and puts the plainness a few kilometres away. I was all for calling in to the Seifried Winery just a few minutes' drive to the right along State Highway 60, but we were running late for the long day's drive ahead of us so I had to abandon the idea. If travelling teaches you just one thing, it is that sometimes you have to roll with the punches. Nelson is there to revisit.

Richmond was soon behind us and we entered the countryside, passing vineyards, nectarine, peach, apple and pear and kiwifruit orchards, glasshouses, and landscape suppliers. We could have stopped at several studios to buy pottery and paintings, even decorative wrought iron work. The atmosphere was one of a very settled community doing what it liked best, a sentiment that was upheld when we came to Brightwater and drove along the main street trying to find the birthplace of scientist Lord Rutherford, the first person to split the atom. The little town is much as it was 100 years ago, the wooden cottages, many of excellent, distinctive colonial design, still occupied. After 10 minutes we gave up and asked directions at the Four Square store. I was astonished at the cheapness of the apples, peaches and apricots for sale there, less than half the price I had paid in Auckland. We were directed to Lord Rutherford Road North, and found a substantial and intelligent monument at the end, right on the corner with the main highway. The memorial is built on the site of the cottage Lord Rutherford was born in, in 1871. He was destined to do well; his mother taught at the local school, mathematics being her specialty! The memorial is circular, to resemble the shape of an atom, with concentric pathways lined with interactive, educational displays about his life and his contribution to science. In the centre is a bronze sculpture of the young schoolboy Rutherford holding a book clearly entitled *Arithmetic Primer*, with rosemary for remembrance planted at his feet. We found it a satisfying and worthwhile memorial to visit.

The self-styled 'Village of Wakefield' further on warned motorists that its garage was the last fuel stop for 100 kilometres. I consulted my map – the next refuelling place is Murchison. I had the most wonderful feeling that the forthcoming two weeks in the South Island would prove to be the better half of our holiday. Already, just 25 kilometres out of Nelson, we were plunged into the sort of blast-from-the-past territory it is difficult to find in the more populous North Island, and which is long-gone in Auckland. Wakefield had a short main street of old colonial buildings, all perfectly in tune with each other, and the smallholdings on the flat land held horses, a few sheep, deer, some dairy cows, small orchards, even a tree nursery. We passed a sign that M. liked, 'Antiques, Sunday Only', outside an ancient, white-painted house. 'Bad luck it's only Saturday,' he smirked, as we sped past. Antique shops bore him *rigid*.

The valley, hemmed in by tall ranges, was utterly scenic. We had the road to ourselves. The fire danger was high, here, as we started to climb to Spooners Saddle and Kohatu Junction to cross the Motueka River which exits in the town of the same name in Tasman Bay. The road south from Motueka to Kohatu is the old Highway 61, 58 kilometres long, and the most direct route to the West Coast from the Abel Tasman National Park.

The descent from the Saddle was quite steep and a sign warned trucks to engage low gear. As we rolled round an awkward bend the fridge door burst open (I must have forgotten to engage the locking pin before we left Nelson) and wine, orange juice and tonic water bottles, and the jam, mayonnaise and Vegemite jars rolled out across the floor, banging together and making a terrible din. There was no place to pull in and stop, so I had the perilous task of moving back to re-stow. It is surprisingly difficult to stay upright in a moving campervan when the road is steep and winding, and I lurched badly from side to side.

The drive was exhilarating, M. utterly captivated with the views. The area was veined on the map with networks of rivers, yet the valley itself was dry, with good, flat grazing for sheep. We came to the very steep ascent of the Hope Saddle and met trucks crawling down towards us, in low gear, an introduction to the driving conditions we would encounter for much of the way in the South Island. I was the lucky passenger on this part of the journey, for while M. concentrated on the driving I was able to look to the left and enjoy the splendid view of the Nelson Lake Rotoroa, and Lake Rotoiti from where the famous Buller River runs down to finish at Westport. The Nelson Lakes National Park is a splendid recreational area. Both lakes offer good boating and trout fishing, deer can be hunted in the surrounding mountains, and Mount Roberts at Lake Rotoiti offers skiing in winter. Fortunately for future travellers, this stretch of road is being upgraded and widened. We descended slowly to Howard Junction, the gorge road following the Buller River between high hills.

We fancied stopping for a cup of tea, and pulled in to an area alongside the river set up nicely with picnic tables, but were driven off by hordes of wasps and had to move on. The Buller River was flat, calm and stony, giving no hint of what I remembered it being in the 1970s when we last drove through the gorge.

We stopped in Murchison, the biggest town on State Highway 6 to Westport, and found the excellent Beechwoods Café, with both indoor seating and a large outdoor verandah. This is the place to stop; there is a tourist shop and the parking lot is huge. I feel slightly ashamed of the food we ordered and ate, every last crumb – two supersize sausage rolls, two large Cornish pasties, one egg and tomato quiche, a large carton of plump hot chips, and one chocomint slice which, together with coffee and an Amstel Light, came to just $23.60! We stayed an hour and read the paper before departing, replete and rested. This was the usual pattern of lunching at our roadside stops, eating the sort of food we never, ever have at home, and which we relished. I threw dietary caution to the winds for four weeks and felt the better for it, and when I got on the scales at the end of the trip I was two kilos lighter than when we set out. The wayside food was always of a high standard (except in Te Kuiti), and very fresh, and I never felt the need to lift the pastry lid on top of a pie to explore the contents before eating.

Murchison has plenty of bed and breakfast accommodation and homestays, and is the headquarters of the New Zealand Kayak School which operates from a house on the main road. There is plenty of fun to be had on the Buller River. White Water Action Rafting Tours situated on the main road behind the Information Centre, (freephone 0800 100 582, www.whitewateraction.co.nz) runs whitewater rafting in Grade 3 and 4 rapids on the river, and has a more family-friendly Grade 2 tour as well. The company also runs a 40 kilometre round trip to the Lower Buller Gorge by jet boat.

The Buller Experience Jet Company, situated in Waller Street (freephone 0800 802 023, www.murchison.co.nz) offers jet boating on the river, and trips depart hourly, every day, weather permitting. If you want to explore the Murchison area in greater depth, but are disinclined to drive yourself, Murchison Day Tours (freephone 0800 888 003) operates tour buses daily through the spectacular surrounding countryside, and the full day tour includes a boat ride on Lake Rotoroa. Half day tours are available by arrangement, and bookings are essential.

There are two campgrounds in Murchison. The Riverview Motor Camp in Chalgrave Street (phone (03) 523 9315) has 30 powered sites, a dump point, and is close to the river. Power sites are $14 for two. Kiwi Park at 170 Fairfax Street (phone (03) 523 9248) has a bush setting, power sites, hard stands for campervans, and a swimming pool. Power sites are $20 for two.

The West Coast was not originally considered an attractive place to settle because of its inaccessibility from the east, its high rainfall, and a very hazardous, rough coastline. One explorer, Thomas Brunner, who had followed the Buller River as far as Murchison before turning back, and who had already, with the noted artist and draughtsman Charles Heaphy, walked in 1846 from Cape Farewell down the coast to the mouth of the Buller River, was determined to explore the territory existing between the mouth of the river and its source to prove that the West Coast could be reached along it. He set out again in 1847. He and his party of Maori guides survived dreadful conditions to forge a way across the rocks, precipices and ravines confronting them, before arriving in Westport six months later. On the way, to combat starvation, they were forced to eat fern root and the roots of cabbage trees, birds, eels and river fish, even rats, and Brunner's dog Rover.

Undaunted, Brunner then set off to explore the coast southwards, thought Okarito one of the most beautiful places he had ever seen, but turned back shortly afterwards, considering the land wild and unsuitable for settlement and cultivation. From Greymouth his expedition travelled along the Grey River, where he discovered a coal seam of very fine quality, to Lake Brunner, and on to the present site of Reefton. He returned back along the Buller River, ill in health and suffering bitterly cold weather, finally reaching Nelson 18 months after setting out from there. It is the epic journey of exploration in New Zealand; I have given you just the bare bones of his travels, and he discovered much more than it is the purpose of this book to cover, but when you look at your road atlas and see the distances and the places covered in such a short time, tamed distances through which you are whizzing in your motorhome in just a few hours, you will realise the extent of his feat.

Later, the geologist and explorer Sir Julius von Haast mapped the extent and quality of coal in the Brunner coalfields and foresaw the future of Greymouth as a busy mining town. Brunner's discovery of the coal seam established the coal industry on the West Coast, and in 1870 the Brunner mine, as it was known, became the first State-owned coalmine in the country. The commercial future of the West Coast was assured for decades, many mines were opened, and The Westport Coal Company became the biggest employer of men in New Zealand.

The Buller River, so difficult for Brunner and his party to follow in 1847, was our side-by-side companion all the way to Westport, 98 kilometres distant. We crossed O'Sullivan's Bridge and entered the Buller Gorge Scenic Reserve, steep, bush clad slopes rising above the road, and saw that the river had assumed a deep, dark green colour. We were looking for New Zealand's longest swing bridge, 110 metres long, and suspended 17 metres high above the river, having been told by a friend that it was a 'must do' experience to cross it. It's a very popular attraction; 50 thousand visitors cross the bridge each year, and we pulled in to the last space in the car park. A word of advice. Before you leave your van, apply insect repellent thoroughly or the wasps, midges and flies will dine off you. The problem is acute; the booking office sells repellent and has flyscreens for doors. The cost for the two of us to cross the bridge and take a short walk around the bush tracks on the other side was $10. You can take the 15-minute Loop Walk as we did, or visit the Ariki Falls, or take the Bushline Walk, or a Forest Walk, and you can return across the river gorge to the car park via the 160 metre flying fox. Details of this popular tourist attraction, which advertises itself in its brochure as being two hours from Nelson, and one hour from Westport, are given in the Appendix.

How did I cope with the swingbridge? Not very well. My Sebago moccasins had the wrong type of sole and I slithered on the chicken wire which covers the planks, so I returned to the campervan and put on my trainers which were the correct footwear for the conditions. The bridge is very narrow. Lots of opposing walkers coming towards you make it wobble badly as their rhythm is not yours, and it is a mistake to get on it if there are lunatic adolescents keen on running and jumping up and down to make it sway and give everyone else a fright. However, I'm still alive, and M. took a reprehensible photograph of me clutching hold of the sides as I walked, so I could prove I'd done it.

The drive continued, this part of the road being full of one-way bridges. There is nothing more annoying than to follow the black arrow announcing right of way over such a bridge, only to find the driver of an opposing vehicle has ignored the red arrow painted on the bridge sign warning him/her to give way. New Zealand is full of old one-way bridges, which might have been a manageable situation 50 or more years ago, but is now an anachronism in this age of mass travel and tourism. We cannot recall crossing a one-way bridge on a main highway in any other country we have driven in. However, I really shouldn't complain. The South Island is networked with swift and turbulent rivers, early barriers to communication and difficult to ford, which before the construction of bridges claimed many lives, so many, in fact, that drowning became known as the New Zealand death.

We reached Inangahua Junction, semi-derelict since its frightful 1967 earthquake. The spectacular White Cliffs on either side of the road are an unusual sight in this region of thick bush and forest. Further down the river, at Berlins, you can book for jet ski tours at the café. 'Blast the Buller River', says the sign as you enter the one horse town. As we entered the Lower Buller Gorge Scenic Reserve, M. said he would recommend this drive along State Highway 6 to everybody, because you get an idea of what New Zealand used to be like, with the sharp-topped, heavily forested hills, and the dark green river with its stony banks swirling below. There is no room for anything else other than the most profound admiration for the men who cut this road, and the others linking the West Coast with the rest of the South Island, through every obstacle, enduring all hardships.

Actually, *I* felt a little let down. My memories of the drive 30 years earlier were those of a thrilling encounter with the forces of nature, where human beings had not quite succeeded in taming the lie of the land. This time, I thought the road had been improved to the point where it was now sanitised from all possible danger, where you never felt you were *on the brink*, and I also mourned the fact that the river seemed to have lost some of its surge and might. Indeed, the only part of the road that is the littlest bit scary is at Fern Arch, where the surface, carved out of the cliff face, narrows to one lane and passes underneath an overhanging rock projection. It was a surprise to leave the somewhat gloomy confines of the gorge and have, at last, a wide sky horizon which promised a fine late afternoon.

Six thousand people live in the coalmining town of Westport and on the coast to its north. The town borders the Buller River, and the streets are laid out in a regimented grid pattern ideally suited to the flat land the town occupies. We drove down the extremely wide and very empty main street, and I saw thankfully, thinking ahead to dinner, that a tavern with a blackboard menu propped outside was open. We seemed to be the only people around and M., scrupulous about stopping at intersections before proceeding on, found he was stopping for nobody. It was hard to believe that this deserted town, obviously designed for a grander life, was once an important sea port. The harbour was carefully planned by Sir John Goode, an English civil engineer who was also responsible for the Greymouth and Timaru ports. The excellent facilities at Westport were instrumental in its popularity as a coal-refuelling stop for the old ships. Coal mining was the lifeblood of Westport and its environs 100 years ago, and its demise as a town dates from the introduction of diesel and oil as alternative forms of energy. Coal has recently become an export commodity, and at present is taken by rail across the South Island to the Port of Lyttelton for shipping overseas, although this arrangement will change somewhat with the proposed redevelopment of the Greymouth port which will enable the direct shipment of coal from there to Japan.

I had selected a local town camp, the Westport Holiday Park at 31-37 Domett Street, to stay in overnight. It read very well in *The New Zealand Camping Guide, South Island* handbook, and we chatted for a while to the pleasant woman in the office as we booked in, paying $21 for the night. Well, we couldn't find anywhere to park, not because the camp was full – it was half-empty – but because it was host to a collection of converted buses and trucks with TV aerials on top, and apparent long-term residents who had their washing strung up on lines between vehicles and awnings even though the camp had automatic laundry facilities. 'Down and out' is the politest description I can give. There were some very weird people hanging around, and we were the cynosure of curious eyes, openly breaking the rule that if there is one thing you do not do in a camping ground, it is to stare openly at anyone even if the temptation is very great. The standard of maintenance of the grounds was low. M. inspected the ablutions, and said that although large they were the worst he had seen so far. The few campervans and motorhomes had miserable-looking people sitting outside at picnic tables, many with a large bottle of gin or rum to the fore, and after circling around the camp twice we drove right out, giving the owner a cheery wave and not bothering to ask for a refund. Whew! That was Westport!

Fortunately, there was a Top 10 camp nearby, the Seal Colony Top 10 Tourist Park at Carters Beach just four kilometres away. The reason we didn't go there first was that the *Camping Guide* had described the Westport Holiday Park as '…a sheltered camp where pockets of bush form natural barriers between grouped sites, with an away-from-it-all environment, you will find wekas in residence… A pleasant leafy retreat, brimful of birdlife.' That is all true; it wasn't the bird life that was the problem, but the local life. I had felt like spending the night at somewhere more *au naturel* than the previous camps at Nelson, Lower Hutt and Taupo, and (shudders) Pauanui.

What a difference at Seal Colony! Seven gleaming white Maui motorhomes were lined up for the night on the large, flat lawn, and were the most comforting sight in the world after the motley collection of vehicles we had parted company with 10 minutes' previously. The camp owner charged us $23.40 including discount, and he was a mine of information about the Top 10 Parks. Apparently, you cannot apply to join; 'inspectors' regularly review all the camping grounds in New Zealand, and if they consider that what is provided fits their camp profile of the best possible locations, standards, and amenities, you are invited to join the Top 10 Holiday Park Group. The grading system runs from one to five, and to qualify for a Top 10 you must be graded four or five. From the experiences we had in 30 days of touring New Zealand, if you want a good camping holiday you either stay in a Top 10 Holiday Park, or you find an idyllic and safe place to free camp beside a lake or beach. I'm sure that many readers will disagree with that remark, but I can only write about our own experiences, and that's the way it *was*. Although we ourselves didn't free camp, we passed many open places in the South Island where it would have been heavenly to have stopped for one or two days to dangle a fishing line in the water 50 metres away.

We had passed the local watering hole, Donaldo's Beached Bar and Café, as we drove along the sole access road to the camp, and we had a pleasant early evening stroll back to it when we had settled in. The café was dinkum Kiwi, one of those gems you find in out-of-the-way places, the meeting place for the locals who sat drinking and yarning on stools outside and eventually drifted off to their own homes for dinner. Tinsel decorations were still on the walls inside and on the Christmas tree in a corner, and might have been there for several years. We sat at a huge table and ordered fried scallops with salad, $13 each, and the roast pork dinner, $10 each. I had a look in the chilled drinks cabinet and unearthed a lonely bottle of Delegats Hawkes Bay Chardonnay 2002 from the back, for which we paid only $22. The roast dinner would have been enough on its own, the portions were so large, and the wine was superb.

Donaldo, if that was indeed him behind the counter, was a burly, middle-aged man who didn't look in the least Italian, I thought, so where did the name come from? I didn't like to ask; it was a nice touch of eccentricity in this lonely part of the world. I told him we'd driven from Nelson via the Buller Gorge and he asked what I thought of the road. 'Disappointing,' I said, 'all the thrill has gone out of it.'

He looked astonished. 'The people from overseas think it's too winding and say they'll never go on it again.'

I told him I remembered it in the 1970s, when it was an adventure to drive it, narrow, primitive in parts, and with a steep drop on the bends to the river below if you didn't take care.

'When I tell the tourists that it's a dream run from what it used to be they think I'm mad,' he said. 'It's good to talk to someone who knew it before!'

We were getting on so well that I thought I should mention that perhaps he had undercharged us for the wine.

'No,' he replied, 'that's given me a good mark-up on what I paid for it a couple of years ago!' What an angel.

Light misty rain that had a taste of salt spray drifted around us as we walked back to the camp along the wide, handsome, grassed beachfront where a few tourists were free-camping by the water's edge, in spite of a sign asking them not to. Who was going to police them in this remote spot?

CHAPTER 18

OFF TO THE GLACIERS

We awoke to the drip, drip of unrelenting rain, the sort of Sunday weather just made for a nice lie-in with tea and toast and the Sunday papers. The van smelled damp, and my sleeping bag was wet at the bottom where rain had entered through the small gap in the window left open for ventilation. M. complained of a very sore throat and put himself onto a course of antibiotics, and, unusually for him, took Panadol tablets regularly throughout the day. We had planned to drive 300 kilometres to Franz Josef and felt quite gloomy at the thought of doing it in poor weather conditions. It would be difficult to enjoy the spectacular scenery, and to leave the campervan to visit renowned tourist spots. But we had to press on. A day wasted waiting for the weather to clear would be a day taken away from somewhere else. I did the outdoor honours under my tiny folding umbrella with the electric power cable and gas cylinder, and we set off for the nearby seal colony on Cape Foulwind, named by Captain Cook for its navigational difficulties but, today, an accurate description of the smell of the seals.

We didn't get very far. The torrential rain had caused flooding on the adjacent low-lying fields, and it seemed unlikely that the seals would come out. We were driving with our headlights on, and felt we were at the end of nowhere, that if we had an accident we wouldn't be found for days. A ray of hope emerged from the mist, the Star Tavern, here in this desolate and remote corner of New Zealand, with a few homestays and bed and breakfast establishments to keep it company. Our sense of isolation was more imagined than real.

The end of the access road is gated, and it is necessary to take the Cape Foulwind Walkway to get up to the lighthouse and to view the seal colony. The walk around the Cape is rated very highly and takes three hours to complete. Two unoccupied campervans were parked at the side, and their occupants were hardier souls than we were, for we decided it was too wet to do the walk and turned our van around. The rugged cliffs, the rocks at the bottom, the sea and the sky were all an unwelcoming dark grey and so, most likely, would be the seals, and thus hard to spot. Pick your day to visit Cape Foulwind – I don't recommend it in the rain.

We took a short cut along Wilsons Lead Road to Greymouth 100 kilometres away. After driving for 12 kilometres, at the junction with State Highway 6 and heading south, amid the total, eerie emptiness of the plain, was a sign which said 'No fuel for 87 km'. That meant Greymouth! 'Talk about closing the stable door after the horse has bolted,' commented M. Memo: keep a full tank in New Zealand.

The vegetation became scrubby, with lots of manuka, as we approached Costello Hill and headed down the other side to the West Coast proper and the start of the world famous drive, revered by New Zealanders, to the Franz Josef and Fox Glaciers, the Haast Pass, and the southern lakes of Wanaka, Hawea, and Wakatipu. This journey has recently been named one of the world's top 10 road trips by the travel authority Lonely Planet (*The New Zealand Herald,* 14 January 2006). The top three road trips were the East Coast of Australia, the Amalfi Coast in Italy, and the lengthy Cape Town to Cairo trip in Africa.

There was no let-up to the rain. The West Coast has the most rainfall in the country, easily explained by the long, high spines of the ranges and Alps running the length of the coast which trap the rain as it sweeps in from the Tasman Sea and cause it to be dumped on the western seaboard. The benefit lies in the exquisite rain forests whose beauty brings a lump to the throat, particularly in Fiordland, which I rate as having the best natural scenery of its type in the world. It was a pity we didn't have time to revisit it on this trip.

Charleston, an old goldmining town, is a relic of the past. In its heyday it was the Thames of the West Coast, with dozens of pubs, dance halls, gambling dens, and plenty of girls. Today you have to get your adventure from taking a tour to the nearby Ananui Caves. Be warned about the stretch of road south of Charleston which turns into a nightmare of appalling horseshoe bends, the surface deeply striated to prevent skidding. We could barely manage 35 kilometres per hour in the wet conditions, but the difficult driving was mitigated by the beautiful bush and ferns lining the road, so utterly, unmistakeably *New Zealand.*

I was impatient to see the Tasman Sea, that stretch of ocean lying between New Zealand and Australia and called 'The Ditch' by local travellers. The road climbed through the Paparoa National Park, mist-clad on the top of the hills, and slow driving in the van, and the nostalgic, heady scent of damp New Zealand bush seeped in through the gaps in the sliding door behind me. Suddenly the sky cleared, little bits of blue appeared, and it stopped raining. The ocean! At last I could see out to the horizon. The nearest landfall from here is Tasmania, Australia. The landscape assumed picture-book West Coast beauty, ruggedness, grandeur, and drama, with vistas of glorious forest, primeval rock formations, swirling water with rough waves breaking on grey sand beaches – none of your white stuff here! – and high, hard-leaved flax bushes framing the road.

If the wild, pounding waves of the West Coast shoreline had not repulsed the Dutch sailor and explorer Abel Tasman, New Zealand might have had a different future. On 13 December 1642 he arrived off the coast near Hokitika, but refused to land because of the rough seas, choosing instead to sail past Cape Foulwind and around Farewell Spit to anchor in Golden Bay. Local Maori repelled attempts to land, so he continued his voyage north along the west coast of the North Island. Several attempts to land for fresh water supplies were abandoned because of the heavy surf, so Tasman sailed into the Pacific to discover islands in the Tonga and Fiji groups, leaving the country to be claimed over a century later by Captain James Cook.

At Tiromoana a smart new bridge has been built across the Fox River (the old one looks more fun to drive over), and the Fox River Caves, up in the hills along the river, are famous. Some very fit young men having a snack by the side of the road were well-equipped with stout boots and suitable clothing and were presumably about to venture inland. The walk to the caves is three hours return.

We drove around Woodpecker Bay, so named, I decided, because an offshore rock bears a decided resemblance to one, and noticed that the ocean had taken on a pale turquoise colour, a good omen for better weather to come. Colour aside, there is nothing in this sea and its shore which remotely resembles the benign beauty of the North Island beaches. Even Baylys Beach north of Dargaville where we had camped for the first night, frightening in its vastness and pounding, gigantic waves, seemed tame compared to the rawness and steely power of this stretch of coastline. If you subscribe to the anthropological theory that geography dictates human character, then the popular conception of West Coasters being hardy, independent, and somewhat of a law unto themselves is explained by their mighty surroundings.

A sign warned us to be careful of penguins crossing the road for the next two kilometres. It wouldn't be difficult for them to land on the beach and scramble up the rocky foreshore and through the short undergrowth to the road. Further on, the bluff above the road showed signs of slippage and motorists were advised to beware of falling rocks. We stopped at a lookout, and crossed the road to the Irimahuwhero Viewpoint, accompanied by a friendly weka. There was a good pictorial information board telling about the 'spectacular limestone landscapes, magnificent stretch of coastline, and a forest that is home to rare native birds' in the Paparoa National Park which comprises '30,000 acres from seashore to the alpine tops of the Paparoa Range'.

Paparoa National Park's most famous limestone features are the Pancake Rocks and Blowholes at Dolomite Point, near

Punakaiki (pron. poona-kye-kee). We were almost there. A short drive high above the ocean, through more bush and ponga ferns, brought us to the Paparoa National Park Visitor Centre, built in 1987, and a credit to the tourist industry in New Zealand. The large centre is run by the Department of Conservation and has all the information tourists and vacationers could possibly need on the National Park and its environs. Hut tickets and track brochures are available, as are topographical and park maps, weather and track reports, activity and transport information; there is even a tide clock with the information that the best time for the blowholes is at high tide with a south-westerly swell. Brochures, at $1 each, are available on all the walks in the Park. There are pamphlets on survival, hypothermia, snow sports, on how to use avalanche transceivers, and on planning trips in the back country. I picked up one entitled 'Dump Stations on the West Coast' – best to be prepared! A comprehensive Westland-Buller weather report was posted on the front door. Showers and cooler winds were forecast for the rest of the day, clearing the next day and becoming fine, with strong gusty winds in exposed valleys expected on Tuesday.

An excellent shop stocked souvenirs, and practical items like thick woollen socks for trampers. For the price of a gold coin an audio-visual display relayed interesting pioneer and early settler history in the district, and the story of the establishment of the National Park. I discovered a large, very beautiful poster of coloured photographs of all the native birds of New Zealand, and had it rolled up into a tube holder for safe transport back to Auckland and our grandsons. Even if you are not interested in viewing the Pancake Rocks, you should stop at the Visitor Centre to gather essential information brochures about the activities and services available to tourists as they proceed down the West Coast.

The large car park, the information centre, the craft shop, and the adjoining cafés were full, and foreign languages abounded. I estimated that about 200 tourists were here. As you might expect, pancakes with fruit, cream and maple syrup were on the menu! We set off across the highway to see the Pancake Rocks and Blowholes, and found a wide tar-sealed footpath, designed for wheelchairs as well as pedestrians. If you want to do only one 'walk' in New Zealand to view native plants, trees and ferns close up, this is the easiest. The carefully-planned path wanders somewhat circuitously through native bush with added plantings of flax bushes near the cliff top to give a truly authentic New Zealand feel. There are plenty of viewing points, and room for everyone. The Pancake Rocks are just that, huge formations which resemble stacks of pancakes, and are quite remarkable geologically. There wasn't much blowhole activity to watch – high tide was one and a half hours away – but the power of the sea, surging through the openings in the rocks, gave an indication of what might be expected if tide and weather were just right.

If you are enraptured by the park and the region and wish to spend time here, *The New Zealand Camping Guide, South Island* recommends highly the large, coastal Punakaiki Motor Camp. Details are given in the Appendix.

The cafés were still full when we returned, so we decided to travel on to Greymouth, 35 kilometres away, for lunch. A short distance along the highway we passed the Pancake Rocks Motel and Villas, a row of terraced apartments of very modern design facing onto a small beach. The Papamoa Motel further on looked down-at-heel in comparison. The Coast is moving ahead, with new homes visible through the bush, and the Rata Café, a modern building standing high off the road to the left south of Barrytown, and famous for its buffalo steaks, advertised a free car park. Does this mean that free camping is allowed? We didn't stop to enquire.

The road was pleasantly flat, with a coastal plain on the right and rain forest and bush on the left. We passed a 30-year-old black Chrysler Valiant car parked deep in the bush at the side of the road. Painted on it in white lettering was the sign 'Private Property Keep Off', indicating, we thought, that it was handy overnight accommodation for the owner. Only on the West Coast…

Nearing Greymouth, the highway became tortuous with very sharp bends, and at Rapahoe, a typical West Coast settlement with about 20 houses, a hotel, and a campground, we could see stretching out to the ocean the flat-topped Point Elizabeth which can be reached by a walking track from Rapahoe. At Rununga, a moderately large settlement seven kilometres from Greymouth, a small hand-lettered sign said 'Party Cakes'. Many of the houses had Sky TV dishes, an entertainment lifesaver (apart from the parties!) in this neck-o'-the-woods, I imagine, where there's only so much hunting and fishing one can do. At the Gumboot Café you can hire trail bikes to explore the surrounding countryside, and it is evidently a popular activity because about 24 bikes were parked in an adjacent lot.

If you use the same road atlas that I did, you will see many acclaimed walkways referenced with the letter W, and as you travel will find many local walks and tracks signposted prominently on the highways. Although I have already given details of some famous walks, it is not within the scope of this book to enlarge on the topic too much, so if you enjoy tramping and walking, and want to explore parts of New Zealand on foot, I recommend buying one of the many guidebooks on New Zealand walks. I have noticed several publications at the Whitcoulls bookstore in Queen Street, Auckland, and one would be a useful addition to your holiday library. The West Coast is a walker's paradise. In the two days we spent travelling to Haast, and from there to Lake Wanaka, we passed dozens of signs indicating marked walking tracks with the distance and return time included. There is usually plenty of off-road parking for campervans, and tourists can easily experience the beauty of our wonderful, unique rain forests in a short space of time. It is worth the effort.

Big boulder retaining banks to stop the Grey River from overflowing during a flood are the feature of the entrance to Greymouth. We turned left over Cobden Bridge and stopped at the Left Bank Art Gallery situated in the old Bank of New Zealand building on the corner of Tainui Street and the Quay. We were looking for some decorative jade ornaments to buy for our apartment in Auckland. In a glass case lay the most exquisite jade bowl I have ever seen, so perfectly proportioned, and such a beautiful colour, that I could have looked at it forever. It was not for sale. Crushed, we drove 100 metres up the street to the Jade Boulder Gallery and found a handsome, rough jade boulder, perfect for our balcony. The owner said it was for sale if the price was so high that he simply couldn't refuse! So that was that. If you want to take a small, exquisite jade object home with you, I recommend seeking out a nephrite jade letter opener, useful as well as ornamental. The Maori word for jade is *pounamu*, and in New Zealand its colloquial name is greenstone. Thirty years ago we had called at a small greenstone factory and purchased a pair of nephrite jade bookends, highly polished, and coloured a rich, lightly mottled, deep green. Good jade, or greenstone, pieces have the merit of being almost invisible in the correct surroundings, but shriek of quality on closer inspection, and our bookends are a prized possession. If I had to choose just one thing from New Zealand to take home to another country, it would be something in jade.

Greenstone is hard, tough, and durable, and Maori sharpened it into adzes and chisels with which to make ornaments, other tools, and fighting weapons, notably the *mere* (pron. may-ray). Fine examples can be seen in museums. Supplies of New Zealand greenstone are limited, the export of unworked stone is forbidden, and most of the jade seen in the tourist shops comes from China.

The Jade Boulder Café, next door, had a large menu featuring very smart food plus classic West Coast offerings including plenty of seafood, and whitebait patties, $9 each and the size of a medium round of pita bread. I was intrigued by a dish of Blackball pork and fennel sausages served on buttery mash with garlic and chives, with two large grilled mushrooms, and onion gravy. *Blackball* sausages? Blackball is a small town further inland, and sausages in New

Zealand do not have regional names. What was so special about these? I had to find out, and we ordered the dish, at $14.95 each.

I thought I'd died and gone to sausage heaven; the food was gourmet, perfectly cooked, and I nearly licked the plate. I had a glass of Montana Cabernet Sauvignon Merlot 2002 for $5, the bottle opened for me. M. ordered a glass of Monteith's beer which came served in a Monteith's goblet, and liked the goblet so much he enquired where he could buy some. 'Just along the road to the right,' he was told. I wondered whether I should have another glass of the good, and very cheap, wine, but said 'no' firmly to myself as I had to navigate us through Hokitika to Franz Josef that night – on the only road that leads there! We called at the Monteith's brewery and ordered six goblets to be couriered to Auckland. They are made in Germany, the home of beer, which probably explains their perfect shape and design, and M. enjoys drinking from them very much. Monteith's Pilsner is in the fridge at present, but he has discovered that Stella Artois also fits snugly into the glass.

We had a view from the café of the Trans-Alpine train entering Greymouth. The carriages looked very old, but were surprisingly full of travellers. The Christchurch to Greymouth railway line is an important transport link bisecting the South Island, and famous for the quality of the dramatic scenery en route.

Greymouth, the principal centre of Westland, is a planned town with the streets laid out in a grid pattern and, like Westport, designed for a larger role in life which never quite eventuated. Somehow it seemed grey, like its name, or perhaps this was because the sky was overcast, but any deficiencies in the colour department were more than made up for by the genuine friendliness and charm of everyone we met there. Coasters are grounded in reality, have a great sense of humour and innate courtesy, and it is a pleasure to tour their region. We stopped for fuel, buying 44.95 litres of diesel for $39.26.

Greymouth's humble beginnings as a harbour port and supply town for the goldminers are evident in the little cottages lining the main road out of town. Even the newer homes are small, crouching below the level of State Highway 6. The road was flat, and we hoped it would continue all the way to Hokitika, 40 kilometres distant.

M. walloped along at 95 kilometres per hour. Shantytown, inland from Paroa, is a marvellous replica of an old goldmining town, and if you are travelling with children it serves as an educational stop where they can learn how to pan for gold. South of Camerons we came to a scary one-way bridge; it was either us, or an opposing vehicle or *train*, and we were on the 'give way' side. We slowed to walking pace, and fortunately nothing was coming towards us. Just over the bridge is a handy café where you can steady your nerves with coffee and whitebait sandwiches.

Kumara Junction is aptly named, for the important State Highway 73 linking the West Coast through Arthur's Pass to Christchurch begins here. The ocean winds sweep strongly inland; the hillside bush was flattened and skewed sideways, and the trees leaned inland. We crossed another ghastly road and rail bridge and arrived at Hokitika to do a tour of the jade factories in another attempt to find something to take home. Alas, nothing. Good jade is *very* expensive.

I had mentally prepared for a night in Hokitika. It was 3.45 p.m., M. didn't look well, and our planned stop, Franz Josef, was another 140 kilometres away. But the sun came out strongly; M. said he felt fit enough, so we pressed on.

Hokitika (pron. hoe-ker-tikka) offers a good illustration of how easily behavioural oddities can occur when gold fever strikes a small place. In *Tales of Pioneer Women*, Lydia Paterson writing *The Romance of Gold* tells of the effect that the discovery in 1864 of gold on the *beach* had on men. She records that 'There were no wharves to which vessels could be moored, so a hundred were run ashore on the beaches and abandoned as soon as the passengers were unloaded', while '...all rushed to the scene of the latest find...' and that 'Some of the vessels were afterwards refloated, some had their engines salvaged, but others were simply left to their fate'. Maori, who '…watched these strange happenings with amazement…' thought pakeha customs were 'beyond comprehension'.

Hokitika became a tent town, with entrepreneurs rushing there to profit from the setting up of dance halls and hotels, and of stores where they sold basic commodities at exorbitant prices, and the author writes that 'Men were said to light their pipes with £5 notes, such was the abundance of wealth'. The beaches yielded enormous quantities of gold above high water mark – all that was necessary to retrieve it was to dig down a few feet into the black sand. A day's work panning a nearby creek or river for gold dust would also yield great quantities. By 1903, over six million ounces of gold worth, then, £25,000,000, had been won.

The neighbouring town of Ross, 15 minutes south, has the distinction of mining the largest gold nugget ever found in New Zealand, weighing 3.1 kilograms, and bought eventually by the New Zealand Government for presentation to King George V. Rumour has it that the nugget was used as a doorstop in the local hotel until sanity prevailed.

The decline of the gold rush left Hokitika a quiet little coastal town, with the Southern Alps on one side, and the never-ending ocean on the other. Today it is worth visiting for its renowned museum, its jade and craft galleries, good cafés, and, especially in March, its phenomenal Wildfoods Festival (www.wildfoods.co.nz), which pumps several million dollars into the local economy. The popularity of the unique festival is such that crowds of up to 20,000 people descend annually on this small town of just 4,000 inhabitants for two days of feasting and drinking. As well as typical West Coast favourite foods such as whitebait, venison and wild pork, you can sample exotica such as deep fried huhu grubs, grasshoppers and other insects, possum pate, goat and hare testicles, muttonbirds, bull penises, colostrum butterballs, wasp larvae, and worm rissoles; nothing that can be dug up, shot, or caught is immune from the inventive cooks who compete for the most adventurous entries, using *every* part of the kill. I feel sick just writing about it. There are about 90 stalls at the festival, and the beer tent is the busiest. Every tourist bed within a 100 kilometre radius is booked well in advance, and campers and caravanners are accommodated in the school playgrounds. Almost all the locals participate in the running of the event, even opening up their homes to total strangers for the night, and this strong community spirit is an important reason for the festival's success.

One of the most outstanding features of the West Coast highway is the number of rivers to cross, hardly surprising when you consider the geography of the region, with the high ranges and Alps sending their surplus water down to the sea. The rivers presented a huge problem to early settlers and travellers in the nineteenth century, for the only dry way across for people and goods was by horse and cart. As the barely-formed main road gradually improved from deep ruts to a smoother surface, passenger coaches plied the coast between the river crossings, where it became necessary to disembark and transfer to a horse and cart to cross, then climb into a waiting coach on the other bank which would drive to the next river, the whole process being repeated again. The journey from Greymouth to Hokitika, just 40 kilometres, took at least two, sometimes three days! It took three days' journey by coach in the 1870s, if all went well, to travel from Greymouth to Nelson via Reefton, a trip that today can be done in under four hours.

We seemed to have spent the whole day driving through remarkable scenic reserves, wall after wall of dense green forests with tiny peeps of the sky above, or hills or ocean in the distance. Just one of these reserves would cause excitement anywhere else – here we began to take them for granted. At the Lake Ianthe Scenic Reserve a sign said 'Rare Birds', and I was reminded of a bird-watching friend in England who would find New Zealand his paradise if he came here. The lakeshore has bush and forest to its edge, and is an excellent place to pull in for a driving rest and a cup of tea.

M. remarked that there's so much on offer in this country, in the way of recent colonial settlement, art and culture, food and wine trails, adventure pursuits, spectacular scenic wonders with the accompanying flora and fauna, recreational land and water sports, and a rich Polynesian history, that he wonders how anyone coming to tour could possibly pack such diversity into a satisfying one-size-fits-all holiday. The short answer is that you can't. Holidays nearly always operate under time constraints. We were realising that even 30 days in a campervan does not give time to 'do' New Zealand thoroughly. We discussed solutions, and decided that tourists who travel a long distance from the Northern Hemisphere must select interests and activities beforehand, and tailor their holiday to suit. On the way around the country, plenty of other attractions can be enjoyed within the holiday time frame and a sense of accomplishment will be achieved. Our English birdwatcher says that his hobby has led him to visit every nook and cranny of Great Britain, and I can recommend New Zealand as a destination for any birdwatcher who is reading this book. Birds, insects and fish were the only inhabitants of the land and foreshore until recent colonial times. All the mammals have been introduced since then, some with disastrous results for ecology, but the bird life is still spectacular and unique to this country.

The highway veered inland, and at Harihari we felt we were on the home run to Franz Josef with only 60 kilometres to go. Harihari has a very large tavern with an adjacent campervan park, and looks a good stop for dinner and some entertainment. At last we were getting closer to the foothills of the Southern Alps. The countryside was peppered with dairy farms, the cows walking in single file to get milked across paddocks of such a bright green that they almost looked artificial. The road became steep and winding, and slowed us down. The recommended speed was 55 kilometres per hour on the bends, and 25 kilometres per hour on the horseshoes. Murray was crouched over the wheel concentrating on his driving, and several motorhomes coming the other way had their drivers in the same position. It wasn't easy. Two cyclists had poles mounted on their safety helmets with rear vision mirrors angled on the end.

We crossed the wide Whataroa River, its pale grey water running down directly from the Southern Alps. Whataroa, a pleasant town, is the official gateway to South Westland and the World Heritage Park. In 1991 the vast area of South Westland, which contains 10 per cent of New Zealand's total land area, was created a World Heritage Park in recognition of its natural landscapes, alongside such other sacred areas as the Mt. Everest National Park in Nepal, the Grand Canyon and Yellowstone National Parks in America, and Serengeti National Park in Tanzania. The World Heritage Highway runs along State Highway 6 from Whataroa to Lake Wanaka, and is an important drive. Unfortunately State Highway 6 covers only a small part of the total Heritage Park land area, but it offers the road tourist a good look at the region, and more discoveries can be made by travelling further south to Lake Te Anau and Milford Sound.

Tours run from an office in the main street of Whataroa to the White Heron Sanctuary north of Okarito, and you can kayak on the large Okarito Lagoon, and the nearby tree-fringed Lake Wahapo which today looked dark and gloomy. Like so many towns on the West Coast, Okarito mushroomed during the gold rush days of the 1860s, and boasted theatres, a church, banks, stores, and the inevitable police station, jail and courthouse. Its claim to fame now is as the home of Keri Hulme who won the Booker Prize for her 1984 novel *The Bone People*, set in New Zealand.

Lake Mapourika, the largest of South Westland's splendid roadside lakes, sparkled in the late afternoon sunlight. There is a good, level-grassed free campsite on its shore with kayaking available at the recreation area at Jetty Bay, at the southern end of the lake. We had our first glimpse of snowy-topped Alps as we drew near to Franz Josef, and the glacier was clearly visible. The last 140 kilometres from Hokitika had taken under two hours, a sterling effort by M. considering the slow conditions encountered from time to time.

We booked into the Franz Josef Mountain View Top 10 Holiday Park, which has a rare five star rating, for $27 for the night (details in the Appendix). It was time for dinner, and the Franz Josef Glacier Hotel where we had stayed 30 years ago was just 500 metres away, still beautifully sited but in need of upgrading and only a vestige of its former self. The barlady told me that $10 million needs to be spent to restore it. We had dinner in the bar, fish and chips with salad for M., and the house special of lamb shanks on mash with mixed vegetables for me. I had a glass of horrible Corbans Chardonnay that should have been put into a cask, not a bottle, but it was only $5. M. was safe with beer. Dinner and drinks cost $39.50 – if only we could dine so cheaply in Auckland! A man playing the pokies won $100 and dithered as to what he should do with his windfall. An interested crowd quickly gathered around him waiting to see if he would shout the bar a drink. I whispered some time-honoured advice in his ear that had been given to my playing companion at the Sky City Casino in Auckland earlier in the year – 'Take the money and run' – and he did!

M. was not well and fell quickly into bed when we got back to the van. I inspected the facilities, found they were unisex, couldn't cope, and went to bed dirty. We got off to sleep to the sounds of a party of 20 young people carousing in the barbecue area.

CHAPTER 19

HELICOPTERING OVER THE SOUTHERN ALPS

It was Monday, 28 February, and we were woken early by the sound of a helicopter powering overhead. The night had been very chilly, there was condensation in the van, and our clothing was damp and cold to put on – awful. I needed a hot shower to warm up, so crossed to the ultra-modern ablution block which I had so hated the night before, and found a spacious room containing a shower, toilet and basin, the only time I encountered this triple amenity on the trip. Perhaps it's what got the Holiday Park its five star rating. There was a fairly clean bathmat, which I didn't use of course, even a dispenser of disinfectant wipes provided to sanitise the toilet seat beforehand. Suddenly the fact that it was unisex didn't seem to matter, it was just so pleasant to have every facility in one private space.

Dreadful hangovers had subdued last night's partygoers, and they packed up their pup tents and departed very quietly. M. felt a little better, in spite of the 292 kilometre drive the day before, but said he didn't feel like taking a helicopter trip up to the glaciers. OK by me!

How quickly things change. We left the camp at 10 o'clock, the checkout time at all Top 10 campgrounds, grateful for the clear sky and sunshine, and drove to the village tourist centre further along the highway. The town was very busy, full of impossibly fit, bronzed young people from all over the world, it seemed, or middle-aged, slightly flabby tourists like us. All the local attractions, including helicopter rides and guides for mountain walks, can be booked here, and the Department of Conservation has an information centre further along on the right should you want specific knowledge of outdoor conditions. The Mt. Cook Ski-Planes company, which flies over Mt. Cook, has an office on the left of the highway.

We decided to inspect the Franz Josef Glacier, and turned left off the highway to drive four kilometres on an unsealed road, to find a sign saying that 250 years ago the glacier came right down to this point. The river which ran alongside the road was evidently carrying away glacier melt, for the opaque water looked like thin grey paint, chilly and unwelcoming.

Free overnight camping is allowed further along by the parking area. Signs warning of car thieves are everywhere, alongside roadside parking spaces and in the parking lot.

The car park was full of campervans and cars, and after looking at an information notice board we decided to take the 20 minute return Sentinel Walk, the easiest option. The bush track was very steep, but well graded and gravelled, and offered a good view of the dirty ice on the glacier. It wasn't very spectacular, being late summer, so I consoled myself when we left by clambering down to the river and retrieving a nice piece of schist for my stone collection at home. The walk up to the face of the glacier takes one and a half hours return; the ice is very slippery and unstable, and venturing onto it is not recommended.

If you wish to take a professional guided climb on the glacier, the Guiding Company (freephone 0800 800 102, www.nzguides.com) operates all year round, and has a variety of options. Call in at The Alpine Adventure Centre at Franz Josef Glacier for more information.

We moved on to see the Fox Glacier, 25 kilometres away, a slow drive due to the very steep, winding road through forested hills and over the Cook Saddle. I began to wish that I had more than two slices of toast and Vegemite inside me as M. swung the campervan round the bends. One just has to get used to these sorts of roads in New Zealand. Electric power cables stretching across a huge ravine below looked like extravagantly long flying foxes, with not a pylon in sight. How on earth is it engineered? By helicopter?

Fortunately, since we were down to a 35 kilometre per hour crawl, there were plenty of gravelled side bays where M. could pull off the road to let faster vehicles go past, judging by the toots a much-appreciated courtesy. It was a relief to see Fox Glacier township, set in a broad, flat plain, from the top of the Saddle, and we descended quickly to the main street, past the large, wooden, white-painted Fox Glacier Hotel, and read a sign at the BP garage stating that it was the last refuelling stop for 120 kilometres, at Haast. Those signs must be good for business.

I felt like a large lunch, so we ordered whitebait omelettes for $16.50 each at Café Neve in the main street, a large salad to share, and coffee and hot chocolate. The omelettes were made with two eggs, stuffed with 100 grams of whitebait, and were excellent value. M. gobbled his food quickly and, mysteriously, disappeared. He returned 10 minutes later looking awfully pleased with himself and said he had gone to the Visitor Information Centre across the road and booked us both on a helicopter ski-plane flight with Glacier Southern Lakes Helicopters (ph. (03) 751 0803, freephone 0800 800 732, email: fox@glaciersouthernlakes.co.nz, www.heli-flights.co.nz) over Mt. Cook, Mt. Tasman and its glacier, landing on the Fox glacier where we could get out and walk around. I froze with fear, and asked what had brought about the abrupt change of mind.

'Well, I'll be 70 years old soon and I probably won't come down here again. It's now or never!'

I couldn't argue with that reasoning, and when he told me the price of the trip, $640 for the two of us, I felt obliged to go. He had settled for the longest flight, the Mount Cook Spectacular with Glacier Landing, Flight Tour 306, which would last approximately 30 minutes.

We were picked up from the Visitor Centre in a van, with four other passengers, and driven to the airfield five minutes away. We had a short talk on safety precautions, climbed into the tiny red and white helicopter where the seats were still warm from the previous passengers – the helicopter does a fast turnaround – and were wafted into the air. I had never flown in a helicopter before, and rather enjoyed it at first as we flew over green fields, but I became extremely nervous when we got higher, and closer to the mountain faces which I felt I could reach out and touch.

The view was sensational, intimate, with a raw drama that groundlubbers like me can never imagine until face to face with it. The pilot hovered over the divide of the Southern Alps and around the soaring top of Mt. Cook, the 'Everest' of New Zealand, then flew over to Mt. Tasman and its glacier, which is the longest in the Southern Hemisphere, giving a succinct commentary so we would know what we were looking at. Mt. Cook is unmistakeable to New Zealanders, of course, but our co-passengers were all Australians. I have nothing but the most profound admiration for mountaineers, now. I wonder what drives them to want to conquer, on foot, such formidable crags and suffer the frightful conditions that accompany their efforts, when it is so much easier to do it from the air. The helicopter pilots choose which glacier to land on according to the weather conditions; we flew across to the Fox Glacier and clambered out onto the slippery snow. This glacier was busy! About a dozen climbers had hiked up, and more were behind them. I was afraid I would skid, and fall, and clung to M. while the pilot took a photograph of us so I could prove to the family that I'd actually done the flight. The intense cold, and fear of breaking a limb, made it a miserable experience for me and I was thankful to climb back into the helicopter for the descent.

Never has *terra firma* felt so good, or trees, the road, even the bridges, looked so welcoming. On the return drive to the Visitor Centre, the van driver, chuckling, made an unscheduled stop outside the hotel to drop us off and I gulped down a double brandy, thankful to have the experience over safely. M., after a beer, said it was his highlight of the trip so far, and much later, as I write this, he still says so.

Alpine Guides Fox Glacier (ph. (03) 751 0825, reservations 0800 111 600, www.foxguides.co.nz) operates year-round guided walks on the glacier. A half-day walk costs $54, the all-day walk costs $85, and the Fox Glacier Heliride costs $245. Minimum ages for children apply, and bookings are essential.

Alpine flying was the brainchild of aviator Henry Wigley. In 1955 he fitted retractable wooden skis lined with Formica on the underneath surface onto his small plane and, with a friend flying another plane overhead who would raise the alarm if he had an accident, landed solo on the Tasman Glacier. He kept the engine running in case the plane failed to start again. Wigley, who believed that the Southern Alps should be enjoyed by all, not just the few climbers who made it to the top, opened up the region to sightseers and was the pioneer of adventure tourism in New Zealand. He was knighted by the Queen for his efforts. Sir Edmund Hillary was the third person to land on the Tasman Glacier in Sir Henry Wigley's ski-plane, and since that early flight 350,000 tourists have enjoyed the experience.

Putting my own small fears aside, I recommend our helicopter flight wholeheartedly, especially if seeing and walking on high snow doesn't form a part of your regular life back home. Grandeur and majesty, sublime views, uncanny solitude, human vulnerability, and the ever-present threat of true danger, are all rolled into the journey. After a few amateur calculations with the help of my road atlas, I estimated that we had flown about 70 kilometres in the helicopter on the round trip to the peaks and glaciers, and as we left the Fox township for Haast Village, I appreciated my safe and settled earthbound existence as I never have before. There are exciting parts of alpine South Island which cannot be travelled into by campervan, and the easiest way to maximise your sightseeing in the shortest time is to take helicopter flights. There are many companies which offer this service and their brochures are available at all Visitor Information Centres.

The flat road across coastal plains was a pleasure to drive on; there was very little traffic, indeed very little sign of human habitation at all, and the conclusion one comes to is that the lack of population has ensured the preservation of the region in its natural state. The farming settlement of Jacobs River has a grand view of Mt. Cook, six houses, and a church, Our Lady of the River, one of the earliest churches in Westland. There is a plethora of small wooden churches in New Zealand, and their importance to the early settlers cannot be overestimated, for they offered a place of faith and comfort in a new land with an uncertain way of life. Some of the most endearing churches are to be found by the wayside, many now closed and in a bad state of repair, the population which kept them alive having moved on. I counted only 10 houses in nearby Bruce Bay, a battered, wild and windy beach held in place by its headlands, and reportedly a good place from which to collect schist and quartz rocks.

We seemed to cross a river or creek every five minutes. The West Coast rivers abound in whitebait, a famed delicacy, during the winter/spring seasons. New Zealand whitebait looks quite unappetising when seen in the fishmonger's window, resembling miniature eels about six centimetres long and a few millimetres wide, of a dark grey, transparent and rather shiny appearance, blobbed together wetly in a bowl. But when cooked in a well-seasoned fritter batter they separate and turn white, and have a delicate flavour and texture unlike anything else. Some cooks prefer just to add them to a well-beaten and seasoned egg, which holds them together as they are fried in large spoonfuls in the pan, and if you buy some for your dinner this will be the easiest way to cook them in the campervan.

Flat land never lasts for long on the West Coast, and we encountered steep, stunningly-forested hills as we approached Lake Paringa, a well-known camping and recreational area. The glacial lake is surrounded by forest and renowned for its beauty and its abundant native bird life, but unfortunately the only glimpse I had of it from the road was through land levelled for a motel.

I was looking forward to driving past Lake Moeraki and reaching the coast proper. The road followed the lakeshore, we reached Knights Point, and saw the spectacular coastline which continues past Ship Creek to Haast and beyond. Ship Creek is famous for its swamp forest, one of the finest in the world, which can be viewed on a 20 minute walk, but you can also undertake a 30 minute Dune Lake walk advertised on a signboard in the township, which affords good views over the coastline and Lake Moeraki. I would head for the swamp forest; it's a shorter walk, and ecologically very important for its kahikatea trees are among the oldest we have, the species reduced now to just two per cent of a type of forest once widespread in New Zealand.

Thomas Brunner made Paringa River the southernmost stopping point on his 18 month journey of exploration of the West Coast. Weakened by nearly a year of near starvation and wretched weather, he decided at this point that there was no land fit for settlement and no hint of gold(!), indeed nothing on the West Coast worth incurring the expense of exploring, so he returned north to Nelson.

We crossed the very wide and often formidable Haast River which looked lazy today, with little rivulets weaving their way through the stony river flats and forming an interesting braided pattern as they did so, and felt we were within reach of what many people consider to be the most exciting and beautiful region of New Zealand to visit. The bridge over the river is the longest on the West Coast, and was one of the most difficult to construct. State Highway 6 veered inland to Haast Village, just three kilometres further on, and our destination for the night. If you want to visit remote beaches, rivers, and forest, take the sealed coastal road which leads through Okuru to Jackson Bay, 50 kilometres away, but before you do so, call in at the South Westland World Heritage Visitor Centre south of the Haast Bridge at the junction with the road to Jackson

Bay for useful information on this unspoilt and accessible region of the World Heritage Park.

At the village we turned right into Marks Road, and booked in at the Aspiring Court Motel and Haast Highway Accommodation where we were charged $24 for the night. The grounds were well sealed, a definite plus in the West Coast climate, the showers were excellent, and the open plan kitchen provided all utensils and plates. There was an adjacent lounge with TV channels 1 and 2, and plenty of tables and chairs. It probably gets quite jolly in winter. Details are given in the Appendix.

Six Maui vans pulled in shortly after us, with more to come later on, and about a dozen touring cyclists performed that astonishing feat of pulling good-sized tents and other bulky equipment from small saddlebags and setting up for the night in about 10 minutes.

The supermarket was two minutes' walk away, and proved to be one of those eccentric stores which are full of goods, but have nothing you really want. I didn't want six varieties of boxed chocolates, or 20 varieties of canned drinks, or cakes or biscuits, or shoe polish or candles, or floppy brown lettuce, moulding fruit, soggy tomatoes, or potatoes which should have been put back in the ground to grow. I wanted steak, or chops of any kind, or good quality sausages. All the meat, which was frozen, looked as though it needed to be simmered for four hours to tenderise it. Perhaps I was just there on a bad day, but I wasn't the only person circling dismally, trying to find food for the evening meal. I settled for the last two packets of Watties Mild Chicken Curry and Rice from the freezer, snaffling them just in time from another camper who had his eyes on them, and managed to find two not-so-awful tomatoes, and a cucumber costing $4.50, with which to make a side salad.

The curry heated up nicely in the microwave, and was delicious. I would buy it again. I opened a bottle of Esk Valley Sauvignon Blanc 2003, and would buy that again, too! The sandflies swarmed in to welcome me to Haast, so we sprayed the van, and retired rather early for the night.

CHAPTER 20

THE HAAST PASS, LAKE WANAKA, AND QUEENSTOWN

The first day of March is also the first day of autumn in the Southern Hemisphere and, through to mid-April, the best time to tour the far South. Then, you will encounter hot, still days, a good hint of coolness in the air at night, a fresh sprinkle of snow on the Alpine peaks, and the start of what I call the autumn foliage season when the deciduous trees, many grown originally from seeds brought to New Zealand by early settlers, assume a cloak of bright colour unknown in the semi-tropical conditions of the north of New Zealand.

We left Haast Village anticipating eagerly the drive alongside the river and over Haast Pass to Makarora at the head of Lake Wanaka. From there we would skirt the eastern shore of the lake, then cross the narrow divide to Lake Hawea and Wanaka township. The 140 kilometre journey would be fairly slow travelling in the campervan, but we should reach Wanaka in time for lunch.

Haast Village itself is just an overnight stop for tourists. We were almost the last to leave the campground, except for a German couple who had draped their duvet and pillows out to air over their outdoor table and chairs in the early morning sunshine, and who obviously wouldn't leave until the job was done. I've always found that a caravan, or in this case the rear of our campervan, gets hot enough during the day when travelling in fine weather to dry off and air damp sleeping bags, clothing or shoes, so I don't see the merit in going to all the trouble that our neighbours were.

The Haast Pass was named after the geologist Sir Julius von Haast, who, in search of gold on the West Coast, crossed it in 1863 after being told it was the ancient greenstone trail of West Coast Maori. If you look at a map of the South Island you will realise its importance as a transport link between Westland, Otago, Southland and Fiordland; it is the only through road. Somewhat surprisingly, the construction of the modern highway that we were about to travel on was not completed until 1965, when it was opened with great fanfare by the Prime Minister, Mr Keith Holyoake. At last, New Zealanders and tourists could see for themselves the soaring snow-capped peaks, deep valleys and ravines, the fast rivers, the forests and the lakes previously only visible at close range to horse riders or trampers. This drive across the Alps is one that every New Zealander likes to say they have done, not because of the degree of difficulty, for in places the road is very steep, but because of the primitive beauty and drama of the elemental landscape. I consider that autumn is the best season to undertake the drive, for the fresh snow on the alpine peaks makes a memorable contrast with the stunning rain forest cladding the steep mountainsides, and the river rushing alongside the road. The prime beech, kahikatea, and rimu forests of South Westland are not found elsewhere in New Zealand; it is a sad fact that after 900 years of human occupation, 80 per cent of lowland forests have disappeared, cleared mostly in the nineteenth century to make way for European settlement.

The highway from Haast Village, flat at first, led along the south river bank and headed inexorably to the distant ranges of the Mt. Aspiring National Park. It was a superlative drive, through nature at its most spectacular, and strangely peaceful because the road was empty at this early hour. We clipped along at a steady 80 kilometres per hour, every few minutes crossing a small stream or creek, some with rather heartfelt names – Roaring Pig, Gout, Serpentine, Chelsea! At Pleasant Flat Bridge we parked in a recreation area and got out of the van to enjoy the million-dollar views of Mt. Hooker and the lush, forested slopes and valleys. Plenty of rest areas are thoughtfully provided along the road for this very purpose. It was surprising to find such an expanse of open country here in what I had imagined to be solid mountain landscape hung with forest.

The road turned south as we left the river flats behind, and seemed to be heading straight up into a mountainside, so enclosing were the ranges. This is considered to be the most dramatic section of the entire highway. The Gates of Haast gorge, where many tourists had stopped, had a one-way steel bridge crossing a mighty canyon filled with huge boulders, where the river ripped and roared along, totally unlike the placid reaches further back at Pleasant Flat. The river becomes a raging torrent when in flood; earlier bridges across the gorge were swept away in 1957 and 1961. Once clear of the bridge, the road climbed suddenly, and deceptively, and the sign 'Runaway Vehicle Ramp 500 m.' for vehicles coming towards us, said it all! The recommended speed on the bends was 45 kilometres per hour, just right for us, for we were high above the gorge and I had a scary view down to the rocks below.

The drive, a once-in-a-lifetime experience for a tourist, shouldn't be hurried. In a small country which boasts of dozens of unique man-made and natural features, this combination of civil engineering which marries so well with the best natural scenery on offer deserves to be enjoyed in a leisurely manner.

A sign indicated a 20 minute walk through the forest to view the Fantail Falls, evidently very popular with tourists judging by the number of empty vehicles parked along the roadside. We crossed the lowest of the three road passes across the Southern Alps, the 564 m. Haast Pass, a former horse trail, where you can take the nearby Historic Bridle Track walk of 1 hour 20 minutes. Colourful, intensely red lichen covered surrounding rock faces and the river stones below, a wonderful contrast with the dark greens and greys everywhere else. The descent from the pass was very steep, and a sign warned trucks to slow down to 20 kilometres per hour. At Davis Flat a sign announced another historic bridle track, and M. remarked that it must have been an awful experience to make the crossing on horseback 100 or more years ago.

Suddenly, unexpectedly, we were in open country, with a wide sky above, and M. sped up to 80 kilometres per hour in relief. In the middle of all this isolation we came to a camping ground for tents, called Cameron Flat, where some new shelters had been built recently. Bush walks abound in this area, and at the entrance to the Blue Pools, a 20 minute walk, seven cars and a campervan were parked. We continued the descent to Makarora, a small settlement with the obligatory café, petrol station and a tourist information centre. It gave us quite a jolt to have left so quickly behind powerful, primitive terrain, virtually untouched by humans, and enter a balmy man-made landscape of large paddocks covered with grazing cattle and sheep, and deliberately planted shelter belts of pine trees. A Transit New Zealand information board said that the Makarora-Wanaka road was open, which gave a good indication of how snowbound it must be in winter.

The sky was grey and cloudless, but with a strangely luminous, even quality to the light, and the driving conditions were perfect. Lake Wanaka emerged to the right, with steely grey, very still water, and an unusual, long, horizontal ribbon of thick white swansdown cloud bisecting the peaks ahead. This northern end of the lake was lonely, with no sign of habitation on either shore. It took just 15 minutes to reach the narrow isthmus between Lakes Wanaka and Hawea, which run parallel to each other, and cross over to journey down the western side of Lake Hawea and on to Wanaka. Lake Hawea had a friendlier aspect, idyllic and very pretty, a pleasant place to have a holiday home, I thought. A sign just outside the township welcomed us to the Otago Goldfields Heritage Trail, but we bypassed the turnoff and stopped for fuel further on. The diesel was expensive, and 48.59 litres cost $44.17.

Wanaka is a gateway to the Mt. Aspiring National Park. We turned off State Highway 6 onto State Highway 84 to enter the town, and parked the van on the attractive lakefront. If you look to the top end of the lake, towards the snow-clad alpine peaks, you will see the view that was used as the backdrop for Gandalf's flight to Rohan in *The Lord of the Rings*. Fans will find locations used in the trilogy quite easy to reach from the town. West from the lakefront to

Glendhu Bay, just before the turnoff to the Treble Cone Ski Field, is a view of the location used for Gandalf's flight to Rohan, and near Tarras, 30 kilometres to the east, the Great East Road and Flight to the Ford scenes were filmed. If you are short of time, Wanaka Flightseeing, located at the Wanaka Airport, will take you on a location flight.

We walked over to Relishes Café where we knew the food was good; I ordered a homemade steakburger with aoli, red onion relish, lettuce, tomato and grilled cheese served on flat Turkish bread, a satisfying luncheon dish which I enjoyed in several different versions as we toured, and M., who said he was starving, packed away the substantial all-day breakfast. The cost, with excellent coffee and hot chocolate, was $35.50.

Wanaka has recently become a boom town. There is tremendous wealth in the area, and new and expensive houses and country estates abound. The town hosts the famous Warbirds Over Wanaka International Air Show, a spectacular event held every two years. A three-day aviation trade expo and flyers market is run in conjunction with the air show. More information can be gained from the website, www.warbirdsoverwanaka.com. Adjacent to the airfield, on State Highway 6 on the way to Queenstown, is the Transport and Toy Museum, a good place to stop if you are touring with children.

The route from Wanaka to Queenstown on State Highway 6 is a rather circuitous journey of 95 kilometres. The alternative route to the west of Wanaka on State Highway 89 which travels alongside the Crown Range and the Cardrona Skifield, and passes through pleasant countryside, is just 64 kilometres long. The road is sealed and quite good, although care needs to be taken on the steep, winding drive on the approach down to Arrow Junction. As a bonus, the road passes the historic Cardrona Hotel where you can stop for lunch in the charming rear country garden.

We've driven on both routes to Queenstown, and time-wise there is nothing much to choose between them. If you intend to visit

Queenstown and then head east via Cromwell to Mt. Cook, or to Dunedin, then you should avoid repeating a drive by taking the Cardrona Road into Queenstown, and the Kawarau Gorge Road and State Highway 6 when you leave. If you are travelling down to Te Anau and Milford Sound, and then returning to Queenstown before going on to Mt. Cook, etc., you should do the same thing, for the same reason. But if you are driving to Queenstown, Te Anau, Milford Sound, and then journeying across Southland on State Highway 94 to Lumsden with routes available from there to Invercargill, Bluff (and the sea crossing to Stewart Island), Gore, Balclutha and Dunedin, then the best advice is to take State Highway 6 from Wanaka to Queenstown.

Does all this sound too complicated? Look at your road atlas and you will see how few the choices are at the bottom of the South Island of New Zealand, nearly at the bottom of the world!

Now, in spite of all the foregoing very sound advice, we took State Highway 6 from Wanaka to Queenstown, and the very next day found ourselves backtracking along the gorge road on our way to Cromwell, Alexandra and Dunedin! It was a question of time and, as I have said, good roads in this part of the country are scarce. The end of the trip was in sight, and we didn't have enough time to travel to Te Anau and Milford Sound and drive through Southland, *and* carry out our aim of traversing Arthur's Pass and the Lewis Pass before returning the campervan to Christchurch. Something had to go, and it turned out to be time in Queenstown and further south, a decision made at lunchtime the following day. There is nothing worse than doubling up on a drive, particularly so soon; if we had thought our time in Queestown was to be just one night, we could have taken the Cardrona Road and avoided repeating the Kawarau Gorge Road 20 hours later.

We sped along State Highway 6, following the Clutha River whose mighty volume of water generates much of the electric power in New Zealand as it winds through South Otago to Balclutha and the sea. The golden paddocks of the flat plain above the river gorge were proof of the dry summers enjoyed in this region. Recently-planted vineyards at Mount Pisa were draped in white netting, an expensive exercise, and I decided it must be done for protection from the summer hailstorms which frequently ruin local stone and pipfruit crops. Along the shore of Lake Dunstan, created artificially by damming the Clutha River at Cromwell and thereby controversially flooding half the town, is a granite monument marking the 45th Parallel. At Lowburn we branched right to take the Kawarau Gorge Road, and drove past the old goldmining centre of Ripponvale where outbuildings and other remnants of the gold rush days have been preserved. The scenery was astonishing; the lush rainforest of Haast had been replaced quickly by dry and dusty craggy hills rising above the Kawarau River, a reminder that east of the alpine divide a different New Zealand exists.

The 53 kilometre Kawarau Gorge Road, for much of its way perched high above the Kawarau River, is a dramatic drive, particularly for the front seat passenger who has a bird's eye view of the rich green, swirling water far below and can warn the driver if the edge of the road and the long drop to the water look perilously close. The road needs to be taken with care when travelling from east to west, as we were. It is easy to misjudge the outer bends and plunge into the river, and the road has a long record of serious, often fatal accidents. The road is steel-barriered in parts above the ravine, but I do not think the standardised barriers are high enough to prevent a tall vehicle like our campervan, or an even higher motorhome, from toppling over the side if a calamity occurred.

The road is host to many enterprises, from renowned vineyards on both banks of the river, to the thrill of bungy jumping off the Kawarau Bridge, to the Shotover Jet Boat rides where the passengers are seemingly hurled at high speed into the rocky cliffs along the river, only to be reprieved at the last second by a flick of the steering wheel by the skilled pilot. Nearing Queenstown, a side road leads past Lake Hayes, one of the prettiest little lakes in New Zealand, to the historic goldmining settlement of Arrowtown, whose main street is carefully preserved in its nineteenth century glory, and whose corner pie shop is, as I mentioned earlier, deservedly famous. Try the steak and onion mince, my favourite, eaten outdoors straight from the brown paper bag. More about Arrowtown later.

The well-known Gibbston Valley and Chard farm vineyards are part of the magical grape-growing landscape created very recently along the gorge. The courtyard restaurant at Gibbston Valley is a popular lunchtime venue for both tourists and locals, and on past visits we have returned to Auckland with a few bottles of pinot noir and chardonnay in our luggage. The winery has a cheese factory and a wine cave, dug deep into the hillside, and offers wine tasting there as well as in the shop adjacent to the restaurant. Five years ago, Chard Farm vineyard was reached by a lumpy rutted road, a *track* actually, terrifyingly narrow and with a sheer drop to the river below, cut into the hillside. I looked across the gorge hoping to find that it had been widened, never mind the ruts, but couldn't tell. On that visit I had come away clutching some good rose wine, hoping I would get back home safely to enjoy it.

I was on the lookout for the Peregrine vineyard, the business end of which turned out to be housed dramatically in a recently-built, modern steel and concrete building. A few years ago I had drunk some Peregrine chardonnay and had nearly died with delight. It's hard to forget a really superb wine, and I was looking forward to visiting their cellar. We bought a case of the excellent Pinot Noir 2001, and a mixed case of riesling and rose wines. We haven't tried the riesling yet, but the pinot noir and rose wines are smooth, succulent, and utterly delicious. It was quite a surprise to the wine world when Central Otago started to produce good wines for it is the world's southernmost wine region, but the alluvial schist soil, cold winters and hot dry summers, plus the shelter afforded by neighbouring mountain ranges, provide the perfect cool climate conditions needed to grow grapes of outstanding quality.

If you want to visit some of the 24 wineries in the region, you will find most of them concentrated along the Kawarau Gorge, around Cromwell and Bannockburn, and between Clyde and Alexandra. The Cental Otago Winegrowers' Association produces a map and information brochure which can be obtained from local Visitor Information Centres.

We made the obligatory stop at the Kawarau Bridge Historic Reserve to watch the brave fools getting their nerves ready to do the A.J. Hackett bungy jump from the high bridge over the river. I delight in seeing the interplay of fear, bravado, panic, and then stoic resolve which passes over the face of everyone before they take the plunge, and I consider bungy-jumping to be one of the very finest of spectator sports!

For *The Lord of the Rings* fans, the entrance to Chard Farm vineyard, opposite the bungy jump, indicates a site of the River Anduin. I noticed that some tourists had stopped their campervans by the side of the road for a look down at the location. If you wish to take a rafting trip down the Anduin past the location of the Argonath, the Extreme Green Rafting Company, (ph. (03) 442 8517, email: bookings@nzraft.com, www.nzraft.com) whose office is located in Shotover Street, Queenstown, will arrange the trip for you. Ian Brodie in *The Lord of the Rings Location Guidebook* which, as I have already written, is a must-have book for devotees, mentions that two trips are run – one with 'action-packed rafting', and 'a softer option which doesn't require wetsuits, for the less adventurous'.

By now, we were intent on getting to Queenstown and setting up camp for the night. We resisted the temptation to turn off at Lake Hayes and visit Arrowtown, one of our favourite places because it is so gentle and *nice*, and kept on the highway past the turnoff to Frankton and the airport, located the Creeksyde Queenstown Top 10 Holiday Park, a five star establishment, in Robins Road, and booked in for two nights for a total of $54.

Queenstown has a reputation for doing things well, and this camp was exceptionally good, the best one we stayed in on our travels around New Zealand. I can think of only one other camping ground in Europe that surpasses it, Camping Girasole situated in the hills behind the town of Figline Valdarno, outside Florence in Italy, and that camp is huge, with its own supermarket, several restaurants, even a hairdresser and medical centre, and really not to be compared with this small and intimate Queenstown camp. Creeksyde claims to be 'The World's First Environmentally Certified Holiday Park', and is run in exacting European style by Tonnie and Erna Spijkerbosch.

The main building is very Swiss Alpine in architecture and decoration. The attractive lounge has comfortable sofas, a wonderful old organ, and a chimney breast painted in central European style with colourful folk figures and flowers. The furniture in the adjacent dining area has wooden tables and chairs which would be at home in any chalet, a change from the bland Formica tops and cold metal frames encountered so often elsewhere. The superb kitchen has four Rinnai gas stove tops, plus microwave ovens, and the attention to detail even includes fresh Steelo soap pads provided at each sink, and containers of salt and pepper, tomato ketchup, mustard and Vegemite on the serving counters. Every possible need is catered for, the beautiful grounds have hard standing for motorhomes, and there is a team of people who seem to do nothing but *clean*. It is the cleanest camp I have ever stayed in. The motorhomes parked around us were all expensive, top-of-the-range vehicles, the standard of camper was very high and, again, we seemed to be the only New Zealanders. Our campervan looked quite humble in comparison with the others. All the region's renowned activities, from bungy jumping, hang and paragliding, skydiving, 4WD trips, jet boating, river surfing, fishing, and side trips to Milford Sound, can be booked from the office. A supermarket and a smart Mediterranean Foods store are adjacent, and the town centre is just five minutes' walk.

We made a bad choice of restaurant for dinner, the Mandarin Chinese Restaurant, up a flight of stairs and overlooking Lake Wakatipu, where the food was awful and overpriced, but the wine, a delicious Allan Scott Sauvignon Blanc 2004 at $29, was not. (The view was magnificent)!

Now to tell you about Queenstown. It is not so much the natural beauty of Queenstown that makes it attractive, it is the *getting there*. You're in love with it well before you arrive, whether you fly in to the charming little airport over the Southern Alps with the lakes glinting bright blue below, or whether you arrive by vehicle and take the rich scenery slowly, smiling with pleasure as vista after vista unfolds before you. It doesn't matter if you approach Queenstown from Mt. Cook, Wanaka, Alexandra, or Te Anau, the drive is stunning, never to be forgotten, past lakes, rivers, fabulous rain forests, mountain ranges, snow-topped peaks, orchards and vineyards, across golden farmlands, or dry tussock high country, through small towns where almost all the buildings are old, in the wooden colonial tradition which is uniquely New Zealand, and where old roses, hollyhocks and dahlias grow in the front gardens; it's all here, in the south of the South Island. It is quite natural, you may think now, that Statistics New Zealand expects a 46 per cent rise in population over the next 21 years in the Queenstown and Lakes Districts (*The Otago Daily Times,* 5-6 March, 2005).

And Queenstown doesn't let you down. The most popular time for tourists who are escaping their Northern Hemisphere winter to visit Queenstown is in the New Zealand summer, when the daytime temperatures are pleasant (although nights can get chilly), when all the roads are open, water sports can be enjoyed on Lake Wakatipu and the rivers, and side trips can easily be made to adjacent tourist attractions like Milford Sound, Lake Te Anau, Lake Manapouri and the Underground Power House at West Arm, which is worth a visit, and Deep Cove. The Mt. Aspiring National Park is a target for mountain climbers and trampers who arrive from all over the world in the summer season. They are a bronzed, very fit and strong-looking bunch of people and lend a touch of rugged outdoor glamour to the town.

Queenstown and its surroundings need to be taken quite slowly, and I recommend a stay of three nights, which will give at least two full days to explore and sightsee properly. The alpine township is small and touristy, and an effort has been made to preserve the original architecture and atmosphere. It hasn't always worked and many commercial buildings are quite out of keeping with the character of the town, but its location and the natural beauty of the lake and mountains make up for it.

The Queenstown Gardens, full of old trees, attractive flower beds and large lawns are situated on a small peninsula to the left as you look up the lake from the waterfront, and are pleasant to stroll in. At the lakefront you can hire boats for fishing, water skiing, or sightseeing around the lakeshore. Queenstown is a very good place to buy outdoor clothing and sports equipment of high quality and practical design. Tourist shops sell hand-knitted goods, and sheepskin rugs and jackets of superlative quality, and will arrange air freight or shipping to other countries.

There is a casino in Beach Street, plenty of bars, cafés and restaurants to choose from, and a pleasant day can be spent walking around the little town, having lunch on the lakeside jetty, taking a vintage steamship ride across the lake to the Walter Peak sheep station for afternoon tea at the homestead and, on return, riding in a Skyline gondola up the hillside behind the town to enjoy the wide view across the lake to the Remarkables Range.

Tourism is the lifeblood of Queenstown and the lakes, and of New Zealand, and you may be interested to know how and when it started. The lack of roads, and rail networks into remote areas, made transport of people and goods on the lakes and rivers an essential part of the establishment of the colony. After all, Maori had been using the waterways as their prime means of travel, communication and exploration for centuries, so the idea was not new. Lake and river cruising expanded quickly, and a paddle steamer service started on Lake Wakatipu in Queenstown in 1868, a service which lasted for 30 years. A commercial paddle steamer service began on Lake Wanaka in 1881, and tourist cruises operated on Lake Rotorua from 1889. Tourists were even prepared to travel down the Buller Gorge to view the scenery! By 1900 many excursions were advertised on Lakes Te Anau and Manapouri, and the steamer TSS *Earnslaw*, launched in 1912, is still in operation on Lake Wakatipu – the lake water is so pure that corrosion of its steel plates is negligible.

I find it astonishing that tourists from Europe and Australia would have wanted to visit New Zealand in its development stages, but they did, and the Government Tourist Department was established in 1901 to cater for their interests.

By 1954 the motor launch had become the only type of commercial vessel in use, and the next challenge, to explore the shallow waterways by boat, was met by C.W.F. Hamilton who invented the jet boat which bears his name, and with its draught of just a few inches enables travel to formerly inaccessible parts of the country.

A favourite drive is the one to Glenorchy, 45 kilometres away at the head of the lake, where the local pub serves excellent fish and chips and you can take a jet boat ride on the Dart River. As you pass through Closeburn Bay, eight kilometres from Queenstown, look across to the pine trees on your left where some filming was done for the finale of *The Lord of the Rings – The Fellowship of the Ring*. Just four kilometres past Closeburn, at Twelve Mile Delta, are a number of tracks to take you to the site of Ithilien.

It is possible to drive further on from Glenorchy to Paradise. On the way you will pass the place where Gandalf rode to Isengard and, further on, a forest site used for the Fellowship entering Lothlorien. The road is listed as 'Other Roads' in my road atlas, but I would expect it to be sealed, though unmarked. If you wish to enter this area, the easiest option is to take an excursion with Dart River Safaris, many of whose guides worked on *The Lord of the Rings*. Dart River Safaris is situated at 27 Shotover Street, Queenstown, or in Mull Street, Glenorchy (free phone 0800 327 853, phone (03) 442 9992, www.dartriver.co.nz). Reservations are essential.

The second drive we love to do, and it is a completely different journey from the one to Glenorchy, is the one along Gorge Road to Malaghan Road, past Arthur's Point to Arrowtown about 20 kilometres away. Once clear of the environs of Queenstown, the road runs alongside flat grazing paddocks against which the slopes of Coronet Peak ski field provide a picturesque backdrop. Arrowtown, situated on the Arrow River, is a pretty settlement, and worth a visit. Many of the old stone cottages are still there, and the short and distinctive main street, viewed from either end, looks much as it did 150 years ago in its goldmining heyday. The old shop facades and some of the interiors have been retained, and it is entirely pleasant to shop for arts and crafts, souvenirs, all sheepskin products, and outdoor clothing. If you gagged at the prices asked for jade on the West Coast, there is a store here selling off-cuts where you can pick up a polished piece to use as a paperweight or, as I do, to add to my stone and rock bowl.

The local museum has admirably re-created the historic pioneering past of the town, and if you wish to enjoy an excellent dinner, Saffron Restaurant has been listed by *Conde Nast Traveller* as one of the world's 100 most exciting restaurants. I haven't managed to dine there yet, but it is near the top of my Unfinished Business List.

The famous Millbrook Resort, near the corner of Malaghan Road and Lake Hayes Road and approached by a long, tree-lined drive, is renowned for its style of villa accommodation set in beautifully landscaped grounds, and its golf course. Lunch or dinner outdoors by the small millstream is an attractive option if the weather is warm. M. and I have stayed there many times, and if you feel like ditching your campervan and having a night or two of luxury, this is a good place to choose.

Two days in Queenstown will pass very quickly. If you have had a lot of hard driving to do in order to cover distance in a short time, as we did, it is a relaxing town in which to rest up and recover. Of course, I am looking at it from the perspective of an older traveller. If you are younger, and fit, or even just plain adventurous, then Queenstown covers the gamut of exciting outdoor pursuits better than anywhere else in New Zealand. In summer, you can now take the chairlift to the top of Coronet Peak, clutching hold of your mountain bike, and bike all the way down to the bottom. Details of 4WD off-road tours and safaris, off-road motorcycle tours, hang gliding and paragliding, sky diving, more mountain biking, bungy jumping, canyon rope swing, fly-by-wire flights, jetboating, horse riding and white water sledging are given in the free Queenstown Visitor Guide, available everywhere (www.queenstownvisitorguide.com).

Queenstown Combos, (www.combos.co.nz) as the name suggests, specialises in combinations of adventure activities that give better value than individually purchased trips. For example, their Shotover Canyon Combo combines a Shotover Canyon rope swing, a jet boat ride on the Shotover River, a helicopter flight deep into Skippers Canyon, and whitewater rafting down the Shotover River, duration a full day, for a cost of $355 per adult. The price includes a sauna and hot shower, and refreshments.

Extreme Air (free phone 0800 727 245, www.extremeair.co.nz) specialises in both hang gliding and tandem paragliding, and charges $185 per glide. Extreme Green Rafting, already mentioned above, which specialises in rafting on the Kawarau and Shotover Rivers, will combine jet boating, bungy jumping, or a helicopter ride with rafting.

Fly-by-Wire, Rees Street, Queenstown (phone (03) 442 2116, www.flybywire.co.nz) has an adventure flight lasting six minutes, billed as the world's fastest ride, '...the closest you'll ever get to taking control of a fighter plane', and '...aerobatics on a leash'. Intending aviators don a red flight suit and a secure harness, and lie face down in an open rocket-style 'plane', which is held by a cable to a support spanning the valley. The pilot directs the speed and direction of the plane as it swoops around the canyon; the record speed is 171 kilometres per hour. Bookings include transfers by 4WD vehicles.

Reservations are essential for the popular Shotover Jet Boat rides which depart from Arthur's Point. You can book at your campground, or by email: reservations@shotoverjet.co.nz. Their website is www.shotoverjet.com.

If you wish to spend more time in the Queenstown-Lakes District and explore on foot the stupendous scenery of the South Island high country, it is worth considering the option of walking the Routeburn Track. The *Lonely Planet Blue List* has included the walk in its Top 10 list of Most Awesome Treks (*The New Zealand Herald*, 10 January 2006). Ultimate Hikes (freephone 0800 768 832, www.ultimatehikes.co.nz) runs a guided three day, two night walk along the track costing $1,090 per adult, and a longer walk, the Grand Traverse, taking six days and five nights, costing $1,475 per adult. M. has walked the Grand Traverse twice in the last decade. Tourists from all over the world do it, many friendships are forged, and no one forgets the experience. Costs include transport, accommodation in fully-serviced lodges, meals, backpacks and rain jackets. You will need your own sturdy tramping boots and suitable clothing, all of which can be purchased at the last minute in Queenstown. The daytime temperatures on the track can be quite warm in summer.

I've mentioned a few of *The Lord of the Rings* sites in this chapter, but there are many more, for a large part of the filming was done around Queenstown. At the Info&Track shop at 37 Shotover Street (phone (03) 442 9708, www.infotrack.co.nz) you can book 4WD excursions, jet boat safaris, and horse treks to *The Lord of the Rings* locations; and at the Off Road Adventure Centre at 61a

Shotover Street (free phone 0800 147 858, www.offroad.co.nz) you can book for a Discover the Rings 4WD Adventure Tour. Trips depart at 8 a.m. and 1 p.m. daily.

If I were a true fan of J.R.R. Tolkien's epic, and had travelled to New Zealand with the express intention of visiting as many of the film locations as possible, I would do nearly everything by helicopter. It is the easiest and quickest way to get to the numerous locations. In his location guidebook, Ian Brodie recommends a local helicopter company, Heliworks Queenstown Helicopters (free phone 0800 464 354, phone (03) 441 4011, www.heliworks.co.nz) which was contracted exclusively to Peter Jackson for aerial filming and transportation of cast to film locations in *The Lord of the Rings*. The company is situated at Queenstown Airport and offers four different *The Lord of the Rings* flights; one of 40 minutes' duration at a cost of $320 per person, one of 1 hour 15 minutes' duration which includes two landings and costs $590 per person, the third of 2 hours 30 minutes' duration which includes three landings and costs $1,230 per person, and the fourth of 3 hours 30 minutes' duration which includes a flight over Milford Sound and has five landings, at a cost of $1,575 per person. Each flight is for two people.

It would be a pity to leave Queenstown without having made a trip to Milford Sound, New Zealand's revered natural beauty spot and a must-see wonder for every tourist. The pictures of the sound and its majestic peaks appear regularly in advertisements for New Zealand and in global travel literature, and it must be one of the most photographed tourist destinations in the world. I have never met a visitor to this country who doesn't rate it as one of the most splendid sights on offer. Independent travellers who arrive in Queenstown should make a visit to Milford Sound a priority.

If you plan to travel Queenstown-Milford Sound-Queenstown, then two days should be allowed for the drive. Don't be tempted to take a day tour bus. The return distance is almost 600 kilometres, you will be on the road for at least 10 hours, and will have no more than two hours in Milford Sound, if you are lucky.

I recommend departing from Queenstown very early in the morning, well ahead of the tour buses which leave at about 7 a.m., and driving directly to Milford Sound on State Highway 6 and State Highway 94. The journey to Te Anau is straightforward, but the road from then on climbs steeply and the narrow Homer Tunnel has a gradient of 1 in 10. Dave Chowdhury, in *Driving Scenic New Zealand: A Guide to Touring New Zealand by Road* gives excellent information and advice on driving in this remote corner of New Zealand, and his book is a worthwhile addition to your travel literature.

The New Zealand Camping Guide, South Island recommends staying at the Milford Sound Lodge (details in the Appendix), but you will need to make a prior booking as only six of the sites have power. The lodge has a restaurant, Internet access, a small shop on site, and no TV or radio. An off-peak cruise on the sound can be undertaken after 2 p.m. when the tour buses have departed for the return journey back to Queenstown. The township is notorious for its sandflies and it is absolutely essential to wear insect repellent and to spray the interior of your motorhome before retiring to bed.

An early departure from Milford Sound the next morning will see you back at the junction of State Highway 94 with State Highway 6 in three hours, from where you can return to Queenstown, or continue east across South Otago and Southland.

You can, of course, fly from Queenstown to Milford Sound, a good option if you do not wish to undertake the long drive there, or are short of time. Glenorchy Air (phone (03) 442 2207, www.glenorchy.net.nz) situated at 91 McBride Street, Queenstown, operates a variety of regional scenic flights as well as flights to Milford Sound. Their four-hour Milford Fly Cruise Fly tour operates all year, and costs from $345 to $370 per person, depending on the time of day you wish to fly. The price includes the cruise on the sound.

CHAPTER 21

A MARVELLOUS DRIVE ACROSS OTAGO TO DUNEDIN TO SEE THE ROYAL ALBATROSS COLONY

I decided to take advantage of the excellent laundry facilities at the Creeksyde campground, hoping that this would be the last wash load necessary before arriving back in Auckland. My minimal clothing had performed remarkably well and my jeans, already worn continuously for several days and destined to remain worn for another 10 days until we reached Christchurch, were still looking good. Blue denim is the most satisfactory fabric to wear when travelling on the road. It is comfortable, sheds creases, is easily sponged down, and doesn't advertise itself unfavourably unless the wearer sports tattoos and body piercings. At 68 years I don't consider I am too old to wear well-cut jeans, and they are a mainstay of my wardrobe. M. now prefers to wear Ralph Lauren chinos in dark navy, and finds they have all the virtues of jeans and can go satisfactorily from campsite to restaurant.

M. spent the morning reading the local newspaper. He can make a newspaper last longer than anyone I know. It was also a sign that he felt tired; I suggested we quit Queenstown immediately and that instead of driving the 290 kilometres to Dunedin the following day as originally planned, we go just as far as Alexandra, 92 kilometres, and spend the night there. This would break the journey up satisfactorily. He agreed, I whizzed across the road to the Mediterranean Foods store and spent $81 on smart food for a quick lunch, and fillet steak, a vegetable dish, and salad ingredients for dinner, and off we went. It was 2 p.m., and we felt we were too far into the day to ask for a night's refund so we drove out quietly.

It felt *so good* to be on the road again! The drive back to Lowburn along the Kawarau River Gorge was soon over, and we crossed the bridge over Lake Dunstan, bypassing Cromwell and its old historic precinct, and joined State Highway 8 to Clyde and Alexandra. This section of the road was built well above the water when the Cromwell Gorge was flooded to create the Clyde hydro-electric power station. We had it completely to ourselves as we drove alongside the bare, rocky, dry hills, lamenting the loss of the productive land which had existed prior to the formation of Lake Dunstan. We stopped at the Clyde Dam lookout, but the information signboards had been vandalised, or else removed, and apart from marvelling at the huge scale of the enterprise, there was little of interest.

Alexandra, in the middle of New Zealand's 'fruit bowl', is one of the hottest places in New Zealand in summer, with temperatures regularly hitting 30 degrees Celsius and over. The local landmark is the Clock on the Hill facing Centennial Drive, and the town is extremely pleasant to visit with that placid aura which pervades so much of the surrounding countryside.

We eventually found the Alexandra Holiday Park situated to the right off State Highway 8 on the way out of town. This very large camp, which holds 4,000 people in summer and is quite well landscaped with plenty of willow trees to provide shade from the summer sun, was a terrible let-down after the previous night's accommodation in Queenstown. It is not the sort of camp where you are likely to see many Maui vans. Only one ablution block had hot water in the showers, so we parked nearby on the lawn, where the grass was too long to make it comfortable to walk on, particularly in the heavy dew the next morning. The ablutions were character-forming, situated in a concrete block bunker with one dim bulb to light everything – economy taken *too far*. The showers had chilly stainless steel walls, a raw concrete floor, and the toilets were dark spooky holes, but fortunately clean (as far as I could see). I decided to skip my evening shower. The charge for two people for the night was $22.

We had driven past the Alexandra Tourist Park in Ngapara Street on our way to this camp, but had been put off by the approach through an industrial area. It might have been the better choice, for it reads quite well in the camping guidebook. I give details of both camps in the Appendix, because Alexandra is the central town in a large region, and a useful overnight stop.

Our Holiday Park, situated by the Clutha River, had many permanent caravans in storage, and several static caravans in our area occupied by elderly people were completely set up for year-round living. Opposite us was a large trailer with four wheels, all mod cons, a Winnebago-style retractable living room which jutted out on one side, a TV aerial, and a little rotary clothesline, doll-sized, erected by the back hedge. An expensive 4WD vehicle was parked alongside. It was obviously a permanent holiday retreat for the couple, in their sixties, and I wondered what brought them, and everyone else, to this camp, year after year. Was it the river? Or the hot summer climate?

Thank goodness I had shopped for dinner before we left Queenstown – there wasn't a restaurant or a store in sight. It's surprising what good steak, oven-roasted mixed vegetables, a rocket and avocado salad, and banoffee pie will do to lift one's mood. M. went across to do the dishes – one pan, two knives, forks, and spoons – because he always likes to chat to the other men in the kitchen. He came back and said they were seasonal fruit pickers, all middle-aged, who were living cheaply at the camp while working in the surrounding orchards.

The next morning was fine and hot with a clear sky. We left the Holiday Park at 10 a.m., without regrets, and drove back into Alexandra to shop at a New World supermarket I had noticed the day before. It was quite an experience! I have always thought that the shoppers in a local supermarket constitute an excellent cross-section of the local population. There was no cross-section this morning, in this large supermarket – *all* the shoppers, and there were many, were elderly. There were no housewives buying supplies while the children were in school, not even one mother with pre-school children! The age of the cars in the car park indicated the age of the shoppers, too. For the first time since leaving Auckland, M. and I, in our well-worn camping clothes, looked smartly dressed compared to everyone else. 'Nippy morning,' said one woollen-wrapped old dear to another as we left the supermarket. I read, later on in Dunedin, that many people of working age live in the city during the week and return to their homes in Alexandra for the weekend. It's a drive of 200 kilometres, just two hours on the good road through Roxburgh and Lawrence.

But for me, the highlight of this supermarket was a neat row of sausages labelled 'Blackball', and I bought several for dinner in the campervan that night. What a treat! This was to be almost the last night I cooked dinner in the van, the last night, in spite of very good promises to myself, being in Kaikoura; both were meals of Blackball sausages, absolutely delicious, and I know that my culinary efforts in the campervan ended on a very high note.

Before I continue describing the rest of the day's journey, I want to mention that if you time your trip to New Zealand in the spring, then the Alexandra Blossom Festival, held at the end of September, is absolutely outstanding, with floats and parades through the streets, and it coincides happily with the recent opening up to the public at Lawrence, 100 kilometres west of Dunedin, of 10 hectares of daffodils planted in the 1890s. The daffodil garden is situated at Wetherstons, outside Lawrence, and directions can be obtained from the Gabriel's Junction shop.

We took State Highway 8 over the bridge behind the town which crosses the Clutha River, green, mysterious and utterly beautiful here, passed a sign saying the road to Roxburgh was open, and were immediately in open country. The absence of dreary suburbs and industrial clutter made it easy to understand why Alexandra is always spoken of in glowing terms. The undulating highway was newly-surfaced, with excellent roadmarkings and views forever over the dry, rather surreal landscape which sprouted unusual rocky outcrops of schist. It was just the sort of country that rabbits love. The wide Clutha River flowed gently on the left, serene and reed-fringed and home to small ducks in the sheltered waters. Rows of giant poplars acted as windbreaks across the wide valley, and evidence of early settlement was everywhere, especially in the stone cottages by the roadside, some derelict, built from the local rock. It was a spectacular landscape in early autumn, and would be even more so in a month or two with snow on the hills. Deer and very woolly sheep grazed in the paddocks; in fact, there were sheep *everywhere*.

M. thanked God that the highway had been reconstructed. We were driving above the old road in parts, and could look down and see how hellish it was. I noticed that the hay was not baled individually, but forced into long turquoise (hideous) plastic tubes through which the outlines of the bales could be seen. Lake Roxburgh, long and skinny with water of the deepest blue-green, which was formed when the Clutha River was dammed for the construction of the Roxburgh hydro-electric power station, appeared on the left, and we descended into the town of Roxburgh.

What a delight! Apricots, plums, green grapes, peaches, nectarines and walnuts were for sale at roadside stalls. A charming house called Walnut Cottage advertised itself as a Bed and Breakfast stopover, and at Tom's Orchard we could have picked our own fruit, a pleasant activity. I often buy the large and luscious Roxburgh apricots in Auckland, and every two years make a double batch of the very best apricot chutney in the world. I feel a recipe coming on!

Apricot Chutney

From *The Constance Spry Cookery Book* by
Constance Spry and Rosemary Hume
J.M. Dent and Sons Limited, London, 1957 reprint

2 ½ lb. apricots, weighed when split and stoned
1 ½ lb. onions
½ lb. raisins
1 lb. brown sugar
1 tablespoon mustard seed
1 level teaspoon chilli powder
1 dessertspoon salt
1 pint malt vinegar
grated rind and juice of 1 orange
½ teaspoon cinnamon
1 level teaspoon turmeric
2 oz. shelled walnuts
grated rind and juice of 1 lemon

Put all the ingredients in the preserving pan with the exception of the walnuts. Simmer till soft and pulpy, add walnuts, and pot.

All the towns of Central Otago have lovely old stone public buildings, and Roxburgh has a fine, white-steepled church and Sunday School building next door. This is a most attractive town with well-kept front gardens where hollyhocks and roses bloom profusely, and a handsome golf course. I have never seen so many golf courses in my life as I did in our drive around New Zealand; every small town has one. M. passed a colourful little bus whose signwriting on the bodywork said 'Hit the road, Jack', a first line sentiment I can thoroughly endorse.

When you look at a map and plot a route across unfamiliar territory, it is easy to tell if you will be crossing mountains or flat plains, or following rivers, or passing through villages, towns or cities. What you cannot know unless you have done some research is what you will actually *see*. This was turning out to be a cracker of a drive across Central Otago, completely different in natural and man-made landscapes, architecture, agriculture, farming and history from anywhere else in New Zealand. Apart from the known tourist centres of Rotorua, Taupo and Queenstown, and, later, Mt. Cook, this was the first time we had seen dozens of campervans on the road, all intent on visiting this lovely rural countryside, well away from the usual routes and famous sights. There was no end to the apple, pear, apricot and nectarine orchards, the sheep, and the tall shelter belts of poplar trees, beautiful plantings of conifers and cypresses, the ravishing pastoral views, and the stately serenity of the Clutha River and the plains in the early autumn sunlight. At Millers Flat, where there is a campground with 75 powered sites and an annual Boxing Day rodeo, tiny two-bedroom cottages lined the road, most of them inhabited and in a good state of repair. It's at times like this that I wish I could paint.

State Highway 8 crossed the Clutha River at Beaumont. We were sorry to leave the river behind, but you are never far from water in New Zealand and at Lawrence we found a perfect roadside pull-in beside a stream with large trees, picnic tables, and mown grass, where we stopped to enjoy a cup of tea and a sandwich in the sunshine. A middle-aged couple pulled up alongside in their own stylish motorhome which they had humorously named 'The Apartment'. M. asked me if I thought we should buy our own motorhome, too. I recollected Brian from Invercargill whom we had met at Ninety Mile Beach. He had purchased his campervan second-hand from a company, Maui, perhaps, since it was identical in size and interior layout to ours, and he and his wife had explored every corner of New Zealand in it. Regular campers are always relaxed, resourceful, positive and happy people, and after just three weeks on the road I already felt better than I had for months. How simple to have one's own vehicle, fitted and equipped to one's own requirements, a holiday house available at a moment's notice to take us to ever-changing venues. The idea was tempting, and as I write this nine months later, even more so! We will see.

The rocky, arid summer land south of Alexandra was just a memory, now. Here the orchards were hemmed in by round, low hills and green pasture, obviously the result of higher rainfall. We'd never ever seen so many sheep. Lawrence is a delightful little town, famous for its gold mining heritage. In 1861 gold was found by Gabriel Read in nearby Gabriel's Gully, and about 15,000 diggers flocked in to mine the area which eventually yielded millions of pounds worth of gold. Errol Brathwaite, in *The Companion Guide to the South Island of New Zealand*, writes that 'Gold was here in such quantities that men were able to tear up clumps of tussock and shake nuggets from the roots'.

Read's discovery of gold brought the unexpected benefit of reliable transport to large parts of the South Island, for an Australian entrepreneur who had run a successful coaching service on the Victorian goldfields seized the opportunity to do so in New Zealand. Mid-nineteenth century roads were no more than rough tracks, but the Cobb & Co. coaches established a fairly quick service between Dunedin and the goldfields, making the journey in nine hours rather than two days on horseback. Transport soon expanded west across central Otago to Queenstown and south to Balclutha, and to Canterbury, and the distinctive red coaches provided an excellent daily service from the main centres. Cobb & Co.'s success inspired other regions to follow suit and pioneer many of the routes travelled on today. Many New Zealand artists have captured on canvas the stirring sight of a team of galloping horses drawing their heavy coach across the dry Otago plains, whipped on by the driver and raising clouds of dust, and the best paintings manage to evoke the spirit of romance and derring-do of those not so distant days.

Although the landscape began to change to manuka scrub country after Waitahuna, the huge sheep population didn't. There were thousands of sheep mustered into large paddocks; I suspected they were due for the abattoir. The 250 kilometre journey from Queenstown to the turnoff at Clarkesville onto State Highway 1, to Milton and Dunedin, had taken us through gorges and barren high country, across rivers, past the modern marvels of hydro-electric power stations, alongside lakes and lush green pastures, past orchards where laden trees blazed with late summer fruit, and across a countryside which reeked of its very early settlement, and where a few human beings shared the land with millions of sheep. It was a heady mix, and very memorable.

State Highway 1 was billed as 'The Southern Scenic Route', and further south from Milton I know that is an apt description, but after the journey we had just completed on State Highway 8 this stretch of road to Dunedin was disappointing. Milton is just another main street town, not exciting, or pretty, with some of its old cottages sadly in need of painting and repairs. Any one of them would be worth a small fortune if popped onto a piece of land in Parnell or Ponsonby in Auckland, and renovated. We crossed the Taieri Plains, prone to flooding by the adjacent Taieri River which was stop-banked in places, and suddenly we were on the outskirts of Dunedin, our destination for the next two nights. The last 50 kilometres had flown by.

Our camp for the night was to be the Aaron Lodge Top 10 Holiday Park (details in the Appendix) and to find it we exited the southern motorway into Dunedin at Kaikorai Valley Concord, and drove along Kaikorai Road for four kilometres. The camp is situated in a light industrial and commercial area, and the entrance is not promising, but it is the only city campground in Dunedin and is very good indeed. The grounds are groomed with beautiful gardens, have 40 power sites, the excellent kitchen facilities and ablutions are spotless, and are protected by covered walkways. We enjoyed our two nights there, for which we were charged $54. Our pitch, at the end of a row of campervans, was adjacent to a rose garden backed by ivy-clad walls, hydrangeas, and hedges. The vans kept piling in for the night, and soon our level was full and later arrivals were directed up onto higher terraces.

As soon as we had parked on our gravelled pitch, I rang Citibus Newton (phone (03) 477 5577) to book a one hour bus tour of Dunedin at 10.15 a.m. the following morning, and a four hour trip to the Albatross Centre at Taiaroa Head on the Otago Peninsula in the afternoon, leaving Dunedin at 2.30 p.m. and returning at approximately 6.30 p.m. The tour of the albatross colony was at 4 p.m., and would take one hour. Tickets for two for the city bus tour cost $30, and for the albatross tour $98, and the buses would depart from the i-Site Visitor Centre in the Octagon.

I always find my fellow campers interesting. We had hardly settled in when a large Apollo motorhome parked opposite, and out stepped four very pretty young women with perfect figures, wearing tiny bikinis, who rushed off to the heated indoor swimming pool. A dozen pairs of male eyes followed them, M.'s included. You don't often see four girls camping together in New Zealand. A curvaceous beauty in the van behind us undid several packets of ham, salami, and sliced sausage, opened a tin of beetroot, laid it all out attractively on a plate on the picnic table, took the tops off two Tui beers, and her middle-aged, rather seedy, Elvis look-alike partner appeared from the kitchen carrying a big pot of mashed potatoes that he had cooked there. I had an idea. I despatched M. across to the kitchen to do likewise, saying it would save our gas, and he had a good time in that essentially male domain talking in English to anyone who understood it, or trying out his fractured German on others! I opened a bottle of Grove Mill Marlborough Chardonnay, nice, but not full-flavoured enough, and pan-fried our Blackball pork sausages bought earlier that day in Alexandra, an age ago. I tossed a mixed salad with a few tablespoons of Paul Newman's finest, and sat down peacefully with a brimming glass of wine to await the arrival of the cooked potatoes.

After dinner we had long, hot showers, our first for two days, and retired happy, and very full, to bed.

The following morning a taxi took us the two kilometres from the camp to the i-Site Information Centre in the Octagon, where we boarded a bus for a superb guided tour of the city. I had never visited Dunedin before, it was about 50 years since M. had, and this was the easiest way to become acquainted with the principal places of interest. M. and I take a bus tour in every new city we visit, and particularly enjoy the hop-on-hop-off style of tour.

We visited First Church, a very fine example of Gothic Revival architecture perfectly executed in Oamaru stone, the somewhat bizarre yet interesting railway station, New Zealand's grandest, with its Royal Doulton wall tiles and frieze, and the famous educational institutions of Otago University, Otago Boys' High School and Otago Girls' High School, all of which were endowed with gold-mining money. We were given some interesting statistics; the population of Dunedin is about 120,000, of whom 25,000 are students, and who bring $2.5 million to the city every week! The bus took us slowly through the seven kilometre long Town Belt, a cool and shady domain which extends across the hills above the city. Here, if a tree falls down, it is left to rot and re-seed naturally in order to preserve the ecology of the area. We visited the Botanic Gardens where every September and October enthusiasts arrive from all over the world to see the rhododendrons in bloom. (There is another very fine garden, the Glenfalloch Woodland Garden, on the Otago Peninsula). Garden lovers will find plenty to interest them in Dunedin. Many private gardens are open for viewing, and a helpful brochure entitled *Dunedin Gardens* giving all details is available at the Information Centre in the Octagon.

Dunedin had a rocky start, for the early occupants of the port were runaway sailors who, with little prospect of employment in the area, earned a living by selling wild pork to the whalers at the Heads. It was not until 1848 that the first of the Scottish Presbyterians who arrived with the intention of setting up the first Scottish settlement in New Zealand under the auspices of the Free Church of Scotland, and who were to elevate the city to its later status, set about transforming the settlement, described as a 'hole', to a liveable town. Otago had been chosen as the most suitable site to found the new Edinburgh of the South, the beautiful scenery of the long, bush-clad harbour having much to do with their choice.

Architecturally, Dunedin is the finest of the four major cities in New Zealand, with perfectly preserved Victorian buildings dominating the inner commercial centre and suburbs. The Scots quickly set about providing the institutions and amenities they had known in their own country, and created a city of 'firsts' with the establishment of New Zealand's first university and girls' high school, first city council, the first public botanical gardens and art gallery, the first cable car, and the first daily newspaper, *The Otago Daily Times*. The first big New Zealand businesses were started there; some eventually shifted their head offices north from Dunedin, but the old firms of Cadburys, Fisher and Paykel, and Speights Brewery still have a presence. By the later years of the nineteenth century, Dunedin had become the commercial capital of New Zealand. It was a vibrant, cultured and progressive city when Wellington, today's capital, was little more than a shantytown; today, it is a university city.

We made a mistake by not visiting the 35-room Olveston mansion built between 1904 and 1906 and incorporating all the skills of the nineteenth century craftsmen who worked on it, and all the more marvellous because, as Errol Brathwaite writes in *The Companion Guide to the South Island of New Zealand*, '…if you've seen larger, grander houses, please do not forget that this house was built in a place which is exceedingly remote from the sources both of its inspiration and its furniture'.

It is a very grand home, designed by Sir Ernest George, a renowned domestic architect of the time, and parts of it, such as the English oak staircase, were shipped out from England. Every architectural and decorative detail is perfect, in its original state, much of the furniture, silver, rugs and ornaments are still in place, and it offers an authentic glimpse, unduplicated elsewhere in the country, of a grand colonial lifestyle. The comforts and innovations incorporated for both the family, and for the staff, were ahead of their time in New Zealand. Even the crockery and cutlery used by the family, and the kitchen utensils used by the servants, are set in their appropriate places. Our bus tour guide waxed lyrical about the historic home, and it was not until I arrived back in Auckland and read about it in a brochure that I realised what we had missed. (Larnach Castle, built in the 1870s and mentioned later in this chapter, is the rival to the grandeur of Olveston.)

At the conclusion of the tour we strolled down the unimpressive main shopping street, George Street, found a foodhall, and had an un-magical lunch at The Magic Wok. You can't win 'em all. The Public Library had a free Internet service, and M. was able to catch up on his emails while we filled in time before our afternoon tour. If you are in this situation yourself, and the weather is wet, the Otago Settlers Museum at 32 Queens Gardens, open seven days, is an excellent place to learn more about the region and its people. The well-indexed photograph gallery is worth visiting if you have ancestors who emigrated to Dunedin, for the staff are happy to help you locate their photos, if they exist. We were told on our bus tour that the Transport Gallery attracts train buffs who come to view the steam trains, one of which, a double-ended Fairlie called 'Josephine', is one of only five surviving world-wide.

At 2.30 p.m. we were seated in a comfortable coach for a tour of the Otago Peninsula. What an afternoon! I boarded in a state of high excitement. I'm not a dedicated nature-lover – I just like being outdoors – but *all my life* I had wanted to see an albatross, and now I was about to do so.

My curiosity had been aroused at college, when we had to study Samuel Taylor Coleridge's poem *The Rime of the Ancient Mariner.* After the albatross, the bird of good omen, has been shot by the Ancient Mariner, the ship becomes becalmed, and the sailors' distress is described memorably, and evocatively:

> 'Day after day, day after day,
> We stuck, nor breath nor motion;
> As idle as a painted ship
> Upon a painted ocean.

'Water, water, everywhere,
And all the boards did shrink;
Water, water, everywhere,
Nor any drop to drink.'

Those lines, with those of Thomas Gray's *Elegy in a Country Churchyard*, and William Wordsworth's *Daffodils,* have remained with me for 54 years, proof of the staying-power of good poetry, and a testament to a thorough education. Cows and daffodils I already knew; how wonderful to be able to see an albatross, at last.

Our bus driver, Richard, who looked 45 years old but later owned up to being 60, was a treasure. For the hour that it took him to drive to the Albatross Centre, he delivered a non-stop commentary on the early history of the Otago Harbour and Port Chalmers. This splendid drive along the coastal road and around the bays to Taiarua Head, and the return journey, also with commentary, high across the hilly spine of the peninsula, is hard to forget because of the degree of difficulty, especially for a bus driver, in negotiating the tight, narrow bends on both stretches. At times I would rather not have had the experience of taking the top road back; if you do, don't sit in a window seat on the left hand side!

Scariness aside, no tour of any length around New Zealand is complete without a visit to the Otago Peninsula (www.otago-peninsula.co.nz). You can, of course, take your own vehicle – the large car park at Taiaroa Head was full of motorhomes – and much of what this country does best can be encapsulated into a day's easy sightseeing. The peninsula is a renowned eco-tourism area and offers opportunities to view not only the albatross colony, but also rare yellow-eyed penguins, many water and wading birds, and seals and sealions. Elm Wildlife Tours (freephone 0800 356 563), a New Zealand eco-tourism award winner, runs small group wildlife tours to view albatrosses, penguins, fur seals and Hooker sealions, as does Back to Nature Tours (freephone 0800 477 0484, email: bookings@backtonaturetours.co.nz), and Wild Earth Adventures (ph. 473 6535, www.wildearth.co.nz) offers sea-kayaking around the peninsula for sightings of all of the above.

Glenfalloch Woodland Gardens in Macandrew Bay are just nine kilometres from the city, and have superb displays of peonies, roses, rhododendrons, azaleas, fuschias, and magnolia trees in the mature gardens which also contain many native trees. The harbourside drive to Wellers Rock is one scenic delight of sandy bays and inlets, lush pastures on the protecting hills, Victorian architecture, and the splendid Larnach Castle, built in the early 1870s, and renowned for its superb plaster ceilings and the grand quality of the wood carving and architectural and decorative accoutrements, including New Zealand antique furniture. The nineteenth century gardens, which are very pretty in spring, have been restored, and as a bonus you can purchase a picnic lunch there to enjoy outdoors. The views over both sides of the peninsula from the castle and grounds are breathtaking. The historic and charming settlement of Portobello has a camping ground, the Portobello Village Tourist Park, at 27 Hereweka Street (ph. (93) 478 0359, email: portobellopark@xtra.co.nz). This is a small, very popular campground just 30 minutes' drive from the city, with excellent facilities. Power sites are $12 per person per night, and the camp is the only place on the peninsula where camping is permitted.

We could have left our tour bus at Wellers Rock jetty and boarded the M.V. *Monarch*, a large, venerable launch, for a one-hour wildlife cruise around the cliffs of the Taiaroa Head to view the albatrosses and other marine activity from the water. Although half the passengers left the bus, I'm glad we didn't. There are plenty of opportunities elsewhere to view aquatic life from the water, but only one place to see the albatrosses close up, on land, at the Royal Albatross Colony. Albatrosses need wind to persuade them to fly, and, for me, wind is the enemy of a comfortable boat experience. We stayed on the bus.

The large Albatross Centre, with its weathered cedar walls and a steel roof painted in an indeterminate olive grey, is skilfully constructed and blends invisibly into its rugged, windswept surroundings. The centre has won the New Zealand Tourism Award for the last five out of six years. H.R.H. Prince Charles was due the next day to see the albatrosses, and when I asked a staff member if everything was ready for his arrival, she rolled her eyes and said they'd had a hectic few weeks, but at least a few things which had needed doing for a long time had finally been attended to. That sounds like the pattern for all Royal Visits!

The centre is run to a timetable, and the endless crowds of tourists are moved along very efficiently. Valuable information is poured forth by photographs, written information, a lecture, and a video presentation, so that by the time you walk up the very steep path on the way to the observatory you will know exactly what you are looking at, and can appreciate the experience. Only about a dozen visitors are allowed at a time into the series of padlocked enclosures that divide the pathway, and a tally is taken frequently, so tight is the security surrounding this rare breeding ground. The day was not particularly windy and we were warned that we might not see the birds fly, but as we were toiling up the path there was a 'whoosh' in the air and one flew immediately overhead, the first flight that day, the guide said. What luck!

The glass-enclosed observatory lookout, closed during the breeding season of 17 September to 23 November, is fitted with plenty of binoculars and a comfortable ledge on which to steady one's elbows. The albatrosses are just a few feet away, and considerable time is allowed for viewing.

Unfortunately, only three birds were 'on site' that afternoon, and I was delighted to note when watching the six o'clock news on television at Omarama the next evening that Prince Charles didn't fare any better either; the one concession to his rank was that he was allowed to walk out onto the tussocky headland which is their habitat, accompanied by a ranger, and crouch down just a few feet away from the birds.

On the return journey the coach took Highcliff Road from Portobello, which, in spite of my fears mentioned earlier, was a thrilling drive above some of the finest coastal scenery in New Zealand. Here we looked out over the bright blue southern Pacific Ocean, and numerous inlets and bays which are home to the peninsula's famed bird life. We arrived back at the i-Site Centre in the Octagon at 6.30 p.m., feeling we had 'done' Dunedin thoroughly, and seen the city and surroundings at their best, in just one memorable day on the buses.

The Italian Café two minutes' walk away up Stuart Street provided a good dinner of calamari with aioli for us both, a porcini and spinach risotto for me, and cannelloni for M., for $55, plus a bottle of Montana Reserve Merlot 2002, very smooth, for $38. A taxi drove us the two kilometres back to the camp, where we discovered a *caravan* had pulled in to a corner site opposite us, and had strung up a load of laundry on makeshift ropes to dry. This was a most attractive and well-run camp and the caravanners should have had the sense to use the laundry dryers and keep their smalls away from public view. Actually, I mention this caravan not because of its exterior decorations, but because it was the only touring caravan we encountered in a camp. All the large vehicles were motorhomes; the caravans were statics and used as holiday homes, and in a month of driving around New Zealand during the busy tourist season we encountered only one caravan being towed on a highway.

CHAPTER 22

TO OAMARU AND ACROSS TO AORAKI MOUNT COOK.

A quick stop before departure from Dunedin the next day at the local Four Square supermarket on Kaikorai Valley Road, not a good example of the genre, where after a tour of the shelves and bins I bought only bread and milk, turned out to be a bonus, for with the end of the trip only one week away I decided henceforth to keep the fridge quite empty so that I wouldn't be tempted to prepare dinner again.

In just 10 minutes we whizzed through the Octagon, past the chic Saturday brunch crowd dining alfresco at Bacchus and Ra Bar Restaurants, and onto State Highway 1, following signs to Timaru on the one-way road system.

M. felt revitalised by his day off from driving, and we pounded along the excellent, well-graded and maintained highway through the rolling countryside north of Dunedin. The land was beautifully treed with pine, oak and macrocarpa trees, and we soon entered Blueskin Bay where the water was so calm that the trees, houses and hills were mirrored double. The pastures had benefited from the wet summer and were very green, with well-conditioned sheep grazing quietly (as they do). We drove through Waikouaiti, a quaint little village which advertised itself as 'The Birthplace of Otago'. The local pharmacy seemed to have closed down permanently, but Eddie Todd the saddle maker was still doing business in a small, red-painted wooden building. There was a petrol station, a pie shop, a dairy, and a 'Tax and More' consultancy. Blink, and you missed it. Yet this was indeed the first permanent settlement in Otago, and dates from about 1838 when a whaler from Sydney named John Jones set up a shore station in the bay, and bought a large tract of fertile land from local Maori. He returned to Sydney and on-sold the land to English migrants who had found the hot Australian summers oppressive. These new settlers established the infrastructure that Jones was seeking of productive farms, food and alcohol supplies, general stores, a Wesleyan Mission, and other accoutrements of a new society, all of which were necessary to maintain his whaling crew and factory processing workers.

The scenery was pastoral, elegiac, holding cattle and sheep, stands of dark pine, small copses of native trees, and freshly-mown hay still waiting to be baled. M. suffered an attack of sneezing and decided to buy some nasal spray, but the only pharmacy we could find in Palmerston, a mid-sized town at the junction of State Highways 1 and 85, was closed, it being a Saturday. At Shag Point, home to seals and yellow-eyed penguins, we entered a wide, open bay flanked by limestone cliffs, with a popular weekend surfing spot at the northern end where the off-road parking was already full of cars disgorging young surfers and families.

Moeraki Beach was a home to pre-European Maori, who named it after the sweet potato, the seeds of which, legend has it, were washed overboard when an ancient canoe travelling from Hawaiiki capsized near Shag Point, and grew into round-formed boulders, a well-photographed geological rarity seen at their best at low tide. We turned off State Highway 1, signposted Kaihinatu, to drive to the beach. M. said I had to see the boulders as they are more famous than the Pancake Rocks. The large car park outside the restaurant and bar, whose rooftop is domed like the rocks, was full of campervans and we had to queue for one to pull out before we could find a place. There was an honesty box at the entrance to the walking track to the beach inviting donations of $2, which I gave, and perhaps it was a good thing to do because the track, particularly on the return leg, was very well maintained and easy to use.

The Moeraki boulders, with unusual 'webbed' surfaces which remind me of giant paperweights, are 4 million years old, the most perfect examples of their kind yet found in the world, and vary greatly in size. They come down from the land and fall into the sea below, which gradually breaks them up. Excavations in the cliff above revealed the shape of a rock which hadn't fallen yet, confirming that the remarkable roundness is not due to the actions of the sea. The beach on which they rest is long and pleasant, and three Japanese tour groups clicked away with their cameras. This would indeed be an easy attraction for a bus tour company to bring them to, with the large car park, restaurant and bar, a 25 minute return journey to see the rocks along an easy walking track, and the added bonus of a short stroll on the firm sand of the beach. Elderly tourists would have no difficulty with the arrangements. However, the rocks are not such a great attraction that a tourist, on a short tour of New Zealand, needs to see them. There are other more significant sights, unless, of course, geology is your passion.

The lunch food at the counter of the restaurant consisted of pre-packed sandwiches, large and doughy filled rolls, and too many cakes, not what we wanted, so we drove on to Oamaru 35 kilometres away. We seemed to have entered red-hot poker and blue agapanthus country, a horrible combination of planting which decorated many domestic roadside boundaries. I know they are both hardy plants which grow well from cuttings and survive dry conditions, but I plead for just one, or the other, to be planted, not both together!

The little town of Herbert, south of Oamaru, had a vintage clothing store, unfortunately closed because it was Saturday. I don't buy vintage clothing for myself, because some of my garments already *are*, but I would have loved to see if anything was for sale from the 1920s and 1930s, an era of elegant dressing, or if the word 'vintage' was merely a euphemism for 'op shop'. I'll never know.

Oamaru, population 13,000, and approached from the south through an avenue of oak trees, is one of the most attractive towns in New Zealand, thanks to its limestone quarries which have provided the stone for the many fine buildings, and also for most of the older public buildings throughout the country. The harbour precinct of well-preserved Victorian buildings built from this fine stone is unique, the atmosphere being such that I felt I should be wearing a crinoline and bonnet as we explored it.

Hungry, we stopped at the nearby Star and Garter for lunch and couldn't believe our luck when two of our favourite dishes were on the menu – fish pie for me, and liver and bacon for M. We almost licked the plates clean. Lunch, which included a glass of wine, a beer, and one coffee, cost just $39.95. There is a move afoot to have Oamaru's beautiful town buildings, the Oamaru harbour, and the harbour precinct declared a World Heritage Site. I asked the café proprietor what she thought of this, and a look of consternation crossed her face. 'It's not the proposition that I'm worried about,' she said, 'it's just that I've got the oldest building in Oamaru out at the back of these premises, and the cost of improving it to World Heritage standard is too much for me. If the plan goes ahead, I may be forced to sell. Also,' she continued, 'once a building is declared a heritage site you can't make any alterations unless they follow the original design. I might have to rebuild and redecorate parts of this café to conform to the original, and who will pay for that?'

We followed her outside through the rear of her café to find a large courtyard and old, attractive stable block which would indeed require bringing up to a suitable standard. I could do nothing but sympathise with her circumstances, and I'm sure she isn't the only owner facing a dilemma if the heritage proposition goes ahead. She has plenty of time to worry, for the list of sites will not be finalised until later in 2006, and the process of gaining World Heritage status could take up to three years.

A drive along the main street of Oamaru is very rewarding. The protected heritage buildings were designed in imposing neo-classical style by fine architects, and built in the creamy coloured local stone. Oamaru is not to be missed, for its consistency of architecture is unlike that of any other town in New Zealand. By the time you reach Oamaru, you will have realised that most towns grew rather haphazardly according to the needs of the time, and many old centres have an impermanent look given by the use of the local building materials of timber and corrugated iron. Not so with this town.

Oamaru has always been prosperous, thanks to its excellent situation on the edge of the Otago goldfields, its rich farmland, and its port. It was a busy commercial centre in the nineteenth century, dealing in meat, wool, timber and grain, and thoughtfully planned with wide streets and a good harbour. Guided walking tours through Victorian Oamaru depart daily at 11 a.m., 12 noon, 2 p.m. and 3 p.m. from the i-Site Information Centre (ph. (03) 434 1656) easily found on the corner of 1 Thames Street and Itchen Street.

Travellers of a literary bent, just passing through Oamaru as we were, but who wish to stretch their legs, might like to try the Janet Frame Heritage Trail which takes about one and a half hours to walk. Janet Frame is New Zealand's most celebrated author. She lived much of her life in Oamaru and used it as the setting for some of her early novels. The i-Site Centre has a brochure detailing the sites used, and their descriptions.

M.'s father and uncles were brought up on their farm, Lyndhurst, which was conveniently situated on the main highway opposite Waitaki Boys' High School, and were educated there during the early years of the twentieth century. The farm is no more, but the well-respected school, with its attractive front façade, is very much there and we were able to drive and walk around the grounds. It gave M. deep satisfaction to visit the school; it was a pity it was closed for the weekend, for a tour of the interior would have shown his family name on the Honours Boards.

It was time to move on. We refuelled the van at a Caltex station where 53.54 litres of diesel cost $44.38, significantly cheaper than that last bought outside Wanaka. At Pukeuri we turned left onto State Highway 83, heading for Kurow and past the Benmore Dam to Omarama, our stop for the night. It was a drive of about 110 kilometres, on a straight highway through unpopulated country areas, and should take about two hours, we thought.

I cannot forget those perfect hours. We travelled past small clusters of elderly houses where the front gardens were crammed with roses, dahlias, tall delphiniums, and hydrangeas of the most outrageous pink, where giant piles of freshly-chopped wood were heaped in back yards ready for the winter fires, and the patchwork of surrounding pastures was divided naturally by low, often tangled hedges. The land was very green, well-irrigated by the nearby Waitaki River, the distant ranges were a greyish blue, and shafts of golden sunlight penetrated the clouds and tinged the tops of trees. I have a painting of a North Otago scene by Peter Beadle, a well-respected New Zealand artist, and the painting could very well have been done on a day like this, looking at the same scenery.

The road was as straight as an arrow, lovely for M. to drive on. We sped through Duntroon, which has a fossils and geology centre, and the rare sight of a working blacksmith's forge, and one kilometre further on came to an interesting cliff formation holding Maori rock drawings. Sadly, Maori art, red or black in colour, which used mostly limestone rock as its canvas and existed all over New Zealand, is fast disappearing. The causes are vandalism, neglect, natural decay, and the drowning of many sites adjacent to hydro-electric power stations. Most of the art is pre-European, but drawings of the horse, which was introduced by Europeans, at Duntroon, suggests that rock drawing continued well into the nineteenth century. The drawings are of common subjects such as fish, birds, including the moa, insects, imaginary monsters, and simple decorative forms, and vary greatly in size. Although considered a national treasure, there is no body entrusted absolutely with the preservation of what remains, and it seems set to become lost forever.

I was looking forward to seeing Kurow. I have a cousin who used to practise as the sole doctor in this very rural area, and he said that payment for his services often took the shape of a side of lamb. It's a little gem of a town in summer, with a fine stone church on the right, and tidy old houses with the usual magnificent blooms in front gardens that I had come to expect in the South Island, but, judging by the surrounding bare hills, it would be bleak and very cold in winter.

We were entering hydro-electric dam territory, with dams across the Waitaki River at Lake Waitaki and Lake Aviemore and the biggest of all at Benmore. These lakes are a stunning bright blue, set off by the pale gold tussock grass along their shores, and the dark green of trees ringing the lakes on the far side. All it needed was a fringing of snow on the high hilltops and the scene would have been fit for a calendar. Some campervans were free camping alongside Lake Aviemore and I envied them their perfect setting, unable to be duplicated readily in a commercial campground. At Otematata, built in 1959 to house workers on the dam projects, there is boat access to the lake, and a few P Class yachts were sailing on the still water. It's a popular, unspoilt holiday spot amid gorgeous scenery, with a tavern and a motel, a café, petrol station and a golf course.

I never knew I had an engineering bent until we went on this holiday, but I have found hydro-electric power stations very satisfactory places to visit. I was agog to see the scale of the construction of the Benmore Dam, and I wasn't disappointed. This is a truly great hydro-electric dam, New Zealand's largest earth-formed dam, carrying an 11 metre wide road along its top, and measuring nearly 700 metres from abutment to abutment. The Waitaki River, backed up behind it, forms the largest man-made lake in the country of 75 sq. km., and is a splendid water lover's paradise with its reaches providing ideal conditions for boating and water skiing, and a plentiful supply of trout or salmon for anglers. The water flows of the Waitaki River from the Benmore Dam provide 25 per cent of the country's electricity. There is an observation point just a short signposted drive up a hill, which gives an excellent view of the dam, its surroundings, and the lake, and from there one can easily appreciate the brilliant engineering. It is not just a concrete mass like other dams; the sluice gates are placed unobtrusively to one side, and care has been taken with the landscaping of the dam itself. The large transmission and 'working' section of the power station cannot be seen from the observation point; all one is aware of are the stunning water views and the sculptural quality of the curves of the landscape. It's a case of man-made being good, and we were delighted we'd come to see it.

There are several campsites at Parsons Rock (Lake Aviemore), Otematata, Sailors Cutting, Lochlaird, and beneath the Benmore Dam. *The New Zealand Camping Guide, South Island* gives full details of these lake-edge camps which all have a boat ramp and toilets but, except for the Otematata Holiday Park (ph. (03) 438 7826), very few frills.

We turned right to drive the remaining 24 kilometres along State Highway 83 to Omarama, and found we were on a Heritage Trail called 'From Ocean to Alps'. The lake-edge campground at Sailors Cutting (ph. (03) 434 8060) was well-patronised by water sports enthusiasts, and the Lake Benmore Holiday Park (ph. (03) 438 9624) which is described in the camping guide as being 'A special treat for motorhome travellers' looked very attractive. It was uncanny to remember that only 24 hours earlier we had been watching the albatrosses. The scenery and surroundings had changed so completely that I felt disembodied and could only liken it to being in a different country, a sentiment which persisted when we pulled into the Omarama Top 10 Holiday Park (details in the Appendix). This camp was unlike any other we had stayed in. It is geared towards South Island holidaymakers who come for the fishing and boating, and the 'overseas' contingent, on this particular evening, was very small. A side fence had a line-up of permanently-stored speedboats on trailers, the predominant vehicles in the camp were SUVs with towbars fitted, and the smart chalets situated in a long row opposite our site were all occupied for the weekend. There were many permanent caravans, some having been there for a long time judging by their appearance. An English couple whose motorhome was adjacent to ours commented that they had never seen so many elderly and outdated caravans as they had in New Zealand!

This large, well-landscaped camp with smooth lawns and large willow, sycamore and cypress trees is well-run, with fine and very clean ablutions, a new kitchen fully equipped with microwaves, fridges and freezers, a good dining area, a fully automatic laundry, and a gas barbecue. There are 94 power sites, and 100 tent sites. It is an excellent overnight stop in a region where first class camps are scarce and, as a bonus, the Heritage Gateway Hotel across the road offers full dining and bar services.

We booked in for the Saturday night buffet dinner and while we were waiting for our table, for the hotel was very busy with two tour parties of elderly trippers, we sat outside at a table on the lawn with our drinks, and breathed in delicious lungfuls of the clear, pure, invigorating country air. The night's menu was nicely countrified, too, with chicken and celery soup, roast lamb and vegetables, and M. came back to the table, shamefacedly, with a high pyramid of ice cream, pavlova, and chocolate sponge cake for his pudding. Dinner with two glasses of wine, plus our pre-dinner drinks, cost just $60.

We got back to the camp to find the most splendid motorhome we had ever seen had pulled in a few yards away. It was German, eight metres long, had a TV aerial, and was equipped with fishing rods and bikes strapped on. The owners were an elderly couple touring the world.

I looked at the odometer the next morning and calculated we had travelled 260 kilometres from Dunedin to Omarama. It had been an easy drive along very good roads, with interesting stops on the way, and I expected that this morning's journey of just 99 kilometres to Aoraki Mount Cook with that famously scenic stretch along the western shore of Lake Pukaki to look forward to, would be the same. How wrong can one be!

The day was overcast, with the sun struggling to break through when we left Omarama on State Highway 8 at 10 a.m. Once away from the shelter of the town, the wind whipped strongly over the vast, rugged, tussocky landscape, true 'man's country', the stuff of stirring advertisements for strong beer and fast cars. A large, barren paddock – although paddock is not the correct word here for the stretch of land continued unbroken by boundary fences for many kilometres alongside the highway – had its dry soil raised into a cloud of dust and looked as though it could never be converted into productive land. Yet in a short while a large 'aeroplane' irrigation system was in play on land to the right, and miraculously the pasture around it had become a lush, bright green, an astonishing sight amidst all the aridity.

The road was a pleasure to drive on, flat, well-graded, and straight. Near Twizel a sign read 'High Country Salmon Turn Right', and about a dozen vans were pulled up alongside Lake Ruataniwha to fish. The fire risk was high on the outskirts of Twizel, hardly surprising, for except for the aberration of that irrigated pasture the land was tinder dry.

Twizel is a small town built in 1968 to house workers on the Waitaki River hydro-electricity schemes. At the conclusion of the construction, many of the houses were bought as holiday homes by anglers and skiers. The town is well-served with hotels, motels and lodge accommodation, and a modern shopping centre, and is a useful stop if you are running short of supplies. If you want to take a scenic flight over the area, the nearby Pukaki airfield offers tourist flights, as do other small airfields in the region.

We turned left onto State Highway 80, unsealed when we drove along it nearly 30 years ago, to drive 55 kilometres along Lake Pukaki to Glentanner and Aoraki Mount Cook. Shallow hills hid the lake from view at first, but a short climb brought us to the top of a crest by Peter's Lookout, and suddenly the lake was *there*, shining, bright turquoise, brilliantly set off by a plantation of dark green pines fringing the water's edge. The colouring of the landscape, with the ochre plains and tussocked slopes, and the misty blue mountaintops with snow in the ridges, was fantastic. In Switzerland similar scenery would be covered with fir trees, chalets with window boxes of geraniums, and grazing cows; here, it is bare and empty, in its original condition except, thankfully, for the tar-sealed highway to The Hermitage Hotel.

Alpine weather can change in a matter of minutes. Suddenly, without warning, a fierce wind swept across the lake, chopping up the surface and pulling and pushing the campervan across the road. M. began to have trouble holding it on the road, and slowed down to a crawl. We were buffeted across our lane, crossing the centre line at times, and very thankful not to be in a higher-topped vehicle. It was frightening. The driver of a lone car approaching us saw we were in difficulty and pulled as far over onto his road shoulder as possible in order to avoid a collision. A drive alongside the lake, which would normally take half an hour, took nearly one and a half hours, and we were very thankful to turn into the grounds of The Hermitage and find a park for the van in the bus parking lot at the rear of the hotel.

We tottered inside to the café for a reviving lunch, very disappointed that Mt. Cook was obscured by thick cloud. Suddenly a monstrous gust of wind shook the windows of the café, and torrential rain, driven horizontal by the force of the wind, lashed the hotel. We would need to leave soon if we wanted to spend the night at Fairlie, a drive of 145 kilometres back along Lake Pukaki and along State Highway 8.

We scurried back to the campervan, hardly able to stand against the wind and the wall of rain, and debated whether or not to continue the journey. I, being a lover of luxury, had been seduced by the warmth and comfort of the hotel and wanted to stay the night; M. felt we should press on. Suddenly, in answer to my prayers, a mighty roar of wind and rain shook the campervan so violently that M. capitulated, saying he didn't want to tackle the drive in the deteriorating conditions. He booked a room for the night, which the receptionist promised had one of the best views of Mt. Cook, and installed himself comfortably on the bed to watch a rugby match on TV, while I installed myself for a blissful hour in the bathroom, emerging clean and shining and ready for drinks and dinner. It didn't matter that we were very casually dressed in our camping clothes, for all the guests were short-term tourists living meagrely out of a suitcase.

The hotel had been rebuilt since we had stayed there almost 30 years ago. Then, it was the comfortable, old-fashioned domain of well-heeled guests there for long relaxation; today, it caters for overnight tour parties, mainly from Japan and Korea, and has large, modern facilities to match. The 'atmosphere' has disappeared, but after three weeks in the van I was not overly fussy about such minor considerations. I wondered if the bar still served its prize-winning Roadrunner cocktail, the recipe for which had been given to me by the barman and which I had made often, over the years, in Auckland. I got a blank look when I enquired, and settled for a gin and tonic instead. Here's the recipe.

Mt. Cook Roadrunner Cocktail

Put into a shaker equal parts of gin, Galliano, grenadine and cream, add ice, shake well, and pour. If it is too sweet for your taste, reduce the grenadine the next time. It is a pretty shade of pink, has a rich medicinal taste, and will do you good.

The dining room was full of Asian tourists and much of the buffet dinner catered to their food preferences, for us a welcome change from our diet of the previous few weeks. Dinner, bed and breakfast cost $313.02, and our very ordinary bottle of wine at dinner was $40. The storm was still raging when we retired to bed.

CHAPTER 23

AORAKI MOUNT COOK TO ARTHUR'S PASS IN A DAY

We must have been mad! This was supposed to be a relaxed, leisurely holiday, yet the day became a race against the clock to make up for our delay at Mt. Cook. I opened the curtains to a perfect view of the snow-clad mountain, shining in the sunlight and looking so close that I felt I could stretch out and touch it. The craggy face in front of us was not unlike that of the north face of the Eiger, with a similar sharp outline and 'spiderlegs' of snow in the ridges connecting to a central 'body'. There was no trace of the storm, just still, pure air and crowds of thrilled sightseers pressing the button on their digital cameras. There's plenty to photograph here, especially a recently erected statue of a youthful Sir Edmund Hillary who trained on Mt. Cook in preparation for his epic climb to conquer Mt. Everest in 1953. Several guests were setting off for one of the many well-signposted walks which can be taken from The Hermitage, the shortest one I saw being the one hour return walk to Kea Point. The entirely pleasant evening in the hotel had refreshed me; I felt quite slim, so helped myself to a large fried slab of hash brown potatoes at breakfast.

Sitting at a table behind us at dinner the previous evening had been a driver of one of the tour buses. With the memory of that enjoyable day on the coaches in Dunedin fresh in my mind, I stopped this morning and said hello. He had time to talk while he waited for his tour party to assemble, and had an interesting tale to tell about his duties as the coach driver, guide and commentator, baggage handler, and general factotum for about 24 tourists during four days, for which he received the princely sum of $14.50 per hour.

Once a week, he said, he travelled from Christchurch to Mt. Cook, to Queenstown, to Milford Sound, and back again to Christchurch with an Asian tour party, the trip involving four days' solid travelling and three nights' accommodation. I was astonished that he could cover so much ground in so little time, and pressed him for more information. I found what he said quite horrifying, used as I was to our comparatively slow pace of travel. His present tourists were Japanese, and had boarded their flight in Nagoya on Saturday night, had landed in Auckland on Sunday morning and transferred to the domestic terminal for a flight to Christchurch. He had collected them from the airport and driven directly to Mt. Cook where they had stayed the night. (This tight schedule explained the exhausted look on the faces of the middle-aged tourists at the table next to us at dinner). He was now about to drive everyone to Queenstown where they would stay for their second night, and on the following day, Tuesday, he would drive them from Queenstown to Milford Sound and back again, for their third night in New Zealand, again at Queenstown. The next morning, Wednesday, they would depart early for Christchurch and catch a late afternoon flight to Rotorua for the night. Thursday was scheduled as an organised 'day off', with a Maori concert and hangi dinner in the evening. On Friday morning they would be driven to Auckland and would fly out later in the day for Japan, arriving on Saturday after having 'done' New Zealand in seven days, with two of the seven nights spent on the aeroplanes.

The driver said the most difficult part of the tour always occurred on his leg, in Queenstown, when jet lag was surfacing and, suddenly, the tourists realised that the trip to Milford Sound took a whole, tiring day in the bus and left no time whatsoever to enjoy the beauty of Queenstown. He questioned the thinking of some travel agencies, and said the Koreans always got the worst deal. Since arriving back in Auckland I have read newspaper reports commenting on the very points he raised, so perhaps a better look at this splendid country will be offered to short stay tourists in future.

This particular tour party would hardly have had time to visit a duty free shop to spend their holiday savings!

M. told the coach driver how scary our drive along Lake Pukaki had been in the gale force wind which had come up without warning. 'Watch the surface of the lake,' replied the driver. 'It will always signal weather changes to you. I moved down into bottom gear at the first sign of wind and drove the final half hour here at a snail's pace. It's the only safe way when that wind comes up.' He wanted to know what sort of vehicle we had, and seemed relieved when he heard. I wondered why he had asked. He replied that he worried when he sat behind a large six-berth motorhome and saw it handled badly, because a heavy vehicle licence is needed to drive one safely due to the exhaust braking system, a provision which does not, unfortunately in his opinion, apply to tourists who *rent* such vehicles.

Today the lake was a calm, milky aqua green, and campervans were heading in droves up to Mt. Cook, having been thwarted in their intentions the day before. The Mount Cook National Park, covering over 28,000 hectares, is conserved in its natural state and is a popular destination for tourists. We arrived quickly at the bottom of Lake Pukaki to enjoy one of the most iconic views in New Zealand, that splendid panorama back up the lake to the Southern Alps and Mt. Cook. It is breathtaking, calendar perfect, is one of the finest views in New Zealand, and is not to be missed.

We were on State Highway 8 heading towards Lake Tekapo, Fairlie, Timaru and Christchurch, signposted the 'Bullock Wagon Trail'. Our plan for the day was to turn at Fairlie onto State Highway 79 to Geraldine, and then take State Highway 1 to Christchurch where we would stay the night before driving across Arthur's Pass to Westland the following day.

The highway to Lake Tekapo and Fairlie crossed the famous Mackenzie Country, named after a Scottish highland shepherd who landed in Otago in about 1847, became a sheep drover for a while, and on a jurney of exploration discovered the vast, flat alpine basin and applied to the Commissioner of Crown Lands in Otago for a licence to occupy it. The Government was willing to sign over 2,500 square miles of land to one man without asking for much payment, because it considered the terrain inaccessible and unlikely to be used. James Mackenzie could not afford to stock the land, so resorted to rustling, was caught and sentenced to prison, and eventually he left New Zealand, abandoning his land. Today, the official discoverer of the Mackenzie Country is recognised as being Michael Burke.

The Mackenzie Country was opened up in the early 1860s, and in the first years there were only four women, all wives of station owners, living in the whole of this immense area. The pioneer families endured unbearable loneliness and arctic winters, and lived in cob or sod huts with thatched roofs, earthen floors, with furniture made from packing cases prettied up with draperies, and open fireplaces on which, if they were lucky, perched a camp oven. They were dependent on local creeks for water, and suffered a difficult journey to reach the nearest town, Timaru. The mistress of Mt. Cook Station, Catherine Burnett, had no other woman to talk to within 30 miles, yet she reared eight children there.

Ours was a grand drive on a flat, easy, perfectly-sealed road, so different from the rough track, suitable only for a bullock dray, travelled over by the first farmers 150 years previously. We had plenty of time to enjoy the wide, high country canvas of soft gold-coloured tussock grassland, the huge bright blue sky, and the backdrop of the Southern Alps. Today, thousands of sheep with unusual dark grey fleeces, looking like round rocks on legs, grazed the dry earth which didn't look as though it could support an ant hill, let alone these vast flocks. Looking to my left across to the Alps, Mt. Cook and Mt. Tasman, I felt enormously satisfied to know I had flown over them in a little red helicopter seven days ago, and *landed*! If your itinerary does not include the West Coast drive and helicopter flight onto the glaciers described in an earlier chapter, you should consider taking a scenic flight from

Glentanner/Mt. Cook airfield over the grand traverse of Mt. Cook and Westland National Parks, which cover over 200 kilometres of wonderful alpine scenery. The flights are run by Air Safaris and Services (N.Z.) Limited, P.O. Box 71, Lake Tekapo (ph. (03) 680 6880, www.airsafaris.co.nz). Flights also depart from Lake Tekapo, if that location suits you better.

The township of Lake Tekapo has a beautiful setting at the southern end of the lake of the same name, and the Lake Tekapo Motels and Motor Camp on Lakeside Drive (ph. (03) 680 6825) has a superb location at the water's edge. The camp looked an excellent place to stay, with attractive terraced sites above the lake, and is described in glowing terms in *The New Zealand Camping Guide South Island* handbook. The township is a good place to stop for a snack, or a break from driving.

We crossed the Lake Tekapo hydro-electric dam control gates, and a road sign indicated that the highway to Burke's Pass, considered the actual gateway to the Mackenzie Country, was open. I could see a foggy cloud over the pass, 18 kilometres distant across the flat plain, and once through the pass, 700 metres above sea level, I was amazed to find that we descended to green hillsides and pastures, plenty of trees, and *rain*, disappointing indeed after the very hot, dry haze of the tussock highland.

At Fairlie we turned onto State Highway 79 to Geraldine, a steep, winding road passing many sheep farms, with evidence everywhere of recent haymaking. It looked like a different planet after the dry hills and plains of Otago and the Mackenzie Country. There were several large deer farms, and a few cattle grazing, but the overwhelming sight was of sheep, and more sheep, hardly surprising, because we were now in South Canterbury and beginning the drive through the Canterbury Plains. We stopped at Geraldine at Plums Café for toasted sandwiches for two, and Thai pumpkin soup for M., a beer, and a pot of tea, a satisfactory lunch which cost just $20. The café had a slightly eccentric air, but we couldn't find another, and it was well-patronised by the locals. M.

decided to top up with fuel and it was just as well he did, because we never reached Christchurch that night. The cost for 42 litres of diesel was $36, and we turned out of town on State Highway 72 before continuing on State Highway 79 to State Highway 1.

If you are travelling north from Timaru to Christchurch, the turnoff to State Highway 72 at Winchester and on to State Highway 73 at Darfield is a more interesting drive. I have not taken State Highway 72, but it is reputed to be fast, safe, and very scenic, and avoids the congested southern approach to Christchurch. However, it meant an extra 30 kilometres driving for M., and as we planned to drive to Arthur's Pass and Westland the next day, it seemed better to take the more direct State Highway 1 to Christchurch.

The road across the Canterbury Plains parallels the coastline and is, as you would expect, flat and very straight, with views to the Southern Alps on the left. This is one of the most fertile regions in New Zealand, and is renowned for the production of exceptionally fine Canterbury lamb, which I have great pride in saying is the best in the world.

A short history lesson! The primary reason for New Zealand's settlement was to provide food for England. The Industrial Revolution in Britain in the eighteenth century had led to a dramatic increase in population in the towns and cities, a rise in individual wealth, and a subsequent demand for food which could not be met from existing agricultural resources. By 1815, England was forced to import food. Captain Cook's voyage of exploration had established New Zealand as a promising candidate for colonisation by Britain, but the early settlers were missionaries, whalers and traders, absorbed with their own work and survival, and not likely to want to till vast tracts of land. The big impetus behind the future settlement of New Zealand came from the desire of the new middle class to colonise a country where they could own their land, become wealthy, and enjoy a standing in society denied them in their own country, all of which could be achieved with the export of their produce to an assured market. Although land settlement and development got off to a slow start, New Zealand eventually became one of England's primary food suppliers, helped by the establishment of refrigerated shipping in 1882, a status enjoyed until 1971 when Great Britain joined the European Common Market.

The results of all this are apparent in the splendid farms of New Zealand, and nowhere more so than on the Canterbury Plains, described in *New Zealand Heritage* (Clive Litt, *Exploring the Hinterland*, Vol. 2. p. 424) on its 1841 sighting as 'an immense plain containing millions of acres of the richest soil'. The soil was so rich that for 30 years wheat could be grown without the application of fertiliser, and when the soil eventually became drained, grass pasture was sown and sheep farmed for export in the new refrigerated ships.

We crossed the wide Rangitikei River, pale grey and swift flowing, to enter Ashburton, a town serving the farming region and rather like Matamata in the North Island, with its wide main avenue and the railway line running down the middle. Popular settlement of the district surrounding Ashburton occurred in the 1850s, and in *Tales of Pioneer Women*, Ethel McQuilkin writes: 'The early run-holders who took up huge areas under pasturage licence were for the most part men of culture, men of vision, many of whom came from the public schools and universities of England' ... '...perhaps the best known was Samuel Butler, who took up the Mesopotamia run, which he immortalised in "Erewhon" '. But, as elsewhere in New Zealand, background hardly mattered when there were no roads, you had to live in a cob house with an earthen floor, cook on the hearth, and put up with a lack of fresh fruit and vegetables. It was not until 1858 that the future town of Ashburton was established. As you drive along the plains today and see the wonderful stands of trees, remember that there were none in those early days. Manuka scrub and tutu roots provided firewood, and it was not for many years that planting began in earnest.

This part of New Zealand looks perfect from the air, a geometric patchwork of fields divided by long rows of poplar and macrocarpa trees, and precision-trimmed hedges, some as high as eight metres. 'Aeroplane' irrigation is popular here. We drove past a farm with at least 300 cows grazing, the larger herds being viable because this method of irrigation grows new grass more quickly.

As we were crossing the Rakaia River, which boasts the longest bridge in New Zealand, M. asked me to work out the distance to Arthur's Pass. 'I'm feeling fine,' he insisted in answer to my astonished look. 'That stay at Mt. Cook did me good and I'd like to continue driving!'

'Er, Christchurch to Arthur's Pass is 160 kilometres,' I said, 'and you've already driven 300 kilometres today. Are you sure you're up to it?'

That comment to M. is always like a red rag to a bull. A study of the road atlas showed a short-cut from Norwood, which we were approaching, to Darfield, and the camping guide listed a campground at Springfield, a little further on, if he flagged a bit. So we turned off State Highway 1 and onto a ruler-straight country road, flat and beautifully sealed, with not a car in sight, and had it to ourselves for the 20 kilometres to Darfield. The pastoral views across the plains were unbroken, and anyone who has travelled here and who sees Canterbury lamb listed on a menu would be foolish not to order it, because they will know that this part of New Zealand is lamb heaven, and that their lamb has had a lovely life getting fat for the table.

Oh, the South Island humour. We arrived at a crossroads with eight roads radiating from it, and a handsome sign calling it 'Charing Cross' – again, not a person in sight. At Darfield we stopped at a dairy for some tonic water, and soon arrived at Springfield and the Kowhai Pass Domain which I had insisted should be our stopping place for the night – NOT! This was the camp of nightmares, utterly basic, lonely, and completely deserted except for one caravan, a permanent fixture, tucked into a dark corner. We could have been robbed, killed, and buried here behind the high hedge and no one would have found us. There was no office, no one to take our $10 power site fee, just a concrete bunker ablution block at the far end of the ground, with stark facilities, and some dilapidated tennis courts. Goodbye!

There was nothing to do but continue. There is a scarcity of adequate campgrounds along State Highway 73. Flock Hill Lodge at Lake Pearson (ph. (03) 318 8196) about 45 kilometres further on had an attractive write-up in the camping guide, but seemed more suited to tents. Ablutions, a lounge, a TV room, and full kitchens were provided, and the descriptions 'set among trees and well-kept lawns…' and 'The atmosphere is of a high country station with deer and stags in the neighbouring paddock…' almost swayed me, but there was no mention of power sites. The Lake Pearson, Klondyke Corner and Hawdon Shelter campgrounds, all near Arthur's Pass, had very basic toilets and drinking water had to be boiled.

Feeling somewhat desperate, I turned to the Maui Motorhomes 2005 guidebook to find The Chalet Tranz Alpine Lodge and Restaurant at Arthur's Pass Village listed, with powered campervan sites available (details in Appendix). This would have to do.

I knew that M., when we set out blithely from Mt. Cook that morning, had no idea that he would drive 430 kilometres to finish the day at Arthur's Pass. We still had 84 kilometres to drive after the abortive attempt to find a camp at Springfield, on a road which climbed from the flat farmland of the Canterbury Plains to the Torlesse Range and Porters Pass, and ran alongside the Craigieburn Range. The last leg of the journey would take us through Bealey and Arthur's Pass National Park, and we expected to arrive at The Chalet at about five o'clock in the afternoon, nearly seven hours' driving along Lake Pukaki, across the high Mackenzie Country, down to the Pacific Coast, along the plains, and then inland back to the alpine divide. Paradoxically, the distance from Mt. Cook north to Arthur's Pass is only about 150 kilometres, as the crow flies!

The climb to Porters Pass crosses the Kowai-Torlesse Tussocklands Park, where the lumpy vegetation looks like green moss-stitch on an old-fashioned woollen jumper. The road is very steep and is not recommended for towing. The landscape is bleak, and very dramatic, with layer upon layer of hills and ranges, each one higher than the last, giving an idea of how wonderful the ski slopes at the Porters Pass Skifield are in winter. Low mist swirled around us at the summit of the pass, 935 metres high. The drive is best undertaken in summer, when the majestic, isolated landscape with its strange rock formations, utterly barren and quite forbidding, can best be enjoyed without its winter snow which looks pretty, but blurs the outlines.

New Zealand has over 300 fine lodges, many world-renowned, which offer top-class accommodation in magnificent locations. Grasmere Lodge, a historic high country sheep station on State Highway 73 near Cass, is such a place; it can be glimpsed from the highway as you drive past, and is famous for its luxury and its cuisine. It is a member of the Small Luxury Hotels of the World group, and a suite for two people costs between $1,500 and $1,800 per night, excluding tax. If you wish to browse, the website is www.grasmere.co.nz.

The highway followed the Trans Alpine rail track across the huge, delta-like valley as we rounded Paddy's Bend. We'd left the bleakness of Porters Pass well behind to swap it for a drive past native beech forest which all but obscured Wilderness Lodge (www.wildernesslodge.co.nz) on the hillside above. The lodge is well-sited on a historic high country sheep station, and as its name suggests invites guests to experience the ecology and wildlife of the region in a wilderness setting. Incredibly, because it looks as though it will fall down in a puff of wind, the old Bealey Hotel, at Bealey, established in 1865, is still in operation for meals and a bed.

As we crossed the Bealey Bridge over the Waimakariri River and entered the Arthur's Pass National Park for the remaining 10 kilometres of drive through the forest to Arthur's Pass Village, a campervan which had been travelling slowly in front of us for some time with an elderly couple who, annoyingly, thought they owned the road, and were committed to preventing all attempts to overtake safely, suddenly stopped without warning in the middle of the road. M. circled around the van and I glared angrily at the twits inside as we went past. Suddenly, also without warning, M. braked too; a fine specimen of New Zealand's native parrot, the kea, the only large bird able to live at high altitudes, was walking down the centre line completely oblivious to the chaos he might cause. They are cheeky birds, those keas, and well-known for their predilection for the rubber seal around car windows! The last few kilometres were adventurous driving, through bush where the trees almost locked low branches overhead, and the recommended speed was just 55 kilometres per hour. M. reduced speed to 40 kilometres per hour as he carefully negotiated the bends. Thankfully, 'Welcome to Arthur's Pass Village' appeared on a road sign, and we pulled in to the parking area in front of The Chalet.

Arthur's Pass has a very small population of just a few dozen people, and is the principal township on State Highway 73 connecting Canterbury and the West Coast. It had been on my wish list of places to visit since I was 24 years old and worked for a group of scientists in what was, then, the Animal Ecology Division of the Department of Scientific and Industrial Research. The West Coast population of stoats, weasels and ferrets was under observation to establish what dangers these mustelids were posing to native bird and insect life, and a small team of researchers regularly visited the region to gather evidence. Arthur's Pass, and the Trans Alpine railway, always seemed to feature prominently in chat around the morning tea table when they returned from a trip, and I formed a picture of a small settlement reached by a difficult road, or by rail, at the mercy of alpine weather, and peopled by rugged, hardy individuals unlike those found elsewhere in New Zealand. I don't think much has changed! This was the most interesting and entertaining night's stop on our tour, one that amply fulfilled all its promise, a place I would loathe to visit for eight months of the year, but which on this late summer's afternoon managed a blue sky, a golden sunset, and serene views to the forested ranges.

The Chalet looks exactly as its name suggests. M. walked past the flower boxes and pushed open the front door to find a young girl who spoke almost no English manning the desk. His query for a power point for the night was met with a blank stare. Power points? What did he mean? She didn't know, he would have to wait for the manager to return – all this in broken English and lots of gesticulations. M. thought she sounded German and tried out his few words on her, without success, so we took matters into our own hands and searched the outside of the building for a power point. They must have been well-hidden because we couldn't see any.

Arthur's Pass has an isolated, spooky air, I think, the front yard of The Chalet was open to every passing bogey, it was quite impossible for M. to continue driving to Otira, the next stop, and I didn't fancy a night without power, so I said I thought we should book a room for the night. M. dredged up the word for 'room', discovered that just one was still available, so he took it, and we locked up the van and moved in. For $110, which included breakfast, we had a huge corner bedroom with three bunks and the most comfortable double bed I have ever slept in, well furnished with a squashy sofa and a TV, and beautiful views from the windows. The rooms with ensuite bathrooms had all been taken, so we were led along the corridor, round a corner, and down a short flight of steps, and shown the communal bathroom we would have to share with others. I promptly sent M. back to the van for a torch! My fears were silly, because when I ventured out at 3 a.m., torch in hand, plastic slides on feet, and no covering robe, I found the corridors all brightly lit, and warmed by central heating.

The Chalet opens into an enormous room with reception desk, group tour dining arrangements, a Swiss *stubli*-style restaurant, the bar, a large well-furnished living area, and two big fireplaces, all merging effortlessly. It is the most welcoming of places, one that I imagine would really rock on a cold winter's night, a haven for wayside travellers like us, the many railway and forest workers in the region, and those who come for the skiing, tramping, and climbing. I settled in with a gin and tonic, and looked at the dinner menu. Whitebait fritters for $25 were featured, and the very pretty and well-mannered waitress/bar attendant said that actually the chef cooked just one per person, big enough to fill the whole dinner plate. I said I thought that would do nicely. We ordered a basket of fries to accompany the enormous fritters, and a bottle of Forrest Estate Chardonnay for $33, and ate (and slept) like kings. It had been a long day.

CHAPTER 24

THE OTIRA GORGE, BLACKBALL, REEFTON, THE LEWIS PASS, AND HANMER SPRINGS

It was disappointing to wake the next morning, Tuesday, and find the weather wet and very windy, for we had hoped to get as far as Hanmer Springs that day. Still nervous from his Mt. Cook experience, M. didn't think he was up to tackling the drive down the Otira Gorge in the poor conditions. We consulted one of the excellent waitresses. She consulted a gang of local workmen who had arrived for breakfast, having slept, I think, in some small cabins adjacent to the lodge. The front desk receptionist came across to help, and another guest, a frequent traveller well-known to the staff, chipped in too. The consensus was that the rain wasn't going to last much longer (it did), the wind would die down soon (it did, once we'd left the gorge behind), and that providing we drove slowly we'd be all right. 'You've only got the viaduct to worry about, really,' chirped the receptionist. What viaduct? We hadn't known till then that there was a viaduct to worry about.

Before we left, I asked both waitresses, young, attractive, and cheerful girls, why they were working in this isolated corner of New Zealand, with little in the way, so it seemed, of off-duty entertainment on offer. 'This is an excellent place to do hospitality training,' they replied. 'We have to be able to cope with everything, and apart from what you see us doing at front of house, we learn kitchen, housekeeping, and managerial skills. The local people are fantastic, and all the tourists who pass through have, like you two, made a special effort to get here and really appreciate what they find.' One lass had been there for two years and was ready to move on, having the attitude that 'if you can do it at Arthur's Pass, you can do it anywhere.' Good luck to her. The receptionist had arrived several months ago for a short working holiday and now had no plans to leave. The Chalet, strongly individual, a place which provides travellers with an all-inclusive ambience and offers splendid value for money, is quite a special place! I'd love to return.

With a lot of cheerful 'goodbyes' we left, climbed into the van, and turned on the heating to warm it up. I glanced around to the side of the building as we pulled out and saw that two motorhomes had parked there for the night. Had they found the power points? We didn't stop to ask, but turned quickly onto the highway anticipating the new day's excitement.

The 13 kilometres of road from Arthur's Pass to Otira was open, as were the next 62 kilometres to Kumara Junction, important to know because although we weren't going as far as Kumara, we would still need to cover the 19 kilometres from Otira township to our turnoff to Lake Brunner at Jacksons.

The Maui Motorhome 2005 handbook expressly states that the road from Arthur's Pass to Otira is not recommended for caravans and trailers, although the gorge is now two-way. The handbook also mentions that there is a length restriction of 13 metres on the road. Having done the journey now, I feel it is quite safe to take the descent from Arthur's Pass to Otira if the towing vehicle is suitable and the caravan is light, but the opposite journey from Otira to Arthur's Pass should not be undertaken under any circumstances. It is *just too steep*, and the climb is long. Watching a heavily-laden truck grind up the viaduct as we were descending, I wondered what would happen if its engine stalled.

The rain was still falling. Arthur's Pass Village was quite deserted with not another vehicle in sight, and our narrow, winding road, with 'Caution Wide Vehicle' signs, climbed quickly upwards towards the pass, 920 metres, where we crossed the regional boundary into Westland. The descent from the pass was steep, we took it slowly, and soon saw an awe-inspiring feat of engineering ahead of us, the famed viaduct, soaring down the gorge. A large sign said '16% Steepness Viaduct – Death's Corner', and there was a roomy pull-off provided for heavy vehicles to engage in a lower gear.

What a drive! We wouldn't have missed the next few minutes for anything in the world. Yes, the high, slender viaduct is very exposed to wind and we crawled along, but not from fear this time, just so we could give ourselves extra moments to enjoy the stupendous engineering. As we got lower, the cliff face above us was steel-caged for rock fall prevention and roofed over with chutes rather like the avalanche-protected railway lines in Switzerland. I was glad we were descending and not travelling upwards, so long and steep was the road. We had been told years earlier that the best way to travel on State Highway 73 is to take a rental car from Christchurch to Greymouth, for then you are facing the fantastic panorama which unfolds in front as you drive along, but that the return journey by car does not provide the same vistas, and it is best to drop the rental car in Greymouth and go back by train, an excellent journey in itself.

Dave Chowdhury in *Driving Scenic New Zealand* writes that the Otira rail tunnel, which ended the era of horse-drawn transport over the pass, was not completed until 1923. The steepest section of rail track in New Zealand runs under the pass. After a train enters the tunnel, gates close behind, a fan sucks the poisonous gases and toxic smoke back to the rear of the tunnel, and the gates open when the train is safely through.

The fast flowing river below the gorge was not very wide, or deep, but it was strewn with huge rocks and boulders, which made me feel thankful that we had steel protection overhead. There was a dark, forbidding aura to the landscape, not entirely due to the rain or the gloomy sky, I thought.

Otira, the town with the highest rainfall in New Zealand, consists of 17 houses and a pub. The entire township is owned by the proprietors of the hotel, who are gradually restoring the old railway cottages, and their hotel. Plenty of people pass through

Otira – cyclists, train enthusiasts, and tourists – and these people keep the town going while the renovations continue.

This area of Westland, well in from the coast behind Hokitika, Greymouth and Westport, was of great economic significance in the nineteenth century due to its rich coal and gold deposits. As I mentioned earlier, coal mining is about to become the lifeblood of the West Coast again, with the forthcoming restoration of the port at Greymouth which will allow the local coal to be shipped independently to Japan instead of having to be railed across the Southern Alps to Lyttelton Port at Christchurch. The region is well off the usual 'Do New Zealand in a Week' tourist track, but is very rewarding to visit because it speaks loudly of the humble, hard-working men and women who lived solid lives, and contributed to the great Antipodean dream of opportunity and prosperity for all, even if it didn't quite occur here.

Judging by the look of the local tearooms, Jacksons is an old staging post, and it is easy to see why for the road from there short-cuts to Stillwater where it connects conveniently with State Highway 7 east of Greymouth, and runs seamlessly to Reefton, across the Lewis Pass to Hanmer Springs and Waipara, from where State Highway 1 takes over for travel either north, or south. We were on our way to Blackball to make a pilgrimage to the town's old general store where a friend of M.'s had started out, aged 21, as the grocer many years ago, had moved to Auckland, and had eventually become a Mayor of Manukau City and been knighted by the Queen – a real New Zealand success story. M., something of a fan for the record books, was also keen to cross the Lewis Pass further on, having already done the Haast, Porters, and Arthur's Passes in the last week.

But first we had to see Lake Brunner. My earlier memory of it was of a terrible night in 1976 with three scared children in a dingy and isolated hotel, the only one, serving dreadful food and situated on the edge of a forbidding, sinister, mist-shrouded lake, with no other habitation nearby, and with weird bird and animal noises keeping us awake all night. We thought we had arrived at the end of the earth. There seemed little reason to return! But how quickly things change. Today, the road is sealed and Lake Brunner is a burgeoning township, which owes much of its success to the influx of holiday homeseekers from Nelson. The mountain backdrop provides stunning views year-round, and the unspoilt lake is renowned for its fishing and water sports. The old hotel has been smartened up, is now a holiday retreat, and spreads attractively across its commanding site at the head of the lake.

The drive along the secondary Tourist Route to Lake Brunner was quite a change, indeed a welcome relief, from the high drama of the Otira Gorge. We could look back to the right, across the cattle-studded plain, and see where we'd come from. This route was a short-cut not only for us, but also for many heavy trucks and trailers. I was quite glad it was a damp day, for it added to the feeling of exploration. There were an astonishing amount of old rusted farm sheds, built from corrugated iron and utterly dilapidated, but still in use. These were the real, very lonely, rural backblocks and I felt that this was a part of New Zealand that hardly ever saw a Maui campervan.

The railway line from Greymouth to Otira circles Lake Brunner. Before the line was built, what is now under an hour's journey from the lake to Greymouth meant days of hard travel on foot and by boat. In *Tales of Pioneer Women*, Lena Dense, the wife of a railway gang worker, relates how they and their children moved to Moana at the head of the lake in 1892 so that her husband could continue constructing the rest of the line. Trees had to be felled to make room for the railway line, and she '...had to take the children out on the lake each day as it was the only place where they were safe from the falling trees'. She tethered them to the seat with her clothesline so that if they fell overboard she '...could haul them in like fish'.

There's still an air of individuality here. A sign at the roadside said 'Historic Miniature Bungalow 400 metres' and M. obligingly turned off to find it. Disappointingly, it was open from 2-5 p.m. on Sundays only. Tourists can arrive at any time – or are there really none here? A sign on a farm gate said 'Private Property. Trespassers will be prosecuted or shot'. My goodness.

Stillwater township where we turned right onto State Highway 7 is a logging depot. We shortly turned left to follow the Grey River to Ikamatua, and followed signs up the hill to Blackball, which has some of the oldest, most dilapidated houses in New Zealand. This place is a *treat* to visit. In the 1860s, it was a goldmining town with all the transience that industry implies, but somehow it has survived on a population of about 400 people, and is justly famous for its sausages and the Formerly The Blackball Hilton, a old colonial West Coast pub in the main street which offers casual accommodation and meals. Its quirky appearance is unlike that of any other hotel in New Zealand, and if it had been near the end of the day, and we were camping locally for the night, I would have gone there for a drink and dinner. It looks an adventurous place to enter.

However, this day we were on a mission. It wasn't difficult to find the general store. M. quickly pulled in, leapt out of the van, and entered. I didn't feel like chatting to anyone, so stayed seated, wishing I had a crossword puzzle to do. Glancing idly out of the window, I saw that we had parked directly outside the Blackball Salami Company! It was my turn to leap out and buy six sausages, the ones we had enjoyed so much in Greymouth, for $2.35. I would break my vow taken in Dunedin, of not cooking in the van again, for these. This is a serious place to shop. The hygiene is perfect, you can look through to a rear factory where everyone is dressed in white, with hair completely covered by large shower caps, and when the girl came out to serve me she washed her hands before pulling on fresh gloves. I wish I could buy Blackball sausages in Auckland.

These remote towns have interesting inhabitants. The manager of the general store told M. he had come to Blackball from Auckland because he couldn't cope with the heavy motorway traffic on his way to and from work each day. He had meant to settle with his family in Westport (thank God he didn't), but had ended up in Blackball, wise man, two years ago. He loved the peace and quiet in Blackball, counted himself lucky if he saw 30 people in a day, and when he fancied a trout for dinner he drove for five minutes to catch one in a nearby river. People would die for less. He told M. that just to give him an idea of the rise in value of local real estate, at Lake Brunner, two to three years ago, building sections of land were selling for $20 to $30 thousand dollars; now they are priced at 10 times that, and it's all Nelson money (as I mentioned earlier on), with people having made fortunes with the astronomic rise in land values there and investing it in Lake Brunner.

They know how to enjoy themselves in Blackball, and liven up their cold winter by celebrating the June solstice in fine style. The town becomes the Mecca for West Coasters who flock in, start off with an early champagne breakfast, and launch into the day's activities which include stilt races, a coal shovelling competition, and, literally, a 'pub crawl' in which competitors crawl on their hands and knees on the sealed road from the Blackball Hilton to the Workingmen's Club, and finish at the village green. There is a blackball lolly-spitting contest – the record is supposed to be 10 metres, which I find difficult to believe – and dancing till dawn at the hotel.

It had been an instructive stop for sausages, a chat, and a look at the Blackball Hilton. We continued to Ikamatua along the country road which paralleled State Highway 7 on the other side of the Grey River. Never be afraid to take a lesser road in New Zealand (coloured yellow in my road atlas) even though it might appear to pass through inhospitable and lonely terrain. Country roads are of a good standard and you will have some interesting drives and that enjoyable, relaxing feeling of being away from it all which is presumably what will have attracted you to motorcaravanning in the first place.

Ikamatua repeated the domestic dilapidation we had noticed in Blackball, and were to find shortly in Reefton. I suppose the inhabitants are growing old along with their homes and don't realise the condition they are in. It is depressing to see once thriving areas falling into decay, victims of regional economic downturn and the inevitable population drift of the young in search of jobs elsewhere, usually in the North Island. Yet, oddly, dilapidation is also picturesque.

The high Paparoa Range and the Paparoa National Park were to our left, with the Pancake Rocks on the coast in a direct line with Reefton. We were certainly making some crazy loops across the central South Island in an effort to visit all the places on our list! We crossed the Reefton Saddle, very tame indeed in comparison with what we'd accomplished the day before and earlier on that morning, and came to a sign reading 'Welcome to Reefton the Town of Light'.

I have never seen such an old town; even the cars parked in the main street are *old* old. The main street, called Broadway and looking as though the buildings are all going to fall down, is quaint, historic, and verandah-ed in practical colonial style, with an eclectic mix of businesses; 'Rags to Retro', the 'Reefton Backdoor Trader' advertising a closing down sale, 'The Rusty Rose', and a sign I thought had vanished forever in New Zealand – 'Milk Bar'. There is a pre-loved clothing shop, the inevitable Government Work and Income Office, a crafts and produce market, a Four Square store, some pubs, the Bank of New Zealand, the wooden, historic Reef Cottage Bed and Breakfast, circa 1887, and plenty of cafés and take-away food outlets.

Although I categorise Reefton as a pass-through place, it is an excellent stop for a short break. We always needed to pull up for an hour at lunchtime to have a rest and a change of environment from the van, and on this day Reefton provided a delightful stopover. We parked near the busy Broadway Tearooms and Bakery. Two hot steak and mushroom pies, two ham and tomato sandwiches, a large slab of ginger slice, a pot of tea and a hot chocolate drink came to $16.10, and our drinks arrived with a free piece of shortbread on the saucer! The food was homemade and delicious. We'd just started on the pies when a local woman put her head inside the door and called out to us at the back of the tearoom 'You've left your lights on in the van!' Indeed we had, a leftover from the misty and wet conditions at Arthur's Pass. But did we look so 'foreign' in our jeans and old shorts that she could pick us out immediately from the two dozen other diners, some of whom were passers-through like us?

Reefton is proud of its heritage, and the tearoom walls were full of evidence of the town's past. It was the first place in the world to have hydro-electricity, in 1886 (hence the sign at the entrance to the main street), and the event was well-documented with photographs and newspaper articles hung behind us. There was plenty to read. Also everywhere were old school and sporting team photographs, many at least 60 years old, a truly wonderful way to record the town's inhabitants over the years.

Reluctantly, we left to take State Highway 7 to Springs Junction and the Lewis Pass. At last the weather had cleared. The road followed the Inangahua River, through a broad valley lined with beech forest and giving beautiful vistas at every turn, but became slow to drive on. A sign recommended reducing speed to just 15 kilometres per hour to take a poorly-graded horseshoe bend. Again, as I had many times before, I admired the engineers and labourers who pushed the roads through the dense bush and forests. There aren't very many major roads in the South Island, and only a handful which bisect it from east to west coasts; after having nearly completed our journey I could understand why.

The trees cleared, the road improved, and we arrived at Springs Junction which links State Highway 7 from Greymouth to Christchurch with State Highway 65 to Murchison and State Highway 6 to Nelson. The junction has good roadside services for petrol, accommodation and meals, and we filled up the tank with 46 litres of diesel for $40.72.

We entered the Lewis Pass National Reserve, hot springs territory, with Maruia Springs, a spa town, advertising a Thermal Resort, and a free camping ground signposted on the left above the Maruia River. The road to Lewis Pass, 863 m., climbed quickly and steeply through the beech forest and there was a sheer, scary drop to the Lewis River below us. Fortunately, the road is being provided with metal crash barriers. We encountered temporary traffic lights that guided traffic from our side of the road, which was dug up, safely around the bends. This road has its own Engineers and Highway Maintenance Depot, with small cottages provided for the men to live in. Amazingly, once over the pass the countryside suddenly became open, with dry, tussock-covered hills of interesting formation, as though a giant hand had patted them out into flat terraces.

We were nearing the end of our big day's journey, and at Hell's Gate Corner turned sharply left to State Highway 7A and Hanmer Springs. A sign said we had entered the Alpine-Pacific Triangle with thermal pools, vineyards, whale watching and dolphins as the attractions. It was all unbelievably different to what we had encountered that day. In six hours we had left the moody mountain wetness of Arthur's Pass and the primeval landscape of the Otira Gorge for flat farmland around Lake Brunner; we had stopped in the quirky, photogenic, and utterly individual old settlements of Blackball and Reefton, driven alongside great rivers, crossed through magnificent beech forest to the Lewis Pass, and suddenly we were in the equivalent of Disneyland, where the fire risk was extreme.

We booked in at the Mountain View Top 10 Holiday Park, Hanmer Springs (details in Appendix) for the next two nights for a cost of $54, as we wanted to rest a little after the day's drive of 310 kilometres and the mammoth journey from Mt. Cook to Arthur's Pass. We walked to the i-Site Information Centre to book our tickets for a whale watch, $250 for two, at Kaikoura at 12.45 p.m. on Thursday, then had a look at the town. The i-Site Centre should be your first port of call in Hanmer. It is an essential place to visit if you wish to undertake outdoor pursuits in the region for it has all the information, and you can make your activity bookings there. The freephone number is 0800 442 663.

Hanmer Springs is an old and extremely beautiful alpine town renowned for its spas, and the large outdoor thermal reserve where the many pools were full this fine afternoon of splashing children, and dedicated middle-aged soakers. The facilities are open daily from 10 a.m. and include seven open-air thermal pools, three sulphur pools, a 25 metre freshwater heated pool, sauna and steam rooms, and private thermal suites. The first bath house was built in 1884 and the springs have attracted visitors ever since. Half a million people visit to swim and soak all year round in the geothermal water which ranges in temperature from 36 to 42 degrees Celsius.

Hanmer was famous for many years as the site of the Queen Mary Hospital, which specialised in convalescence from nervous disorders. M.'s father had been a patient there for three months in the 1920s, recovering from a laboratory chemical explosion in which he lost one eye, and became, for a while, completely deaf. The hospital has closed down so a memory lane visit was not possible for M., but I know he was pleased to see it.

The town is sheltered by its backdrop of rugged mountains, and the air is very pure. This high land behind Hanmer is where the New Zealand mountaineer Mark Inglis, who lost both lower legs to frostbite in 1982 on Mt. Cook, is training for his assault on Mt. Everest in May 2006. New legs which will reduce the impact on his stumps during descent are under construction in Christchurch.

There are many forest walks to take in the area, on over 50 kilometres of tracks. The walks vary from half-hour ambles to easy one-hour walks, longer walks taking up to three hours. Hanmer Forest contains some of New Zealand's oldest exotic plantings, and the shorter walks have interpretation stops which identify the tree species. The forest is full of native birds, and if you hear a bellbird singing, you will remember its pure sound forever. Outdoor enthusiasts can also try horse-trekking, mountain biking, quad biking, and jet boating on the Waiau River.

Hanmer has become a favourite holiday town for the residents of Christchurch. Smart new houses, motels, and ski chalets are everywhere, and its principal *raison d'etre* is obvious from the street names; we passed Cheltenham, Bath, Harrogate and Leamington Streets on our easy walk into the town centre. There are plans to extend the thermal reserve and pools, so popular have they become. We sat outside on the wooden deck of a pleasant bar in the thermal reserve and had our usual beer and gin and tonic, and a short stroll around the shops, and decided to have dinner at the Hot Springs Hotel adjacent to the campground and leave the Blackball sausages for another night. We should have stuck with the sausages, for the entrée of scallops and the main courses of roast lamb and beef were both ghastly, almost inedible, a $41.88 waste of money. Don't go there.

Fortunately the camp, the closest to the town, was exceptionally good with excellent ablutions and facilities, a large choice of level sites, and well-treed with silver birches and willows. A motorhome had pulled in next to us while we were at dinner. A nice red mat reading 'Welcome' and a sparkling white step stool were outside the door, and I could swear I saw a potted geranium on the kitchen bench. Germans?

The dream of many townies is to visit a high country station. Somehow that descriptive phrase conjures up images of a tough, hardworking, colourful, exciting, unorthodox life lived to the full, regulated by weather, the seasons, and the demands of animals, where the well-furnished, large and gracious homestead reeks of the history of the occupants and of unending hospitality, and the daily housekeeping routine for family and farm workers takes place on a scale unimaginable to a city dweller. *A River Rules My Life* written by Mona Anderson (published by A.H. & A.W. Reed, Wellington, 1963) had immediately captured the imagination of New Zealand women when it was published; in that first year, her book had five printings. She had gone to Mount Algidus Station, one of the most isolated sheep farms in New Zealand, its 100,000 acres (40,000 hectares) located in the foothills of the Southern Alps alongside the mighty Wilberforce River, her Rubicon, as a young bride completely unaware of the hardships in store and what would be expected of her for the next 23 years as the Missus of all she surveyed. This was the first time that life in the high country from a woman's perspective had been recorded in such detail, and the book was an instant bestseller. It is still sought today in second hand bookshops, and I treasure my copy, a 1964 edition, inscribed 'To Maureen, from Mum and Dad, Birthday Greetings'. The powerful and minute observations of everyday life in this sort of community have stayed with me over the intervening years, and when I glanced through the road atlas after having finalised our campervan bookings and realised that Molesworth Station was not far from Hanmer Springs, I wanted to see it, to capture both the romance and the reality of a way of life so foreign to my own.

Molesworth, 202,350 hectares (500,000 acres), and world famous, is New Zealand's largest station. It is now owned by the New Zealand Government in order to protect its status as a unique High Country Park, and the Department of Conservation has the lease to farm the land. The station is located in Southern Marlborough to the west of the Kaikoura Ranges, and is the size of Stewart Island to the south of New Zealand. Early attempts to farm sheep in the barren mountains and tussock flats met with failure, so a mix of sheep and cattle was tried. Today the station farms cattle only, and is able to support 10,000 head.

An article in *The New Zealand Herald* on 8 January 2005 stated that the Department of Conservation would open the only access road for about 10 weeks until early March for private tourists, and I had immediately decided to go. Alas, a closer study of the road atlas showed that the Molesworth Station Road from the locked gate at Acheron House was suitable for 4WD vehicles only. A friend who had done the trip confirmed this; it would be difficult to drive there in our campervan because the road, which is not much more than two tyre tracks in the hard, gravelly earth, runs alongside the Acheron River and there are many little streams to ford. There was also the question of whether our insurance with Maui Motorhomes would cover us in the event of a breakdown; I discovered that the Automobile Association will not attend in these parts, and that there is no mobile phone coverage.

We had allowed ourselves a spare day in Hanmer Springs and could have booked a guided day trip to Molesworth Station. Looking back now, I wish we had, for it was an opportunity presented, but missed, particularly as we had planned to set the alarm clock to depart early on Thursday morning to reach Kaikoura in plenty of time for our 12.45 p.m. whale watch. I think we were probably fatigued by the cracking pace we had set ourselves; we had been on the road for almost four weeks and had driven from the top to the bottom of New Zealand, and now the deadline was looming for the return of the campervan in Christchurch on Saturday afternoon and our flight from there back to Auckland the following day. However, Molesworth will always be there to visit later on.

If you are interested in seeing this representative example of a way of life particular to the South Island of New Zealand, you should take the opportunity to do so. The i-Site Centre in the town will give you all the necessary current information. Trailways Safaris (ph. (03) 315 7181, mobile 025 201 45361), which is operated by the owner, takes 4WD tours right up the valley to the Molesworth Homestead. The full day tour costs $129 per person and includes lunch and refreshments and tours are available from October until the end of May. Bookings are essential. Details of all the tours available from this company can be read on www.hanmerview.co.nz/molesworth.html.

Hanmer Springs Helicopters (ph. (03) 315 7758, reservations 0800 888 308, email hanmerheli@xtra.co.nz) operates a 50 minute Historic Stations and Alpine Ranges scenic flight over Molesworth and St. James Stations, with a landing on St. James Station, for a cost of $385 per adult, and $220 per child. The company is located off State Highway 7A a short drive south of Hanmer Springs.

M. felt stiff and sore the next morning, maybe another reason why we didn't attempt a tour to Molesworth, and decided to have a massage. It worked. He was eager to see more of Hanmer Springs so we drove around looking at the new residential development on the hillside, and had a very good lunch at the busy Springs Deli Café of lasagne roll, salad, and wonderful coffee, for $28.50. Suddenly, as we backed out of our parking space in the main street, we had had enough of Hanmer Springs. M. said he wanted more action, which shows you the reviving power of a good massage. I consulted the road atlas and we headed straight out of town for Kaikoura, not bothering to return to the camp to cancel that night's booking or to remove the upturned bucket that the proprietor had lent us to indicate we would be back on that pitch later in the day. The freedom!

At the end of State Highway 7A we turned left onto State Highway 7, signposted Culverden and Christchurch, and at Mouse Point took a short cut across to Regional Route 70 and Waiau. Kaikoura is only 136 kilometres from Hanmer Springs and we expected to be there in the late afternoon.

Waiau township, alongside the wide Waiau River, has the last fuel stop for the next 75 kilometres, with a hardware store, café, hotel, and food store if you need supplies. We turned left to Mt. Lyford, Hawk Hills, and Kaikoura, rather than take the eastern road across to State Highway 1 at Hawkeswood, because we didn't want to have to double back on that 50 kilometre stretch when we drove from Kaikoura to Christchurch in two days' time.

Regional Route 70 is a back country road serving the farms along it, at times very hilly and winding, and, according to the road signs, icy in winter. If you want isolation, this is the road to take. I was reminded of a grouchy interview I had read very recently in a South Island newspaper where the heinous statement was made that the only distinguishing feature of New Zealand, the principal tourist drawcard, is the lack of population.

At first the farmland was gentle, utterly rural, with tall rows of macrocarpa and poplar trees and good fencing outlining the pastures. In spite of its claim to be part of the Alpine-Pacific Tourist Route, we didn't meet anything else on the road except a few farm vehicles and a huge herd of black cows with their calves walking along in front of us on their way to the milking sheds. We couldn't make much progress for a while, until one calf became frightened by our van and began to run, with its mother in fast pursuit. Suddenly most of the herd took fright and separated to either side of the road, and although we felt we were in Pamplona running with the bulls we got through, easily outpacing them. I hoped that all the exercise hadn't churned their milk to butter.

The road climbed to Mt. Lyford Village, an alpine resort set in high country tussock land. The slow driving continued across the Whales Back Saddle to Hawk Hills, where the fire danger was extreme and a total ban was in place. When we arrived at the Kahutara River, we found that it had completely dried up. M. said he wouldn't take Route 70 again, because its only merit is that it is off the beaten track, and he's seen enough farms in New Zealand to know what they look like. Oh dear! That's the reward for being the navigator.

At last we arrived at Kowhai and the coast at South Bay, and the blessed relief of State Highway 1 for the remaining five kilometres to Kaikoura. It was 30 years since we'd visited Kaikoura, and what was once a transit stop for petrol and a cup of tea between Picton and Christchurch, with a narrow main street running alongside the rocky sea front, has become a bustling tourist town. The old main road is now a smart esplanade lined with motels, and plenty of cafés where people sit *chicly* outside sipping their lattes. Such is the pulling power of whales.

We booked in to the Kaikoura Top 10 Holiday Park at 34 Beach Road for the next two nights, for $54 (details in Appendix). We were allocated a site which would be ours for the duration of our stay, a sensible recognition of the fact that the local taxi service and public transport are somewhat limited and campers need to take their vans out to drive to the Whaleway Station, yes, that's what it's called, which is situated at the side of the old Kaikoura railway station. This is an excellent camp, divided into sheltered bays with thick, attractive plantings of pittosporum, coprosma, flax, cabbage trees, and other native plants which grow well in coastal areas. The pitches are gravelled, and separated occasionally by a small lawn set with a wooden picnic table.

The whales have put Kaikoura on the map. We drove out immediately on an orientation tour to see where we had to go the next day, and found the town seething with backpackers and cyclists, and motorhomes parked everywhere.

I bought a few potatoes and mashed them, and fried the Blackball sausages. A sweep around the back of the fridge brought forth two tomatoes and an avocado, I opened a tin of asparagus saved for emergencies, and was able to use up the last of the tomato ketchup and Paul Newman's finest. Although I had reneged on my earlier promise made five days previously not to cook again, I was glad I had because it was a fitting farewell tribute to our campervan kitchen, and proof that a reasonable dinner can come out of the most unlikely places!

CHAPTER 25

WHALE WATCHING AT KAIKOURA, AND THE END OF OUR JOURNEY IN CHRISTCHURCH

On Thursday we left the campervan in the huge parking lot outside the Whaleway Station, situated on the beachfront adjacent to the camp but necessitating a short drive to get there, and found that 12.45 p.m. was just a check-in time for our trip. The weather had deteriorated, the sea had lost its early morning calm, and there was some doubt as to whether the trip would take place. If it did, we would be called for a bus departure at about 1.30 p.m. and driven to South Bay, 10 minutes away, to board the boat which would take us out to the whales.

I don't like sailing on an empty stomach, so went through to the cafe and ordered a steak sandwich and coffee. Murray, who had done such a sterling job of driving the campervan around New Zealand, and is a *real* man, settled for a wedge of quiche. I had a moment of hysteria when my food arrived, for the super-size platter was covered with two thick slices of bread cut lengthwise along the loaf, piled with lettuce, on top of which was about 400 grams of steak cut into thin strips and fried to brown perfection with an equal quantity of sliced onion rings, topped with a good spray of barbecue sauce, sliced tomatoes piled on top of that, then a layer of mayonnaise, and plump hot chips on the side! I begged M. to help me eat it, but he was very happy with his quiche. I am ashamed to say that I scoffed the lot. The total bill came to $25.50, with coffee, and the ingredients in my steak sandwich would have fed three people in any other café. Even if you're not whale watching, it is worth going there just for the food and the very good coffee.

That huge, delicious and self-indulgent lunch turned out to be symptomatic of the excellence of the whole whale watch experience. We were lucky, for it was decided that our boat would go out, although it would be the last sailing for the day as the 3.30 p.m. trip had been cancelled because of the worsening weather. The company is consistent in its desire to make every whale watching experience a safe and pleasant one, and although our trip was smooth and uneventful, I noticed on the way back to shore two hours later that the swell had increased and white caps had appeared on the top of the waves. The later sailing would have been difficult for crew and passengers.

The comfortable coach took us all to the departure point at South Bay wharf, we walked down the gangway, and took our seats in the fully enclosed cabin of the boat for a 10 minute talk on safety procedures and what we could hope to see when out on the water. People who were prone to sea-sickness were asked to move to seats in the centre of the cabin where they would have a more stable ride. The very modern whale watch catamarans are purpose-designed and built, with the length of a boat, 20 metres, not exceeding the length of a fully-grown sperm whale. I thought this an excellent idea when we eventually came alongside a whale, as it gave a feeling of scale and a way of measuring the huge, glistening, 50-ton bulk in the water just 50 metres away. The ratio of passengers to deck space has been carefully calculated to ensure that every person has a full view of the whales; no one has to elbow aside another passenger in order to take a photograph.

While the captain took the vessel out to the whale ground, we watched an informative screen presentation and listened to an energetic, likeable crew member who knew everything there was to know about the Kaikoura coast and what is known as its 'grand canyon of the sea world' which attracts marvellous deep sea creatures, and was an authority on the local sperm whales. I say 'local', because he and the captain could recognise the individual characteristics of the three whales we saw, and had pet names for them. They all looked the same to me, but this clever young man could spot small differences in skin tone, or tail formation, or habit.

Suddenly, well out from shore, the captain stopped the vessel, left the bridge, and put a long pole down into the water. This was a sounder and showed whether any whales were lurking underneath. She moved the boat a little further along the coast, sounded again, pronounced whales present, and we all filed out onto the decks to watch the water. One surfaced, lay in the sun for a while, then turned its tail up in the air and dived down without a ripple, the smoothest manoeuvre imaginable. We were all ecstatic, particularly a party of Japanese tourists; I hope they could understand English because our guide never stopped talking and, for me, his brilliant and often humorous commentary was a highlight of the trip.

We were in a group of three whale watch vessels, all packed with tourists, all circling around for the best viewing positions. We had four sightings of whales altogether, one of them, called Tony, surfacing twice to have a look at us. Somehow our guide could tell when they were ready to dive, and told us the exact moment to get that all-important photograph of the aerial tail flip before the whale became completely submerged.

The excitement of whale watching lies in the trip on the water, the expertise, knowledge, and charm of the crew, and in being able to get so close to these huge creatures. *Live the experience*, for the photographs will be disappointing; there's nothing very inspiring about a snapshot of a whale's tail in a sea of water, except for the memories it brings back. Incidentally, the company will refund 80 per cent of your ticket price if a whale is not sighted.

It was time to move further along the coast to the Barney Reilly rocks to view a fur seal colony basking there in the sun, plus two newborn seals which had not been there yesterday. We moved amongst a large pod of five or six hundred dolphins and watched the graceful creatures leaping around us for nearly a quarter of an hour then, reluctantly, agreed with the crew that it was time to turn back to Kaikoura. We were back in the camp by 4 p.m., having had a worthwhile afternoon in which we learned a lot about Kaikoura and its history, sperm whaling and the coastal waters, and saw up close three good examples of local marine life, an experience which most people around the world will never be lucky enough to enjoy.

If you intend to whale watch at Kaikoura, remember that you can include sightings of fur seals and dolphins as well in the one trip and it is not necessary, unless marine creatures are your delight, to undertake sightings of them elsewhere. Details of Whale Watch Kaikoura are given in the Appendix.

If a trip on the ocean doesn't appeal, or you cannot spare the three hours it takes for the total whale watch experience just described, Kaikoura Helicopters Ltd. (ph. (03) 319 6609, mobile 027 437 2300, email: kk.heli@worldofwhales.co.nz, www.worldofwhales.co.nz, operates 30 minute whale watching flights on demand from the Whaleway Station.

Maori culture has undergone a huge renaissance in the last 30 years, and Maori tourism is booming. The local Ngati Kuri tribe operates Maori Tours Kaikoura (ph. (03) 319 5567, reservations 0800 866 267, email: info@maoritours.co.nz, www.maoritours.co.nz), which are recommended for tourists wanting an authentic cultural experience that combines the natural, spiritual and social history of the tribe. Tour groups do not exceed eight people, and the tours take 3 hours 30 minutes.

Dive Kaikoura (ph. (03) 319 6622, reservations 0800 728 223, email: divekaikoura@xtra.co.nz, www.scubadive.co.nz) situated across the road from the Kaikoura Visitor Information Centre at 94 Westend, operates seal swimming trips, will take you diving off the coast and, if you are a beginner and wish to learn, runs four-day instruction courses.

A cup of tea was called for while we debated dinner. I felt I would be ready to dine lightly off fish at 8 p.m. On the recommendation of the camp manager, we took a taxi to the White Morph restaurant (ph. (03) 319 5676), a fine dining establishment overlooking the ocean at 94 Esplanade a few kilometres south of the camp. The walls were painted in one of my favourite colours to dine by, a rich aubergine, and I immediately felt relaxed and happy even though our clothes, which had been through a rugged month, were not quite on a par with those of the other diners, particularly an ex-Prime Minister seated with his friends in a quiet corner. What followed can be described as one of the best dinners I have ever had, capped off by a gesture well beyond the call of duty by the *maitre d'*, the wife of the chef/owner.

Guests at an adjacent table were tackling a large and exquisitely presented seafood platter, and M., who does not like *fish* fish, beamed when he saw a crayfish perched on top. The *maitre d'* said it was not your normal New Zealand platter, because everything was poached in the appropriate *court bouillon* with nothing deep fried. That was fine by me – I'd had enough fried food at lunch. Well, it was a sumptuous feast of crayfish atop creamy potato, poached salmon fillet, hapuka, prawns and scallops, steamed mussels, and as a contrast, chilled hot-smoked salmon which was completely unlike its poached counterpart. Two different cold mayonnaise-type sauces were served with the fish, and the usual lemon wedges. The delicacy and lightness of the dish was superb and we ate everything, including a side salad, which the *maitre d'* was reluctant to provide as she said the platter was sufficient on its own. (M. found room for a dessert). The food was plain, and perfect, and on writing about it now I am tempted to try to reproduce it myself for friends who won't mind sitting up to the table in advance, forks at the ready, while I carry it in, still steaming, from the kitchen. The platter, salad, dessert, and one tea cost $143.10, and the Stoneleigh Sauvignon Blanc, a pleasant choice, was $38.00. This dinner was our most expensive on the trip, and easily the best.

It was 10.30 p.m., and M. asked for a taxi to be called. Alas, the sole taxi on duty in Kaikoura that evening was on a half-hour journey to a farm in the hills behind the town, and wouldn't be back for almost an hour. Dismay! Mrs *Maitre d'*, to my regret I do not know her name, offered at once to drive us back to the camp in her own car, would take no refusals, and left the restaurant, with its scattering of late diners, to look after itself while she did so. It was an act of unparalleled kindness which these two coming-up-for-elderly campers will never, ever forget.

It was a very cold night and the campervan was rocked occasionally by sharp gusts of wind. Snow had fallen on the Kaikoura Range behind the town, but the air the next morning was just medium-crisp and it felt good to be on our way for the last day of travelling. I put on make-up for the occasion, the first for 28 days! Regrettably, a tornado had flattened parts of Greymouth on the West Coast the day before, and the morning newspaper was full of photographs and stories of the tragedy.

The Pacific Ocean to our left as we took State Highway 1 south to Christchurch, 190 kilometres distant, shone bright blue in the sunlight, with hardly a ripple on its surface. At 9.30 a.m. there was no traffic in front of us and we felt like kings of the road. The narrow highway is carved out of the cliff face and follows its contours. It is not made for speed, so the kilometre distance is not a good guide to the time it will take. There is a campground at Omihi Reserve which has power points, toilets, and fresh water, and the adjacent camp at Goose Bay (ph. (03) 319 5348) which also takes bookings for the Omihi Reserve, is a good stop if you wish to enjoy fishing and diving off the raw, rocky shore.

The road eventually turned inland, tucked in alongside the high, dry hill farms of North Canterbury, and became much less exciting although very steep with plenty of sharp bends. It was slow driving in the van, but safe, with good wide shoulders on both sides of the road, quite unlike the Alpine-Pacific Triangle route on the far side of the hills which we had used two days previously and which I cannot recommend unless you want a back country experience. Perhaps it might improve when there is snow on the peaks to make it more 'alpine'.

Sheep were everywhere, always all gathered in one huge paddock ready for shearing, or dipping, or slaughter, I don't know.

We re-crossed the Waiau River which we had met further upstream on Tuesday when taking State Highway 7 to Hanmer Springs. Here the river was wide and stony, a dirty grey colour, a flat contrast to the beige countryside elsewhere. The wide vistas were broken by tall shelter belts of the usual poplar and pine trees, and M. remarked as we approached Cheviot that the hay must be good this year.

Cheviot is a pleasant country town with a few cafés, all services, and a Four Square supermarket, and marked the beginning of groomed countryside which was to last all the way to Christchurch. Judging by the names of local towns – Phoebe, Mina, Ethelton, and Greta – I decided an early settler with foresight must have farmed his daughters out to other nearby landowners, keeping the holdings in the family, as it were. The superb and very large plantings of grapes, which stretch up into the hills on the left of the highway, are reminiscent of the Champagne countryside in northern France, and Waipara, at the junction of State Highway 7 from the Lewis Pass, and State Highway 1, is renowned for excellent wine of the same name. In Auckland I have drunk bottles of Waipara Springs chardonnay and sauvignon blanc, and if your holiday route, or timetable, does not include a visit to the vineyards along Raupara Road in Marlborough, this will be a satisfactory winery to visit. It operates a casual restaurant, and is located at State Highway 1 (ph. (03) 314 6777, www.waiparasprings.co.nz).

We stopped at Amberley's Country Café on the main road for lunch and a break from the van. I ordered macaroni cheese and salad and, unbelievably, the 'salad' was generous helpings of rice salad, potato salad, and pasta salad, all piled onto one large lettuce leaf, with a small wedge of tomato on the side. Talk about a carbohydrate hit! It cost $11, and the accompanying coffee was excellent. This seemed to be a well-known truckers' road stop, and the take-away food was planned accordingly. All the self-service counter food was individually plastic-wrapped, something I had not seen before – salad rolls, slices, biscuits, huge slabs of sustaining fruit cake, massive muffins, and well-filled sandwiches – and I watched several drivers pull in, grab a hot pie, and fill a large bag with the rest of the food which could be unwrapped and eaten later in the cab, still perfectly moist and fresh, while driving along.

Nothing seemed more important than arriving in Christchurch as soon as possible. We bypassed Kaiapoi, described as a historic river town, crossed the wide and swift Waimakariri River last seen on our way to Arthur's Pass, and at Belfast, on the outskirts of Christchurch, turned left onto State Highway 74 which is the city ring road, following signs to City Centre and Lyttelton. I had a large map of Christchurch city so the Meadow Park Top 10 Holiday Park, at 39 Meadow Street, Papanui (details in Appendix) was easy to find.

This excellent camp takes second place to the Creeksyde Top 10 in Queenstown, but not by much. The grounds are level with large, superb specimens of sycamore, chestnut, oak, willow and birch trees, and conifers. The ultra-modern automated ablutions have to be tried to be believed. It is possible to wash one's hands and exit from the toilet block *without touching a tap, a lever, or a door handle*. If you are a New Zealander reading this book and wish to take your children to Christchurch for an inexpensive holiday, you should investigate the range of moderately priced cabins, chalets, and tourist flats for hire. The park offers plenty of entertainment for children, from the heated indoor pool and water slide, a toddlers' pool, two private spas, an adventure playground, a trampoline, and a games room and TV room. The camp is a short walk from Papanui Road, a main transport link which runs directly into the city. Luggage storage is available, and small valuables such as wallets, passports and airline tickets can be stored safely in the office. The camp operates a mail and message service, a dry cleaning collection service, has an Internet kiosk, and is a 10 minute walk from the excellent Northlands Shopping Centre.

We paid $27 for our powered site for one night, and parked underneath a sycamore tree which gave welcome shade. It was mid-afternoon and suddenly we had nothing to do, and several hours to fill in. The van wasn't due to be returned to the Maui depot by Christchurch airport until 5 p.m. the next day, Saturday, 11 March. We'd given ourselves a spare 24 hours just in case something went wrong at the last minute. It was an unaccustomed situation. Here we were at the end of the trip, a moment I had at times longed for, particularly in the helicopter flying over the Southern Alps, or when coping with sub-standard facilities at Pauanui and Lake Taupo, or the few times we ate dreadful food at Whangarei, Te Kuiti, Queenstown and Hanmer Springs; yet, when I thought of the high times, of the places we had seen, the energy we had expended and the fun we had had doing so, I felt quite sad it was coming to an end.

There was nothing for it but to start packing up and cleaning the van. But first, the antique shops at the nearby Merivale shopping centre beckoned. M. nobly dropped me there while he called on a pharmacy colleague, and the half-hour spent doing what I like best restored my good humour. A large gin and tonic on return to the camp – large because we were trying to use up the last of the gin – made us disinclined to tackle the chores, so we opted for an early dinner at the Phuket Thai restaurant at Papanui. For $33.50 we had a delicious dinner of curry puffs, a favourite, followed by beef and prawn dishes in green curry coconut sauce, plenty of rice, and drank our remaining bottle of wine, an excellent Allan Scott 2002 Chardonnay.

Christchurch, known locally as the Garden City, is a good central point from which to plan trips to Kaikoura, Hanmer Springs, Waipara Valley, Banks Peninsula and Akaroa and, if the weather is appropriate, to ski at Mt. Hutt and jet boat on the Waimakariri River. The city is the prettiest in New Zealand, with the willow-treed Avon River, curving gently through and crossed by many ornate bridges, well-incorporated into the overall design. The Christchurch Cathedral in Cathedral Square is built in the English Gothic Style and is small by cathedral standards, but is attractive and well-proportioned, very much a community church, and family legend has it that my great-grandfather worked on it as a builder when he arrived in Christchurch from England with his family. There are other fine stone buildings adjacent to The Square, notably Canterbury University, the Canterbury Museum which has an excellent ornithological section, and Christ's College, one of New Zealand's most famous boys' schools.

Errol Brathwaite in *The Companion Guide to the South Island of New Zealand* writes that Canterbury was founded by the Church of England with the intention of transposing an '...English community, possessing English ideals and English institutions, and completely free of poverty and crime', and that 'The Canterbury Association, which conducted the scheme's business in England ... was headed by the Archbishop of Canterbury himself, with a board consisting of bishops, peers of the realm and wealthy men'. This was not to be a haphazard colonisation. The land was intended for settlement by the upper middle, upper, and professional classes at a price of three pounds per acre, and Christchurch was planned as the principal settlement, the *crème de la crème* of future Canterbury society arriving in the First Four Ships in 1850. The strong British heritage is evident, for Hagley Park is the central feature of the city, and the orderly layout compares well with other South Island towns settled in the mid-nineteenth century. The street names such as Gloucester, Worcester, Hereford, Cambridge, Oxford, and St. Albans give the clue, and there are dozens more like them. Even the pretty river which winds through the city and gives it such charm is named Avon.

But as in the rest of New Zealand, no matter how well born, the life of a colonist was not easy. In *Tales of Pioneer Women*, John Deans gives an account of his grandmother, the redoubtable Jane Deans of Riccarton, arriving in Lyttelton Harbour in 1853 as the new wife of John Deans, one of the early settlers who, with his brother, was mainly responsible for proving the suitability of Canterbury for settlement. You may not agree with the grandfather in this respect when his grandson records that upon landing, their effects which included 'furniture, all household requisites, a water wheel, threshing mill, and dog-cart, had to be taken round by whaleboat to Sumner, up the Heathcote River, and thence by dray to Riccarton', a journey of two months. Riccarton, now an inner city suburb, was, in 1857 a place of 'luxurious cornfields' … 'with fine hedgerows of gorse and broom', and the racecourse was already well-established as a social centre of the district.

Unfortunately the adjacent plains, while suited climatically to sheep grazing, were swampy and full of tussock, and the land, which was supposed to make fortunes for the settlers, sold only very slowly. Experienced Australian graziers, tired of wrestling with unsuitable weather conditions in their own country, were invited to invest and their wealth boosted the development of Canterbury. The colony still remained strongly British, though, and today Christchurch is a quiet, conservative city, where good taste and manners reign supreme and it is considered inappropriate to flash one's wealth, where a good navy blazer and a tweed jacket will get a gentleman through most occasions, and where a pearl necklace can still be worn without looking old-fashioned. A recent survey found that Christchurch is the city most preferred by Aucklanders as a place to live after their own, and it is my choice, too.

Christchurch is a city of quiet amusements. It is billed as the world's aerial gateway to Antarctica, and The International Antarctic Centre has twice been judged the best attraction in New Zealand. It is an indoor experience, and is located at 38 Orchard Road near Christchurch Airport (freephone 0508 736 4846). The Tramway central city tour (ph. (03) 366 7830), which includes the driver's commentary, is a pleasant way to tour the principal attractions of the central city. It departs from Cathedral Square, the Art Gallery, the Arts Centre, and Victoria Square, and is free for children under 15 years. The Arts Centre on Worcester Boulevard, a short walk from Cathedral Square, is open seven days and specialises in locally-made crafts including bone carving, woodcraft, leatherwork, knitwear, and weaving. Make sure you visit the Botanic Gardens in Hagley Park, and include a drive to Mona Vale Homestead reached from Fendalton Road, continuing along Mona Vale Avenue which has splendid old homes set in manicured gardens lining the Avon River.

The Christchurch Gondola, situated at 10 Bridle Road (ph. (03) 384 0700, www.gondola.co.nz) is only 15 minutes' drive from the city centre and gives spectacular views over Lyttelton Harbour which was formed from the crater of a drowned volcano, and Banks Peninsula, and across the Canterbury Plains to the Southern Alps. The Sign of the Takahe, a well-known landmark above the Cashmere Hills, is worth a visit to admire its baronial splendour and the impressive array of British heraldry.

Rugby fans can take in a match at Jade Stadium, one of the principal sports grounds in New Zealand, and the scene of past clashes between the All Blacks and The Lions. By the way, if readers are considering attending the Rugby World Cup matches in New Zealand in 2011, they should book a motorhome, the interisland ferry, and campground sites well in advance. I don't want to alarm you, but in June 2005, about 1500 campervans full of British fans were expected to descend on Christchurch for the Lions-All Blacks test match, to take up just 840 available camp sites.

I recommend highly taking a side trip to Akaroa Harbour on Banks Peninsula. The small French-favoured seaside town has the Akaroa Top 10 Holiday Park, and details are given in the Appendix. If driving there from the Meadow Park campground, the quickest route is along Papanui Road, skirting Hagley Park along Rolleston Avenue to arrive at Brougham Street, State Highway 73, and to turn right to the Southern Arterial Motorway which ends shortly at the junction with State Highway 75. Follow signs to Banks Peninsula and Akaroa.

An alternative, and much more scenic exit from Christchurch is given by Dave Chowdhury in *Driving Scenic New Zealand.* Take Ferry Road from Cathedral Square and High Street to Sumner on the coast, and follow Evans Pass Road, turning right onto the narrow Summit Road which winds along the Port Hills to Gebbies Pass and joins State Highway 75 by Lake Ellesmere. This second route is a good one to take, although the driving is more difficult, if you do not wish to take the Christchurch Gondola, or view Christchurch from The Sign of the Takahe, as it makes both those trips superfluous.

State Highway 75 continues to Little River, past an excellent lookout point where the full panorama of the Akaroa Harbour is laid out in spectacular fashion below, through Devauchelle's Bay, and on to Akaroa. You should allow at least two hours for the high route across the Port Hills, a little less for the direct route from the city.

Early attempts by the French to claim Banks Peninsula came to nothing after the signing of the Treaty of Waitangi which gave sovereign power to Britain. Those settlers who had arrived expecting to found a French colony stayed on, and Akaroa developed into a French/British settlement not seen elsewhere in New Zealand.

The small and picturesque Akaroa township trades a little on its erstwhile French beginnings, and is a delightful place to visit in summer. Many Christchurch residents have holiday homes here. Watch for a local fishing boat to pull in to the jetty, for you will be able to buy fresh fish for your dinner at night. Try the flounder. If your frying pan is not big enough, the Akaroa Top 10 camp has a gas barbecue outdoors.

You can swim with dolphins at Akaroa. Akaroa Dolphins, at 65 Beach Road (ph. (03) 304 7866, email cruise@akaroadolphins.co.nz, www.akaroadolphins.co.nz) runs nature cruises around the harbour, as does Akaroa Harbour Cruises and Swimming with Dolphins, Main Wharf (ph. (03) 304 7641, email akaroa@blackcat.co.nz., www.blackcat.co.nz, freephone 0800 436 574).

There are several good cafés along the waterfront, and *Driving Scenic New Zealand* recommends the Waterfront Eaterie.

Our neighbours in the motorhome next door watched in amazement the next day as the great, therapeutic chuck-out began. Out went the old pillows, cushions, and hand towels I had packed for this express purpose, knowing they were too bulky to take back with us on the plane. Out, too, went the crackly old radio, the clothes I knew I really mustn't wear again, accumulated magazines and newspapers, the few fridge contents, and unused paper plates and cups and my old breadboard.

Out came the five soft holdalls stored away under a bunk before we left Auckland, and into them, somehow, went the two sleeping bags which refused to lie flat, all M.'s shoes, three pairs of which he had never worn on the trip, and the rest of our gear. We were hopelessly overweight due to our extensive medical kit, heavy torches, the computer, and unused wet weather clothing. I turned the smallest holdall into my cabin bag and filled it with my large journal, travelling literature, maps, and all the brochures we'd collected on the way, and it was so heavy I couldn't swing it over my shoulder, nonchalantly, at all.

We worked like demons to clean and shine the campervan. I am a careful housewife and found it difficult to toss out half a packet of laundry powder, the almost full container of Jif cleaner, some tinned food supplies, and half-used jars of Vegemite and jam. Murray emptied the waste water and cleaned the toilet cassette, an unpleasant task for which Maui Motorhomes charges if it's not done, found a hose somewhere, and washed down the outside of the van.

We returned the van at noon, well ahead of its scheduled time of 5 p.m., with a full fuel tank, in its original pristine condition, and undamaged except for the small shatter on the windscreen incurred after leaving Pauanui (which didn't seem to worry the people at Maui at all), so that we didn't lose our Vehicle Security Deposit of $220.

The charm, efficiency and professionalism displayed at Maui in Auckland are all to be found in their Christchurch depot. Our numberplate was checked and matched against records, the odometer read, and our luggage removed into the reception area by a cheerful young man who complimented us on the excellent condition of the van. No worries there! To our astonishment a file was produced with every single detail of our original booking and of the changeover of vans in Auckland, and the distances travelled in both were calculated at 4,725 kilometres, on which we had to pay $116 diesel tax. I know that a mistake was made in our favour. I had recorded faithfully every morning before we set off the odometer reading of the day before, and had already calculated that we travelled 5,442 kilometres. However it would be a nuisance to prove, to leaf through the untidy pages of my daily journal, add it all up, and eventually pay more diesel tax, so after an initial honest 'Are you sure? I thought we had travelled further than that,' I let the matter rest.

A taxi was called, and after many thankyous and goodbyes we bundled our gear in and were driven to the Crowne Plaza hotel in the city centre. A late lunch cost $47.50, the seafood dinner buffet cost $100.50, and our room, at a Weekend Special rate which included breakfast, cost $195.00, a total of $343.75. M. flopped onto the bed to watch some rugby, I commandeered the bathroom, and we gradually wound down from the exertions of the morning.

As a last gesture towards the great pies of New Zealand I ordered a chicken pie for lunch the next day at Christchurch Airport before our early afternoon flight to Auckland, and M. had a square of pizza. It is hard to believe that food could be so awful. My pie, of dry, chewy pastry, was filled with a small and solitary lump of stringy stewed fowl, and a few tablespoons of over-salted, gluey cornflour yuck. M. had a mouthful of his pizza and left the rest of it alone. The cost for this disgraceful example of food which included very bad coffee and a small bottle of lemonade was $18.80, and is a good reason on its own to avoid Christchurch Airport. Arrive there with a full stomach, please!

The weather in Auckland was balmy, so very much warmer than that of the South Island, and by five o'clock we were sitting down at home with a beer and a gin and tonic as though we'd never been away.

CHAPTER 26

CONCLUSION

Now for the statistics.
Our 30 day tour of New Zealand cost **$13,560.79.** We spent 24 days on the road, averaged 226.75 kilometres per day, and travelled **5,442 kilometres.**

Charges were as follows:

Transport

Hire of Maui Motorhome		$7,407.00
30 day hire	$5,946.00	
Full cover insurance	1,140.00	
Vehicle Security Deposit	220.00	
One-way fee	180.00	
Pre-paid gas	25.00	
Diesel Recovery Tax	116.00	
	$7,627.00	
less recovery of security deposit	220.00	
	$7,407.00	

Cook Strait Ferry Crossing	
Lynx Interisland Ferry	290.00
Air New Zealand Return Flight to Auckland	79.60

Fuel

Diesel, 504.31 litres, at average cost of .831 cents per litre		419.41
Campground charges		
27 nights @ average cost of $25.16 per night		679.50
Sightseeing		$1,104.00
Waitangi Mission House	$20.00	
Waitomo Glowworm Cave	56.00	
Buller Gorge Swingbridge	10.00	
Helicopter Flight	640.00	
Dunedin Bus Tour	30.00	
Tour to Albatross Colony	98.00	
Whale Watch Kaikoura	250.00	
Meals and Drinks		2,052.82
Food and Groceries		460.69
Emergency nights in hotels: dinner, bed and breakfast		551.02
Hotel, Christchurch, last night		343.75
Taxis		170.00
	Grand Total	**$13,560.79**

A neighbour asked me on return why we hadn't just toured in our car, and stayed in motels, if we wanted to see New Zealand. Well, that wasn't the purpose of the trip; we were on a mission to establish our preference for one sort of camping vehicle over another next time we undertook an extensive journey through Europe. Having very recently, during the writing of this book, travelled for six weeks by car in Italy and France, staying in hotels, I appreciate now as never before the advantages of camping, whether in a caravan or motorhome, over that mode of travel – the surety of accommodation, my own surroundings, no constant packing and unpacking, and ready access to excellent camp laundries. Three cotton T-shirts and a nightdress entrusted to the laundry of our four star hotel in Rome, already well-worn and with all the shrink taken out of them, came back two sizes smaller and had to be thrown out, an annoying experience when travelling with minimum luggage.

After 30 days in our campervan, we decided that this mode of travel would not suit us on longer journeys. We came down overwhelmingly on the side of caravanning.

When we tour Europe, we like to take at least six months to do it, to travel slowly, set up camp for a week, and tour the surrounding countryside on day trips by car before moving on to the next place that interests us. It is a leisurely and fulfilling way to explore a country. Our caravan is our base, our haven, a miniature kitchen/living room/bedroom set up ready for return at the end of a day's sightseeing, a place into which we step thankfully each night.

Motorcaravanning is a completely different experience. It is a fast and efficient way to travel through a new country if time is short and you wish to be masters of your own universe. Motorhomers pull into a camp at night and leave in the morning to travel to the next place. Very rarely do they sojourn in one camp for a few days, unless good public transport is at the camp gate, because they have to drive their van out to get anywhere and so choose to move on.

M. and I were frustrated by the constraints that 30 days' hire placed on us. Although a small country, there is so much to see and do that two months should, ideally, be allotted for travelling around New Zealand. Tourists who spend just three weeks here, the average length of van hire, according to Maui Motorhomes, will need to plan their itineraries carefully in order to maximise their experiences and get full value for the cost of the holiday. Motorcaravanning is not cheap. Its advantage lies in the versatility it offers, and the time it saves.

Apart from sorting out our own travel preferences, one other vital fact emerged from our holiday. New Zealand, with its difficult geography and the limits that places on road construction, is most emphatically not suited to extensive touring by caravan, particularly in large parts of the South Island or the Coromandel Peninsula. It is just too hard. In our month on the road, in peak summer touring time, we encountered only one caravan being towed, and saw only one caravan which had arrived in a camp, in Dunedin, to set up. Caravans in New Zealand are holiday homes, often towed to a beauty spot like Lake Taupo, or an activity centre, like Omarama in the South Island, and left there for several years, to be reclaimed from the storage fence and towed onto a suitable pitch for family use during the summer holidays or on long weekends.

Camping tourism in New Zealand favours rapid motorhome travel. Many of the best town and city camps, the Top 10s, have marked pitches suitable only for motorhomes, where vehicles can be parked quite closely overnight to make maximum use of the land. The excellent locations, superior facilities and efficiency of operation by this chain of camps makes short-term motorhoming a pleasant way to tour.

The conditions of a camp are crucial to the behaviour of the campers. I have been appalled, and then become hardened, to the flamboyance of other women in European camping grounds, to gross breaches of good taste and lack of consideration for the sensibilities of others, often brought about by a poor standard of amenities which unfortunately seems to bring out the worst in some people, so I think I am in a good position to comment on what occurs in New Zealand. I can say that in 30 days of touring and using camp facilities, I never saw a single example of inconsiderate behaviour. Indeed the female campers, from all over the world, were models of decorum and followed the New Zealand code of respect for one another's privacy. I put this down not only to the calibre of the tourists, but also to the excellence of the Top 10 Holiday Parks, where every requirement from superb kitchens and laundries, and critical ablution block requirements like adequate sanitary disposal and toilet paper, clean showers with plenty of hot water, hygienic bench tops with soap dispensers and hot air hand dryers and even, in some camps, hair dryers, was available. Not once in those camps did I enter a toilet or a shower left in a mess by the previous user, and most campers, particularly during the morning rush hour when the pressure was on to make way quickly for the next person, wiped the handbasin and surrounds clean and dry before leaving. Everywhere, small courtesies ruled.

And the high standards were not confined just to the Top 10s, although I believe they have been instrumental in raising them elsewhere. I have been very honest in my assessment of the camps we stayed in, and for every non-Top 10 that was poor, there was another one that was a pleasure to visit.

New Zealand is completely geared to tourism. The sector earns $17 billion annually, is this country's biggest export earner bringing in nearly 19 per cent of export earnings, and employs directly or indirectly 10 per cent of the workforce (*The New Zealand Herald*, Friday, 2 December 2005). Tourism is expected to increase markedly over the next few years, but there is a long way to go before these lovely islands become overcrowded; a city the size of Dunedin is touring *all the time*, and you hardly notice it!

The UK Conde Nast *Traveller* Awards 2005 gave New Zealand the ultimate accolade, that of voting this country the best holiday destination in the world, beating Thailand, Australia and

Italy to take the top spot. The poll was taken of 30,000 Conde Nast *Traveller* readers, and New Zealand scored top marks for scenery, environmental friendliness, and safety.

When I first started out to write this book, I thought it would be no more than an informative guide to roads, routes, campgrounds, and attractions on the way. I did not expect to be *sucked in* to the diversity of this magical landscape, to the opportunities on offer to experience the thrills of a lifetime, whether those thrills are just enjoying good food and wine, or adventure tourism, or cultural heritage, or merely appreciating the people and the ravishing scenery. Those who have read the book to this conclusion will have realised that I included more, and became more rhapsodical, as I went along. I have tried very hard to curb my enthusiasm and to present an unbiased description of our journey; the truth is, that I can't. I have fallen in love with my own country.

In my life I have been fortunate to get to know many of the oldest of western civilisations, often travelling along cheek to cheek, as it were, by caravan, a very intimate way to see a country. But New Zealand still has a rawness, a feeling of just beginning to come to terms with its Polynesian and European heritages, of mixing them together while including, now, many other races from around the world. You will have realised that I became fascinated with this country's early history as we travelled. Driving through old towns and settlements, many of them still as they were a century or more ago (which is remarkable when you consider that so many of the buildings are of timber), made me want to know more about the reasons for their early establishment and the people who endured great hardships to settle there.

When I was at primary school in the 1940s, we were taught almost nothing about our early history. England was our Mother Country, people still called it 'Home', so we learned British history and progressed to the history of Europe at college. The rest of the world, and New Zealand, was a mystery. This trip has been a learning experience, for I found I could not lightly separate a place from its past and needed to know much more in order to understand it. I have included very small snatches of the history of New Zealand's settlement so that you know how and why some important regions developed and realise, as you drive through, that most of what you see has occurred in the last 150 years, or less.

Because we're so newly-developed, the layers of civilisation don't run deep. The past is within the anecdotal memory of a large part of the population, and it is not often that you can visit a country and trace its early origins in what is still around you, visibly. We are changing all the time as we mature as a nation, but paradoxically our history has become more important as we progress.

It was the histories of women that interested me. Most who arrived in New Zealand in the nineteenth century had been residents of cities all their lives and had no idea of the trials ahead of them. Many were totally unfitted by their early life and training for the rough and arduous life of a settler in a new country, when their education at home had consisted of such accomplishments as French, drawing and music, but lacked any training in housekeeping. These women came to a colony which had no amenities, no formed roads, no shops, and often no close neighbours. They frequently had to cook in the open, had to break in their own land, and were dependent too often on erratic supply ships to bring basic stores needed for survival. I marvel that they didn't return home on the next ship, that they had the stickability to survive their difficult lives, and to persevere in setting New Zealand up to be the super country that it is today.

We travelled for a month, whisked ourselves from major attraction to major attraction, lamented loudly when we couldn't fit some places into our crammed itinerary, and except for a few poor meals and ablution facilities, couldn't find anything to grizzle about. Not that we were trying! I knew that I lived in a scenic wonderland, but I had not expected New Zealand to be so devastatingly beautiful. Other, older countries rely heavily on historical 'place' or on centuries of exquisite architecture to provide their beauty and tourist drawcards. We don't have those benefits.

There is a danger that one could think the scenery of New Zealand is the norm everywhere, that the astonishing views, looking like a perfect painting, are to be found elsewhere. They're not. The film trilogy *The Lord of the Rings* took the world by surprise when it was released for the quality of the unspoilt scenery to be found here. A sizeable tourist industry has grown up in places near the film locations, as fans from around the world, and people wanting to see if the real thing is as marvellous as it looks on the screen, flock in.

When we arrived home, M. asked me the question: 'What part of the trip did you enjoy the most?' I didn't have a quick answer. Mentally, I reviewed every day, every detail, and nothing sprang to mind. Yet everywhere we had been, every single experience, had been governed by people. We were tourists in our own country, living the life of anyone from overseas who had hired a motorhome to tour in. Our experiences had been the same as those tourists, for we had travelled the same routes, done the same things, seen the same attractions, and had had a wonderful time. What had made it all so memorable?

I replied, after a while, 'I enjoyed most *meeting the people of New Zealand*!'

New Zealanders have an abundance of humour, resourcefulness, gentle sophistication and quiet good manners, and are this country's greatest strength. No matter how pure the air, or pristine the landscape, or thrilling the activities on offer, it is the people one meets on the road who make or break a journey. When you come to visit us you will see what I mean.

APPENDIX

Note: New Zealand Information Network
Ph: (03) 366 0644
Email: info@newzealandnz.co.nz
www.newzealandnz.co.nz

Transport

Maui Motorhomes and Rentals
36 Richard Pearse Drive, Private Bag 92133, Mangere, Auckland, New Zealand
Reservations: 0800 628 446
Phone/Fax: (09) 275 4748
Email: direct@maui-rentals.com
www.maui-rentals.com

Pacific Horizon Motorhomes
Cnr. State Highway 1 and Grays Road, Plimmerton, Wellington
Reservations: 0800 808 881
Ph: (04) 233 8881
5 Aintree Avenue, Mangere, Auckland
Ph: (09) 275 9349
Email: reservations@pacifichorizon.co.nz
www.pacifichorizon.co.nz

Kea Campers
36 Hillside Road, Glenfield, Auckland
Freephone: 0800 520 052
Ph: (09) 441 7833
Email: reservations@keacampers.com
www.keacampers.com

Interislander Cook Strait Ferries
Freephone: 0800 802 802
Facsimile Call Free: 0800 101 525
www.interislander.co.nz

Campgrounds and other accommodation

Note: The order of listings corresponds to our progress around New Zealand.
* Denotes camps and hotels we stayed at.

The website for Top 10 Holiday Parks is www.top10.co.nz

Baylys Beach Holiday Park*
Seaview Road, R.D. 7, Dargaville
Ph/Fax: (09) 439 6349
Email: baylysbeach.co.nz
www.baylysbeach.co.nz

The Park Top 10 Ninety Mile Beach*
West Coast Road, Waipapakauri, Kaitaia
Reservations 0800 367 719
Ph: (09) 406 7298
Fax: (09) 406 7477
Email: ninetymilebeach@xtra.co.nz
www.ninetymilebeach.co.nz

Omapere Tourist Hotel and Motel
State Highway 12, Omapere
Ph: (09) 405 8737
Fax: (09) 405 8801
Email: omaperehotel@ihug.co.nz
www.omapere.co.nz

Matauri Bay Holiday Park
Matauri Bay, R.D.1, Northland
Ph/Fax: (09) 405 0525
Email: matauribayhp@actrix.co.nz
www.matauribay.co.nz/camp.html

Kingfish Lodge
Whangaroa Harbour, Whangaroa
Ph: (09) 405 0164
Fax: (09) 405 0163
Email: fish@kingfishlodge.co.nz
www.kingfishlodge.co.nz

Kerikeri Top 10 Holiday Park and Aranga Backpackers
Aranga Drive, off Kerikeri Road, Kerikeri, Northland
Reservations: 0800 272 642
Ph: (09) 407 9326
Fax: (09) 407 9897
Email: mail@aranga.co.nz
www.aranga.co.nz

Whangarei Top 10 Holiday Park*
24 Mair Street, Whangarei
Reservations: 0800 455 488
Ph: (09) 437 6856
Fax: (09) 437 5897
Email: whangareiholiday@actrix.co.nz
www.whangareiholiday.co.nz

Tutukaka Holiday Park
R.D.3, Whangarei
Ph/Fax: (09) 434 3938
Email: tutsholidaypk.@igrin.co.nz
www.tutukaka-holidaypark.co.nz

Puriri Park Top 10 Holiday Resort
Puriri Avenue, Orewa, Auckland
Reservations: 0800 787 474
Ph: (09) 426 4648
Fax: (09) 426 6280
Email: info@puriripark.com
www.puriripark.com

Orewa Beach Holiday Park
State Highway 1, Orewa, Auckland
Ph: (09) 426 5832
Email: obhpark@rodney.govt.nz

Auckland North Shore Top 10 Motel and Holiday Park
52 Northcote Road, Takapuna, Auckland
Reservations: 0508 909 090
Ph: 418 2578
Fx: (09) 480 0436
Email: info@nsmotels.co.nz
www.nsmotels.co.nz

Manukau Top 10 Holiday Park*
902 Great South Road, Manukau City
Reservations: 0800 422 673
Ph: (09) 266 8016
Fax: (09) 268 4209
Email: info@manukautop10.co.nz
www.manukautop10.co.nz

Dickson Holiday Park
Victoria Street, Thames
Ph: (07) 868 7308
Email: info@vacationz.co.nz

Shelly Beach Top 10 Holiday Park*
243 Colville Road, Coromandel
Reservations: 0800 424 655
Ph. (07) 866 8988
Email: shelly@world-net.co.nz
www.shellybeachcoromandel.co.nz

Waihi Beach Top 10 Holiday Park*
15 Beach Road, Waihi Beach, Bay of Plenty
Reservations: 0800 924 448
Ph: (07) 863 5504
Fx: 863 5515
Email: info@waihibeach.com
www.waihibeach.com

Te Araroa Holiday Park
State Highway 35, Te Araroa, East Cape
Ph. (06) 864 4873
Fax: (06) 864 4473
Email: bill.martin@xtra.co.nz

Waikanae Beach Holiday Park, Gisborne
Grey Street, Gisborne
Ph: (06) 867 5634
Fax: (06) 867 9765
Email: motorcamp@gdc.govt.nz

Gisborne District Council (for camping permissions)
Fitzherbert Street, Gisborne
Ph: (06) 867 2049
Fax: (06) 867 8076
Email: csgis@gdc.govt.nz
www.gdc.govt.nz - click on Tourism Eastland

Papamoa Beach Top 10 Holiday Resort
535 Papamoa Beach Road, Papamoa
Reservations 0800 232 243
Ph/Fax: (07) 572 0816
Email: resort@papamoabeach.co.nz
www.papamoabeach.co.nz

Rotorua Top 10 Holiday Park*
Pukuatua Street, Rotorua.
Reservations 0800 223 267
Ph: (07) 348 1886
Fax: (07) 348 1867
Email: stay@rotoruatop10.co.nz
www.rotoruatop10.co.nz

Waitomo Top 10 Holiday Park*
Waitomo Caves Road, Waitomo Caves
Reservations: 0508 498 666
Ph: (07) 878 7639
Email: stay@waitomopark.co.nz
www.waitomopark.co.nz

Lake Taupo Top 10 Holiday Park
28 Centennial Drive, Taupo
Reservations: 0800 332 121
Ph: (07) 378 6860
Email: office@taupotop10.co.nz
www.taupotop10.co.nz

Top 10 Hutt Park Holiday Park*
95 Hutt Park Road, Lower Hutt
Reservations: 0800 488 874
Ph: (04) 568 5913
Fax: (04) 568 5914
Email: info@huttpark.co.nz
www.huttpark.co.nz

Nelson City Holiday Park*
230 Vanguard Street, Nelson
Reservations: 0800 778 898
Ph: (03) 548 1445
Fax: (03) 548 2670

Pohara Beach Top 10 Holiday Park
Abel Taman Drive, Takaka, Nelson
Reservations: 0800 764 272
Ph: (03) 525 9500
Email: pohara@xtra.co.nz
www.pohara.com/paradise

Seal Colony Top 10 Holiday Park*
Marine Parade, Carters Beach, Westport
Reservations: 0508 937 876
Ph: (03) 789 8002
Fax: (03) 789 6732
Email: holiday@sealcolonytouristpark.co.nz
www.top10westport.co.nz

Punakaiki Beach Camp
Main Road, State Highway 6, Punakaiki, Westland
Ph/Fax: (03) 731 1894
Email: beachcamp@xtra.co.nz

Franz Josef Mountain View Top 10 Holiday Park*
State Highway 6, Franz Josef
Reservations: 0800 467 897
Ph/Fax: (03) 752 0735
Email: bookings@mountain-view.co.nz
www.mountainview.co.nz

Aspiring Court Motel and Haast Highway Accommodation*
Marks Road, Haast
Ph: (03) 750 0703
Fax: (03) 750 0718

Queenstown Top 10 Holiday Park 'Creeksyde' *
54 Robins Road, Queenstown
Reservations: 0800 786 222
Ph: (03) 442 9447
Fax: (03) 442 6621
Email: creeksyde@camp.co.nz
www.camp.co.nz

Milford Sound Lodge
535 Private Bag, Te Anau, Milford Sound
Ph: (03) 249 8071
Fax: (03) 249 8075

Alexandra Holiday Park*
Manuherikia Road, Alexandra
Ph: (03) 448 8297
Fax: (03) 448 8294
Email: alex.hol.park@xtra.co.nz

Alexandra Tourist Park
Ngapara Street, Alexandra
Ph: (03) 448 8861
Fax: (03) 448 8276
Email: alex.touristpark@xtra.co.nz

Aaron Lodge Top 10 Motel and Holiday Park*
162 Kaikorai Valley Road, Dunedin
Reservations: 0800 879 227
Ph: (03) 476 4725
Fax: (03) 476 7925
Email: stay@aaronlodge.co.nz
www.aaronlodgetop10.co.nz

Omarama Top 10 Holiday Park*
State Highway 8 and 33 Junction, Omarama
Reservations: 0800 662 726
Ph: (03) 438 9875
Fax: (03) 438 9680
Email: omarama.holiday@xtra.co.nz
www.omaramatop10.co.nz

The Hermitage, Aoraki Mount Cook*
Mount Cook, New Zealand
Reservations: 0800 686 800
Ph. (03) 435 1809
Fax: (03) 435 1879
Email: enquiries@hermitage.co.nz
www.mount-cook.com

The Chalet Tranz Alpine Lodge and Restaurant*
Main Road, Arthur's Pass, Canterbury
Reservations: 0800 506 550
Ph. (03) 318 9236
Email: thechalet@arthurspass.co.nz
www.arthurspass.co.nz

Mountain View Top 10 Holiday Park*
Main Road, Hanmer Springs
Reservations: 0800 904 545
Ph. (03) 315 7113
Fax: (03) 315 7118
Email: mtview.hanmer@clear.net.nz
www.holidayparks.co.nz/mtview

Kaikoura Top 10 Holiday Park*
34 Beach Road, Kaikoura
Reservations: 0800 363 638
Ph/Fax: (03) 319 5362
Email: kaikouratop10@ihug.co.nz
www.kaikouratop10.co.nz

Meadow Park Top 10 Holiday Park*
39 Meadow Street, Papanui, Christchurch
Reservations: 0800 396 323
Ph: (03) 352 9176
Email: meadowpark@xtra.co.nz
www.meadowpark.co.nz

Akaroa Top 10 Holiday Park
Morgan Road, Akaroa, Banks Peninsula
Reservations 0800 727 525
Ph: (03) 304 7471
Email: akaroa.holidaypark@xtra.co.nz
www.akaroa-holidaypark.co.nz

Crowne Plaza Christchurch*
Cnr. Durham and Kilmore Streets, Christchurch
Ph: (03) 365 7799
Fax: (03) 365 0082
Email: hotel@crowneplazachristchurch.co.nz
www.crowneplaza.com

Attractions and Activities

Lion Red $250,000 Fishing Contest
The Organiser, P.O. Box 7, Kaitaia
Ph: (09) 406 7056
Fax: (09) 406 7252
Email: info@snapperclassic.co.nz
www.snapperclassic.co.nz

Fullers Bay of Islands
Paihia
Maritime Building on the Waterfront
Ph. (09) 402 7421 (every day 7 a.m.-9p.m.)
Fax: (09) 402 7831
Email: reservations@fboi.co.nz
Russell
The Strand
Ph: (09) 403 7866
Auckland
Bay of Islands Travel Centre
Downtown Shopping Centre, 11 Customs Street West
Ph: (09) 358 0259 (every day 7 a.m.-9 p.m.)
Fax: (09) 302 1444
Email: reservations@boitc.co.nz
www.fboi.co.nz

Fullers Cruises and Tours, Auckland
Ferry Building, 99 Quay Street, Downtown, Auckland
Ph: (09) 367 9111
Fax: (09) 367 9148
Email: enquiries@fullers.co.nz
www.fullers.co.nz

Coromandel Coastal Walkway
316 Tiki Road, Coromandel Town
Ph/Fax: (07) 866 8175
Email: njstrongman@xtra.co.nz
www.coromandeldiscoverytours.co.nz

Kauri 2000
18 Coghill Street, Whitianga
Ph: (07) 866 0468
Fax: (07) 866 0459
Email: kauri2000@paradise.net.nz
www.kauri2000.org.nz

Johansen Guiding Adventures
Damian Johansen and Sharon Johansen
P.O. Box 76, Pauanui Beach, New Zealand
Ph/Fax: (07) 864 8371

Marlborough Wine Tours
Ritchies Deluxe Wine Tour
Freephone: 0800 500 511
Email: blenheim.depot@ritchies.co.nz
www.ritchies.co.nz

Highlight Tours
(Ph: (03) 577 9046
Email: highlight.tours@xtra.co.nz
www.highlight-tours.co.nz

Marlborough Wine Tours
Ph: Cherry Wilson (03) 578 9515
Mobile: 027 248 1231

Abel Tasman Kayaks
Abel Tasman National Park, Marahau, R.D.2, Motueka, Nelson
Freephone: 0800 732 529
Ph: (03) 527 8022
Email: info@abeltasmankayaks.co.nz
www.abeltasmankayaks.co.nz

Kaiteriteri Kayak
Motueka, Nelson
Ph: (03) 527 8383
Email: abeltasman@seakayak.co.nz
www.seakayak.co.nz

Southern Exposure
Abel Tasman National Park, Moss Road, Parahau, R.D.2, Motueka, Nelson
Freephone: 0800 695 292
Ph: (03) 527 8424
Email: info@southern-exposure.co.nz
www.southern-exposure.co.nz

The Sea Kayak Company
506 High Street, Motueka, Nelson
Freephone: 0800 252 925
Ph: (03) 528 7251
Email: info@seakayaknz.co.nz
www.seakayaknz.co.nz

Abel Tasman National Park Coast Track
Abel Tasman Coast Track Booking Desk
Motueka Information Centre, Wallace, Street, Motueka
Ph: (03) 528 0005

Department of Conservation
Cnr. King Edward and High Streets, Motueka
Ph: (03) 528 1810
Email: motuekaao@doc.govt.nz

Department of Conservation
62 Commercial Street, Takaka
Ph: (03) 525 8026
Email:goldenbayao@doc.govt.nz

Department of Conservation website:
www.doc.govt.nz

Buller Gorge Swingbridge Ltd
State Highway 6, Upper Buller Gorge
Ph: (03) 523 9809
Email: swingbridge@bullergorge.co.nz
www.bullergorge.co.nz

Whale Watch Kaikoura
Whaleway Station Road, Kaikoura
Reservations: 0800 655 121
Ph: (03) 319 6767
Email: res@whalewatch.co.nz
www.whalewatch.co.nz